DYING TO

Spiritual Case Story of a Secular Counsellor

DAVID MIDGLEY

Published in the United Kingdom 2006
by Free Association Books
London

British Library Cataloguing in Publication Data
A catalogue record for this book is available from the British Library

Produced by Bookchase, London
Printed and bound in the EU

ISBN 1853439835

Arthur and Agnes (Peggy) with Paul and Caroline, 1963

Paul and Caroline, 2004

For

Paul and Caroline

In loving memory of

their grandparents, my parents,

James Arthur Midgley
(born 30th March, 1892 – died 6th August, 1967)

and

Agnes Midgley (née Garnham)
(born 6th June, 1900 – died 26th May, 1993)

Contents

Acknowledgements

Almost everyone mentioned in this book deserves to be acknowledged because they have all contributed in some way to my 'case story, as I have called it. But there are a few people I must mention in particular because, without them, there might have been no book at all!

The first is Dr Ian Stewart, a Teaching and Supervising Transactional Analyst, co-director with Adrienne Lee of The Berne Institute at Kegworth, near Nottingham, and the author of several books on transactional analysis. It was under his sponsorship and guidance that I eventually qualified as a Certified Transactional Analyst. The second is Gordon Clarke, an Education Psychologist, a member of the Association of Christian Counsellors and founder of Christian Fellowship Ministry, based in Stockton-on-Tees, who was for some years my supervisor. Ian and Gordon are both professional counsellors of quite different background and outlook, the one secular and a humanist, and the other religious. They represent the two 'horns' of the dilemma described in this book, to which I eventually found a resolution.

I also acknowledge the help of my friend and PA, Paul Nash who, for the past couple of years, has done for me all those things I have been increasingly unable to do for myself, as motor neurone disease has deprived me of both mobility and the power of speech. In addition to changing light bulbs and emptying the shredder, he has telephoned people I could not speak to personally, done much of my shopping and solved problems with the computer, especially in the collection and preparation of photographs for the book, and been my indispensable go-between with Trevor Brown, managing Editor of Free Association Books, and his associates, to who I am also indebted.

Finally, I acknowledge my debt to my wife Betty who has been my unfailing support throughout our long and happy marriage, when I seem to have been always 'messing about' writing in the study, when proper husbands would have been domestically far more useful!

Preface

The need for professionally trained and experienced counsellors is increasing. This development is dictated by the stresses of living in our crazy Western world and these stresses are escalating at an alarming rate. Time was when job security could almost be taken for granted and everyone could look forward confidently to a guaranteed pension on retirement. But that is no longer so. Neither is the expectation that children will have the same set of parents at sixteen that they started with; nor many other traumatic social changes that are happening against a background of crime, terrorism and environmental change. Uncertainty and insecurity are endemic and the counselling profession is growing in response to this situation, filling a role that traditionally has been the province of religion.

My own religious background has been as a very conventional mainstream Methodist; but my professional training in social casework as a probation officer, followed by the discovery of transactional analysis as a means of getting to know myself, faced me with many conflicts that needed a solution – or, at least, a resolution. This book is an account of how – contrary to all my expectations – I became a professional counsellor and psychotherapist.

To read what follows just as an autobiography would be to miss the point altogether. I have subtitled the book *Spiritual Case Story of a Secular Counsellor* but it is far from being an academic case study. It is a case story of which I myself am the subject and I have told it in a way which, I hope, will encourage readers to identify with me and, perhaps, experience vicariously my experiences, especially in the course of some of the personal therapy I did as an essential part of my training to become a clinical transactional analyst. Not only that, but also the experience of facing a Final Exam board, not just once, but twice!

The early part of the book records my own experience of the laying of the foundations – or, rather, of the foundations being laid, because I was not consciously aware of what was going on. Taken one at a time, these events might look like pure chance, a series of remarkable co-incidences; but in retrospect it does not feel like that. Some people might attribute the course of events to 'fate', the inevitable destiny that befalls us all and over which we have no control. Others might think in terms of 'the guiding hand of God'. Or perhaps these events were what the great psychologist C.G. Jung would have ascribed to the influence of the Collective Unconscious. Eric Berne, the originator of transactional analysis, to whom I owe so much, found the ancient Greek concept of 'Physis, the force of Nature, which eternally strives to make things grow and to make growing things more perfect', a useful frame of reference.

Call it what you like, there does seem to have been something at work that has endowed my life with meaning and purpose, almost in spite of myself. I was going somewhere, even though I did not know, for a long time, where it was to be. This sense of direction and of meaning and purpose is what I count as the spiritual dimension of life, which more and more counsellors and psychotherapists are now taking into account. All this is set against a background of family life, an early career that had no goal except fantasies of becoming a successful novelist, and the simultaneous exploration of that 'spiritual dimension' that led, in due course, to my having at least some understanding of what life is really all about – for me, at any rate.

Finally, I record what dying is like! I don't mean the actual event, of course, but the process leading up to it in the context of a neurological disorder that is slowly and inexorably depriving me of both speech and mobility and the ability to do anything except think and, maybe, meditate.

I am enjoying it immensely!

Prologue

TRAINS

From the window seat I could look across the garden and the hedge to the trees beyond the hedge and see trains passing, or the smoke rising in urgent puffs above the trees. The sound was clear and exciting, even if muffled by the windowpanes. In small gaps between the trees, curtained by branches festooned with chestnut candles, pink and white, the very trains themselves appeared, briefly liveried with sparks and polished woodwork, increasing in speed beyond the little summerhouse or slowing down toward the station and the sea.

I am not yet three years old, so this is fantasy as much as memory, for who would let conker trees grow beside a railway line! But memories are like dreams. They are usable, as dreams were later to those who came to me in their confusion, looking for a new direction for themselves. So 'I am the train'. I am going somewhere, one way or the other – to the station and the sea, the beach, sand pies and castles and coloured paper flags; or else the other way to God alone knows where, to places unimagined, unimaginable, anywhere. Station after station after station – junctions and points and new directions.

Is there, in fact, some power, some force, some mysterious morphic field, some God who's drawing me from where I was at two years old, from where I am at more than three score years and ten, to where I ought to be? That is the question to explore. The trains, my father, mother, brother. School and writing from the age of ten; adolescent puzzlement and lack of self-esteem; Dad's accompanist at only ten years old – *When Song is Sweet* and *Trees* and *Bless this House*. Betty at six and nine and ten and holidays together, Saltburn, Whitley Bay. The war; evacuation, all too briefly, to a heavenly place before parental love or need or economics called me back, hungry for the heavenly place again.

What stations punctuate those seventy years or more, what formative events, relationships, experiences, lie on the route from where I was to where I am, to where I ought to be? What would I become – a Secret Service man, an athlete, actor, musician, travel agent, salesman, nurse, preacher, television presenter, probation officer, counsellor and psychotherapist, writer, publisher . . . ?

God alone can know.

Part One

LAYING THE FOUNDATIONS

1

SEEDS AND WEAK BEGINNINGS

My family name of Midgley, when traced to its roots, actually means 'a dungheap in a clearing'. That is not much of a start in life for someone who is not only dying to live but also dying to be significant. I never wanted to be just anyone! So I was delighted to find a plaque in the parish church at Haworth, home of the Brontës, commemorating an earlier David Midgley who was not only Lord of the Manor of Haworth in 1723, but actually lived at Top Withens, the supposed site of Wuthering Heights, my favourite novel!

This book is not a novel, neither is it an academic case study. It is a narrative 'case story' of which I myself am the subject. I don't know whether any professional counsellor has previously risked so much self-exposure in a book, though we all have to face up to it in the course of our training. Fame enough to justify an autobiography does not come to many in my profession, no matter how successful we are at helping people straighten out lives that have got into a mess. What does come to most of us, however, is a sense of fulfilment and that, above all else, is probably what makes this story worthwhile. It explores the things that happened along the way, many of them seemingly trivial; but they are things that undoubtedly contributed to me becoming 'Me', rather than someone entirely different.

One of the things I discovered, when I set out to find whether I was directly related to the erstwhile Lord of the Manor of Haworth (and I wasn't!), was that Simeon, the name of my grandfather, was a family name recurring several times down the generations. I believe I should have been christened Simeon, after my grandfather, but for reasons that are not entirely clear (but probably connected with my grandmother's refusal to attend my father's wedding to a 'factory girl'!) I was not given it, not even for a middle name. Why I should regret not being called Simeon is a mystery to be probed only by analytically minded people, because it means 'obedient'. Well, that's not much to be proud of either when, so many significant people have gone off and done their own thing – like Copernicus, Columbus and dear old John Wesley.

My name, David, means 'beloved'! That might not sound very promising, when so many significant people suffered all sorts of childhood abuse, deprivation and neglect; and I suffered none of those things. My father, a bluff and down-to-earth Yorkshireman who is a major player in this story, would have dismissed the whole question of names and their meanings as 'summat an' nowt'. But I have a hunch that names can sometimes influence the kind of person one becomes. And so can the experiences of our parents, which influence their attitude toward us.

My father was the youngest in a family of four children, two sisters and two brothers. His father died when he was only eighteen, leaving him as head of a household of women, his elder brother having emigrated to America. Their mother was an autocrat who refused to attend the weddings of her children because she deemed their chosen spouses 'unsuitable'. On the 'distaff' side, my mother was a depressive personality and the fifth in line in a family of seven girls, four of whom never married. Their father died young as well. So my father was surrounded by women throughout his adult life; and so, of course, was I throughout my developmental years. Both my grandfathers died before I was born. This abundance of women is, I believe, one of the significant background factors in the formation of my Life Script, as I shall call it.

However, the very first event that launched me onto this path of my life, I did not learn about until I was a pensioner, by which time my mother was widowed and in her eighties. She told me, not long before she died, that when I was only a few months old she had left me in my pram and in my father's care whilst she went shopping. As a child bereft of his mother I began to cry. My father, who was not the most patient of men, rocked the pram for a while and made soothing noises but to no avail. My crying got louder and my father got more and more agitated. Eventually, in despair, he leaned over the pram and, at the top of his powerful voice, bawled 'Shut up!'

And I did, instantly!

'Heck,' said my father, when he told my mother about it on her return from the shops, 'I thought I'd killed him.' He told the tale to others afterwards, laughing about it with what I have learned to call a Gallows Laugh – that is laughter at something that is not really funny, because laughing somehow makes it seem OK. I have no conscious memory of this event, of course; but it is probable that nothing that happens to us is forgotten entirely. The unconscious memory, I guess, would reinforce the significance of the family name I was never given but, oddly, have always wanted: Simeon, meaning 'obedient'.

In the rest of this chapter I shall describe only those important events that are retained in my conscious memory as dramatic and, for me, sometimes quite traumatic snapshots. I have found, in professional practice, that few clients could recall much of what happened to them before the age of eight and this holds true for me as well. However, I have one important memory snapshot of an event when I was only seven years old and it is not at all traumatic That was the time I first met Betty, who was then only six. Our family had been invited to have tea with our friends the Duttons, who were then living in Bank Crest, Baildon, not too far from our house in Bromley Road, Shipley. The scene is in the kitchen at Bank Crest and six year old Betty is standing near the door into the hall. Just behind me is her brother Keith, aged three, who is sitting on the potty! That's all. I do not imagine that I actually fell in love with Betty at that tender age (and she certainly did not fall in love with me!) but I somehow knew for certain that she was mine; hence the memory.

It is crucial for the understanding of my Script that at the age of eight I started piano lessons. Nothing remarkable in that, of course but the reason, in my case, was so that I could become my father's accompanist. Although he worked in the textile industry in a responsible managerial position at Salts Mill, Saltaire (now a major Bradford tourist venue and the home of the famous David Hockney art exhibition) my father was also a trained singer. He was a semi-professional tenor who was well known in the Aire valley and round about, for his concert work, particularly as soloist in church performances of Handel's *Messiah*, Mendelssohn's *Elijah* and other popular oratorios. I was sent to have piano lessons so that I could grow up to be his accompanist.

I learned quickly and before I was ten years old I could play the accompaniment to several of the simpler ballads my father sang – *Just for Today, Because, Bless this House, I'll Walk Beside You* and many others. We had a second hand, but quite good quality, upright piano in the lounge at our house at 5 Bromley Road, Shipley. My father would sing to his own reflection in the mirror that hung over the fireplace, whilst I sat at the piano – with my back to the audience, so to speak. It was this sitting with my back to the (albeit imaginary) audience that was the problem. I always loved playing for my father and was, in fact, quite proud to do so; but for a child dying to be significant this was soon not enough. I began desperately wanting to be a solo pianist, ideally with an orchestra to accompany me! I did, of course, play piano solos, as I grew older, but I never felt to be properly appreciated. I chose showy, and usually noisy, pieces like Chopin waltzes and studies and, in due course, *The Warsaw Concerto*, after the film *Dangerous Moonlight* was released during the war. But, even though I could soon play it all through from memory, the orchestra was never more than a figment of my imagination. And, of course, I played too loudly! I was constantly being told to play quietly. Myra Hess's arrangement of *Bach's Jesu Joy of Man's Desiring* was very gentle and my parents' favourite. But all that, of course, was a long-term development rather than an event.

The next significant and memorable, and quite traumatic, event took place in the prog. Progging was the autumn collection of polled trees and branches to be piled on a piece of spare land near my home in preparation for the Plot Night bonfire. In this pile of prog we children made a den. The entrance was low to ground and quite inaccessible to grown-ups. Even we kids had to get on our hands and knees and crawl into the secret place we had created. Here we could be safe from adult intrusion. We could share our secrets, plot and plan adventures. And explore. We were young and small and curious. We were learning about the world and about ourselves, especially about our bodies. Girls were different from boys. Boys who had a sister knew the difference but even they did not know what it signified. And I had no sister. Boys had an appendage between the legs; girls, another boy had told me, did not. Why? And why should they always be covered up, even on the beach, in the sea on holiday? Why were such parts spoken of in curiously hushed tones? Why was any reference to them 'dirty'? All of us kids were filled with curiosity and none of us could ask our parents or other grown ups because of the hushed tones, the sense of naughtiness and dirtiness and guilt. And so we asked each other.

There were five of us – me and Robert, who were about the same age; a girl called Gwen; Joyce who was a bit younger, and Godfrey who came later. Godfrey was a big boy, about twelve, I think, and at a big school. He was not in the den when the adventure started.

'Don't you have a little man, Joyce? I've got one.' 'You haven't!' 'Yes, I have.' 'Let's see it, then.' 'All right . . . ' So buttons were undone, the little man exposed – a small and unpretentious thing. 'What have you got, then?' 'Nothing.' 'Don't be daft, you must have something.' 'I haven't.' 'What do you wee through, then?' 'There's a little hole.' 'A hole? Between your legs?' 'Yes.' 'Let's see it.' 'No . . . ' 'Go on . . . ' 'I can't put it out like you can. There is nothing.' 'There's a hole. You said so.' 'It's nothing.' 'You've got to let us look. I let you look at mine.' 'Somebody might come.' 'Nobody can come in here, can they? Who do you think might come?' 'No-one . . . I suppose.' 'Well, then . . .'. Maybe a pause. Then, 'All right,' said Joyce and with a defiant expression, pulled her knickers down to her ankles and sat on the ground with her knees apart, ready for inspection. The flat, uninteresting thing was exposed to view. There was a sort of smell with it. Robert and I reached out to touch. 'Stop it . . . It tickles . . . ' Giggles and laughter.

'What's goin' on, then?'

We froze in shock and horror and Joyce's knees suddenly clamped together.

But it was not a parent. It was Godfrey, who we knew. He was one of us. We were relieved. Godfrey had already shown me and Robert his thing, which was much bigger than ours and had no skin over the end of it. He had shown us how he could make stuff squirt out of it. We were relieved it was only Godfrey. He too reached out to Joyce and she let him touch, grinning mischievously and biting her lip.

'Now you,' said Godfrey. 'Come on, get it out.'

And so it all began. There was sunlight percolating through the woven branches overhead and they were watching curiously, waiting in expectation for the stuff to spurt out but it never came. There was growing anticipation, rising wave upon wave, reaching out towards something intensely pleasurable, even beyond the pleasure of the chase, faster and faster and higher and higher. And laughter because there had to be something to hear, to express, to acknowledge the experience. And all of them watching! Another time . . . another time . . . It needs to be bigger . . . You need to be older . . .

* * *

When I was five I started school at Salts kindergarten. The Salt High Schools, which had grammar school status, had been founded by Sir Titus Salt for the better education of the children of his managerial staff. The children of the other employees went to Albert Road Infant and Junior Schools until they were eleven when, if they passed the County Minor exam, they would be eligible for a free place at Salts or another grammar school. However, there was provision for managers' children to go to Salts Kindergarten, which consisted of two class rooms in the Girls' School up to the age of about eight, and after that to the Juniors which was in the adjacent Boys' School. My father, eager to do the best for me and no doubt to reflect his managerial status, paid for me to attend Salts Kindergarten and then the Juniors.

It was in the Juniors, with the encouragement of Mr Bennet, a young, Welsh teacher, that I manifested my first disposition to become a writer.

He himself had written the school play, presented to the parents on Speech Day, and I had a small part in it.

I think I must have told Mr Bennet that I thought I could write a play, so he encouraged me to do just that. It was called 'Robbery at Buckingham Palace' and had a cast of robbers with names like Bill and Dick, and secret service men who are all known by numbers. There isn't a 007 amongst them but the idea was much the same. It was, I think, inspired by stories in *The Adventure*, my favourite weekly, which occasionally included in its pages free gifts of secret codes and instructions for making invisible ink. I think I learned more shady business from *The Adventure* than I learned a few years later at The School of Military Intelligence! All stations along the Way! My teacher was so impressed with my efforts at writing that he rushed off to show it to the Head. So at 10 years old I decided to become a writer.

I was a good little runner and we young Juniors were included with the Big Boys on the school sports day, held in Roberts Park, that had been presented to the village by Sir James Roberts of the mill, following the Salt family. I was eight years old and, being very young and rather small, I was given a few yards 'start' in the 100 yards handicap race. And I won! I still have a tarnished silver medal to prove it. But a more significant 'station' on my journey came at the end of the same day. The mile race was always run last and the little boys were, of course, given plenty of start. We ran four times round the cricket pitch in Roberts Park and by the end of two laps most of the little boys, and some of the big ones, had dropped out, exhausted. But little Midgley battled on round the third lap and the fourth. Even after all the other boys had passed him Midge, as I was known, was still running, puffed but determined to complete the course. Everyone else had long since finished when I eventually arrived at the finishing line, to the gracious, good-humoured applause of parents, teachers and school friends lining the track. When the school met again for morning assembly the Headmaster, G.H. Parkin, commended me publicly for my spirit but declared that in future 'these babies' would not be allowed to take part in the mile race. Needless to say, I was angry and humiliated – and not for the last time either! If there's one thing that still causes me an excessive amount of distress, it is humiliation. Here was I, at eight years old, striving to be 'a big boy' and even my success was rewarded with a put-down!

When I was about eleven years old and the boys who had passed the County Minor exam had joined us, the science teacher, 'Spike' McGill, started a 'science society' and invited our class to appoint a representative to its committee. To my delight and astonishment they appointed me by a clear majority vote! When I told my mother and father I had been appointed 'science society representative' they were very amused. It was the impressive title, and hearing me say it, that amused them, rather than the appointment itself – which was what pleased me and did something for my deficient sense of self-esteem. For some weeks after the appointment I was required to recite my title to visiting aunts. 'Come on, David, what's that posh job you've been given at school?' my mother would say, proudly showing me off. 'Science Society Representative' I would say, to please my mother. They would laugh and I would squirm and again feel humiliated, not knowing then that 'Strokes' (as I later learned to call 'units of recognition') were not to be accepted if they were Negative Strokes or the kind you didn't want.

My school career was far from illustrious and little of significance happened to me at school between that first sports day in 1935 and the last one in 1943. I wasn't even much good at football. Because I was small they used to put me in goals and then get on with the game at the other end of the pitch! Later, when the war started, I had a school allotment and was allowed to 'dig for victory' instead of playing football or cricket.

As I got bigger and my hormones began to flow (which, of course, was all too soon in my case!) I got infatuated with one or two girls. But 'nothing happened' as they say on the soaps. In fact it was quite exceptional for anything to 'happen' in those days of universally agreed ideas about right and wrong and no readily available protection against disaster. People did, of course, 'do wrong' but that it was a deviation from 'right' was never questioned, even by the doers.

I enjoyed the respect and affection of the school staff and had plenty of friends so that I received an abundance of 'Unconditional Strokes', as I later learned to call them; that is, I was loved and Stroked simply for being me. I did not have to 'deserve it'. Most of the people I worked with later as a counsellor or psychotherapist had been denied 'unconditional Strokes'. They had always felt the need to 'prove their worth' and frequently had finished up with emotional problems a great deal worse than mine!

But whatever Strokes I received as a child, somehow my academic ability never flowered. School Reports always spoke of unfulfilled potential with familiar 'could do better' comments. The essential problem, I now know, was that I never had any expectation of doing well. My self-esteem was disturbingly low and whenever it got Stroked (as in the Science

Society appointment) the Strokes were soon discounted by well-meaning people who were not well-endowed with empathy and could not feel my feelings. Eventually, I began to see some advantage in being a child who wasn't really expected to achieve very much. This negative expectation became a part of my 'Script', my Life Plan and, in due course, it had to be dealt with, along with my experience in the prog, in the context of that personal psychotherapy which is required of all who aspire to become psychotherapists themselves.

My father must have been very jealous of my role as his accompanist. I remember one occasion, when I was playing one of my own solo pieces, he came into the room and said, 'Come on, lad, let's have a song.' I was irritated because I was enjoying myself and for once refused to defer to him. He was extremely angry, threw my hands off the keyboard and slammed down the piano lid, saying, 'If you're not going to play for me, you're not going to play at all!' I think I stormed out of the room and nursed my own anger in private – probably in the attic that had always been my playroom. I had quite a decent tenor voice myself as I grew up and sang in the chapel choir but my father never gave me any encouragement or suggested that I take singing lessons. I guess he was afraid I might turn out to be even better than he was. My mother also had a good singing voice and could have done well if encouraged and trained. But she, too, suffered the same rejection. I did play for her occasionally – Purcell's *Nymphs and Shepherds* comes to mind. But she was rarely allowed to perform if my father was there. He seemed to need all the limelight for himself! My mother also played the violin – though, again, she got no encouragement to play except when my father was out (probably at the Masonic Lodge) and I got her to have a go. Her music teacher had been Handel Parker, the chapel organist at Saltaire, when she was a girl, and the composer of the famous hymn tune *Deep Harmony*, which is still sung world-wide to the words 'Sweet is the work, my God, my King.'

My brother Philip was born when I was six and a half years old. Philip was no serious competition for me as a child. In fact, I was more of a problem to him than he to me. For six and a half years I had been an only child, spoilt and indulged, and had abandoned mother's knee on my own initiative long before Philip came on the scene. In fact, I was never very fond of mother's knee and I'm sure this was a disappointment to her. In her old age she told me how, as a tiny child, I would never let her cuddle me up but always wanted to scramble down and go my own way. Oddly, though, I remember often being cuddled up on my father's knee. But I have a strong feeling that as he cuddled me he imagined me to be a little girl! As I have said, he lived in a world of women and I'm certain that, proud as he no doubt was of having sons (especially one who could accompany him as he sang!) he really would have preferred a couple of daughters. In fact there were three little girls, who all came from families where there was not much money, who would sometimes be taken on holiday with us, so that my father had some temporary, part time daughters. Madge Fillingham went to our Sunday School; Peggy Nuttall, who was related to my mother, lived in South Elmsall where her father was a coal minor; and Margarette Knight, who was at the National Children's Home and Orphanage at Bramhope, near Leeds. We lost touch with Madge but still maintain contact with Peggy and Margarette, now in their eighties, both of whom married and had children.

When I was ten years old and Betty nine, our families went on holiday together at Saltburn, so Betty and I began to get to know each other a bit better. Peggy, who was a few years older than me, joined us for that holiday. My relationship with Betty was far from romantic, though even at ten years old, I think I would have made it so had I got any encouragement. The following year, 1938 when there were already rumours of imminent war, our families went on holiday together again, this time to Whitley Bay. But I got no further, at the age of eleven, pressing my suit with Betty! She tolerated my company, in the absence of anyone more congenial, but seemed not to think I was up to much. I must have put her on 'hold' and indulged myself instead in the realms of fantasy.

I was twelve years old when the Second World War broke out in 1939. The threat of invasion by Hitler's armies was very real and bombing was expected. There was national panic and thousands of children, mainly of wealthy parents who could afford it, were hastily evacuated by sea to America, Australia, South Africa and other countries considered safe. Many others were packed off to live with relations or other well-disposed people, in the English countryside. Philip and I were evacuated to the village of Grange-in-Borrowdale in the Lake District. This was organised with my cousin Annie, who was about twenty years older than I, and who took refuge there with her small son John. The choice of location was decided by arrangement with Ellen Coates who lived with her husband Nathan at the house called Grange View. This is on Grange Fell, beside the Rosthwaite Road, and more or less opposite the end of Grange's beautiful double-span bridge. For many years it has had a gift shop attached to it and they still do Bed & Breakfast, as Ellen did in 1939. Ellen had, in fact, been the cook at Hollycroft, Uncle George and Auntie Lizzie's lovely home in Stavely Road, Shipley, until she married

Nathan and settled in Grange. I suppose they rented the house, which would have been a pretty expensive property even then.

Grange-in-Borrowdale became my idea of heaven, despite the rain which came in full Lakeland force so that the River Derwent burst its banks one weekend and we could not even get out to attend the little Methodist Church in the village (a mere hamlet, really) at the other end of the bridge. But much of the time it was fine and I was allowed out unsupervised to explore the countryside, whilst Annie was busy looking after John and Philip, who must have been six or seven.

Our evacuation lasted only three weeks. By that time no bombs had fallen on Shipley or anywhere nearby, the initial panic had subsided and my father, no doubt weighing the safety factor against the cost of keeping us at Grange, decided we might as well go home. I'm sure he and my mother were missing us because we were, in fact, a happy family. I don't know how Philip felt about coming home so soon from this extended September holiday, but I know I was deeply disappointed. Just before the decision was made, Annie had been to see the head teacher of the village school at Rosthwaite, just up the road from Grange, and I, at any rate, was looking forward to going there. But that was not to happen and back to Shipley we came.

I must have been about thirteen or fourteen before I began to take school seriously. Suddenly, I began to pay attention, in German lessons particularly, but history and physics fascinated me as well. My biggest problem was with maths. My father struggled bravely with the 'problems' I was set for homework but I never really got the hang of it. Oddly enough I coped quite well with mental arithmetic but algebra, and later trigonometry, just defeated me. My friend Raymond Fielding, who was a year ahead of me at the same school and was somehow committed to being my mentor, sometimes did my maths homework for me, perhaps trying his hand at being a teacher (which he was to become) but in my case he was not a conspicuous success! Raymond, whom I knew from Sunday School, was an only child of not-very-well-off parents and liked to think of me as the little brother he never had. It was a role I did not accept at all readily since I myself was the 'big brother' in our family, though not, on reflection, a very useful one. Nevertheless, I preferred to avoid the 'little brother' status!

Raymond lived with his Mum and Dad in a back-to-back terraced house in Thompson Street, Shipley whilst I lived in Bromley Road, Nab Wood. Ours was also a road of terraced houses but we had small gardens back and front and (before they were removed for 'the war effort') wrought iron railings and gates – a much more 'desirable' area of middle class people in professional and managerial jobs. Raymond's father was, I believe, a warehouseman, a humble enough job, but he was a man of sterling character, a quiet and unobtrusive Christian and a loyal Methodist who had distinguished himself for bravery in the First World War and had been awarded the Italian Croix de Guerre. His influence on Raymond's development must have been profound, even if unobtrusive. Raymond's mother's influence, however, was far from unobtrusive. She was a little woman with big ambitions for her only son. She had adapted to the predominantly middle class folk of Saltaire Methodist Church (including the Midgleys) by declaring to her growing son (in effect, even if not in so many words) 'You're as good as any of that lot, our Raymond, and better than some.'

I learned many years later to regard such Parent 'messages' as potent and positive 'scripting' which would set the recipient on course for a successful career. My own messages were much more confused and it took me years of determined effort to unravel them and find a clear direction. Raymond, however, knew from the age of five where he was going. When his mother collected him from the Infants' School at the bottom of Thompson Street after his first day there, he told her on the way home, 'Mum, I'm going to be a teacher.' And he was. He was a clever lad, got a good School Certificate and went into the Sixth Form at Salt's to pass the Higher School Certificate before his call-up papers arrived and he was drafted into the Royal Navy. On release, after service in India, and being what my father called a 'top notcher', he got a place at St John's College, Cambridge, from which graduated in due course and followed it up with a Teaching Certificate. He went on to become Head of English in a Boys Grammar School in Poulton, Lancashire. I have no doubt he could have become a headmaster but he was in two minds about abandoning the classroom for the demands of administration and so continued teaching until the school became co-educational and changed its character, when he settled for early retirement, gardening, golf and conducting a local choir.

There were, of course, stations along the way for Raymond as there were for me, but he did not set off to go 'God alone knows where', as I did. In fact, he eventually decided, to my considerable distress, to believe that there is no God, anyway, and no direction or purpose in life other than what one worked out for oneself. I do not know at what stage in life I began to believe that I was surely going somewhere; and even if I didn't know where it was, God did.

* * *

I was thirteen years old when Patch joined the family, in consequence of a manipulative, heart-rending letter I wrote to my father. My Aunts Edith and Emmy, who worked at the family shop in Titus Street (which supplied the nearby Salt Schools with iced buns to be bought and eaten at 'break') had some responsibility for this. The letter (which I still have, my mother having preserved it) reads, 'Dear miserable Dad, You wouldn't let me have a kitten, then you wouldn't let me have a budgie and now you won't let me have a dog. I have never been more unhappy. With love from your miserable son, David.' When my father read it he wept! He shed tears quite readily in certain circumstances when most men would have preferred to keep a stiff upper lip and not let their feelings be revealed. It was, I suspect, his disposition to do this that gave me permission to do the same. It is, and always has been, a confounded nuisance and a source of great embarrassment to me, but every counsellor and trainer with whom I have shared the problem has envied me my emotional freedom! So I was lumbered with the problem until well into my seventies, when it got worse as a feature of motor neurone disease. I was then prescribed fluoxetine, better known as Prozack, the antidepressant 'happy pill'. Thereafter I could sit through *Songs of Praise* without shedding a tear!

Anyway, I got my dog. She was about six months old, a rough haired terrier of doubtful parentage. She had a pointed nose and a brown face but was otherwise mostly white. However, she was already named Patch because of a black patch on her back. She became my constant companion. When I think of Patch now, and my very close relationship with her, I recall also the mothers of delinquent children on whom I reported, as a probation officer, to the Juvenile Court. They would confess their adolescent sons' burglaries, thefts and other delinquencies and then add, to give proper balance to the report, 'but he's very fond of animals'! I never wound up in Juvenile Court as a child but I sometimes wonder whether it was by good luck rather than good behaviour!

It was shortly after we got Patch that my Granny – my mother's mother – died. She was just eighty five and the three 'girls' who still lived at home wondered what to buy her for a birthday present. They decided that two pairs of Chilproof combinations would be very acceptable for an old lady. This one-piece garment, popular at the time for both old people and children (in fact Betty and I both recall having worn 'comms' when we were kids) consisted of a vest-like top with short sleeves and rubber buttons from the neck down to the waist. Below that was attached the pants in the same warm material – short ones for kids but long ones for the elderly – to ensure winter warmth in the days before universal central heating. The pants part was divided down the middle at the back, to facilitate going to the lav, and the split could be fastened with another rubber button. When it was Granny's birthday my Auntie Edith, who had a great sense of fun, stuffed the two pairs of comms with screwed up newspapers so that they almost stood up like headless people. When these were 'walked' into the room to be presented to Granny she laughed so much she could not stop laughing. At eighty five she was much too frail for such unstoppable hilarity and they had a job to get her to bed. The next morning when they took her a cup of tea, they could not wake her up. She had literally died of laughing!

* * *

I have often wondered what course my life might have taken had I been programmed with the kind of positive, life-enhancing, self-esteem promoting messages that my friend Raymond had. Mixed with the many non-verbal messages assuring me of love and security that I received, I also picked up, intuitively as swell as verbally, messages that seemed to be almost the opposite of Raymond's. 'Don't get too big for your boots,' my father would say on the rare occasions when I achieved something and was inclined to be a bit proud of myself. Or, 'Nay, lad, use your common sense! University's only for t'top notchers.' Raymond, in stark contrast to me, he regarded as a top notcher, at least potentially. So when my time came to take the School Certificate exams I failed – just as I had failed the County Minor at the age of eleven. I expected to fail, so I failed! Only top notchers passed, I had come to believe, because only they expected to. As it happened Betty failed as well, which, I must confess, was something of a relief. But Betty's headmaster (she went to a different school) suggested she take the exam again in October, when it was held at Leeds University for external students. So I decided to do the same thing. We both swotted like mad and re-sat the exam. On the day the results came out, the postman rang the bell of our Bromley Road house early that morning and my father ran downstairs in his pyjamas to sign for a registered envelope. It was my School Certificate. I had passed with Credits in English Language, Germans, Physics and Art and Passes in History and Geography. Far from spectacular! Betty passed as well; in fact she did better than me and got a Distinction in English Literature.

Raymond, a year or so earlier, had seemed to get Distinctions in practically everything. But my father was so thrilled that I had had passed at all, that he rushed into my bedroom with the good news, leaned over the bed and kissed me! I was close on seventeen and not accustomed, even as a youngster, to being kissed by my dad. But that kiss is one I have never forgotten and I treasure the memory of it. But what would have happened – or, more particularly, what would not have happened – to the course of my life, if I had not taken the exam again and passed it?

Another close friend at this adolescent stage was Kenneth Wilcockson. He went to Belle Vue Grammar School in Bradford and, academically, was streets ahead of me. He too seemed to get Distinctions in everything. But we were good friends and, with Kenneth, I always seemed to be the leader. Nevertheless, when he was called up into the Navy, Kenneth was soon commissioned. Sadly, we lost touch but I heard not long ago that he had died and the notice in the *Yorkshire Post* had said he was an admiral. Another top notcher!

The one spectacular event during my last year at school was again on the School Sports Day. I was a 'possible' for the Victor Ludorum, though everyone expected that Arthur Dolphin would win it. Arthur became well known as a mountaineer and an associate of Chris Bonnington. Sadly, he died young in a fall on Mont Blanc. At school, Arthur was a year or two ahead of me and excelled at anything athletic. However, I had already won the 100 yards and the 220 yards and got placed in some other events so when the time came for The Mile at the end of the day I was already a serious contender but neither I nor anyone else expected that I might win. I got off to a good start and made a steady pace for the first three laps, but as we went into the fourth and final lap I realised that I had quite a lot of energy in reserve. Dolphin, of course, was in the lead, and several boys were ahead of me. I knew I could overtake most of them to ensure another House point by being in the first ten so I saved my final sprint for the last half lap and then shot ahead, passing others including Longbottom, who was another contender, until I was only a couple of yards behind Dolphin. He was aware of my pounding feet and I remember him glancing over his shoulder to see who this upstart was! I gave it everything I'd got. I could do it, I could win. I could!

But I didn't. Not quite. With the spectators, parents, boys, staff and quite a few girls who came to watch, all roaring their encouragement, I came in only a split second behind the great Arthur Dolphin. I collapsed at the feet of history master John Stanley Mathers, gasping painfully and my heart thumping like a pile driver.

Nearly, but not quite! That was me. I had no expectation of winning, even though I clearly had the ability.

* * *

School Speech Day was an important event, held at the Victoria Hall, which was immediately opposite the school in Victoria Road. The boys all arrived in time for a 'bun fight' in which we were all treated to free iced buns from my late Granny Garnham's shop in Titus Street. Later, when parents had arrived and filled the auditorium, a school play was presented (such as the one that had inspired me at the age of ten to write 'Robbery at Buckingham Palace'), the boys sang things like Upidee-I-dar, the headmaster, Mr Parkin (known to us, of course as Piggy), resplendent in gown and academic hood, made a speech extolling the school's academic and sporting achievements during the course of the year and, finally, certificates and prizes were distributed. The really bright boys went away bearing piles of learned-looking books and the ones who had simply 'made it' received their School Certificates or, in the case of the 'top notchers', their Higher School Certificates. I was ordered to line up back stage with the rest of my class and wondered just what would happen, as I had already received my School Certificate through the post. Names were announced in alphabetical order and each boy walked onto the stage to receive his certificate from the Chairman of the Board of Governors. But when it came to the Ms my name was not called. I was alarmed and disappointed. But finally, when everyone else had been called, I heard the headmaster calling 'Midgley'. As I walked onto the stage, before an audience of several hundreds, I heard myself being identified as 'the most improved boy in the class'. The Chairman of the Governors shook my hand warmly, congratulated me on a splendid effort and handed me a 'pretend' roll of white paper with nothing on it! I was utterly bewildered and had no idea why the audience should be applauding me. Neither, I suppose, had they, since nothing was said about my having passed the exam at the second attempt. Whatever the headmaster's intention might have been I was embarrassed and humiliated. How can a boy be identified 'the most improved' without the implication that he was the most in need of improvement! This experience of what was, for me, public humiliation, particularly when I felt that I well deserved proper recognition, was etched not only onto my memory but also, I now know, into the very neurones my brain was made of!

Unfortunately, my School Certificate was not good enough for matriculation; that would have required at least five Credits in the correct groups of subjects. One more in any subject and I would have made it and been eligible for entrance to one of the Northern Universities. Nearly but not quite – again!

My father spoke to an old mate who worked as clerk in the Surveyor's Department of Baildon Urban District Council. They needed a junior clerk and I got the job. The paid me twenty-five shillings a week of which, I think, I received nineteen and sixpence after deductions, all of which I gave to my mother. She gave me five shillings back for pocket money.

I did not stop long at the Baildon surveyor's office. A vacancy occurred for a junior clerk in the Education Department at Shipley Town Hall, which was more convenient and more interesting and I applied successfully for that. I stayed there until my call-up papers arrived.

Grange in Borrowdale, the 'heavenly place' to which David and Philip were briefly evacuated at the outbreak of war

Betty and David on a joint family holiday, Saltburn, 1937

Betty and David's wedding, 1952, with Margaret Town (Maid of Honour) and Raymond Fielding (Best Man); Allan Heap behind.

Golden Wedding 2002

In our Prime

Close friends for over fifty years
David in wheel chair (2003) with Raymond (far left), Betty, Chris Fielding, Ray Ogden, Doreen and
Philip Waterhouse. (Sue Ogden is behind the camera)

2

ADVENTURES OF A NOBODY

The circumstances of my childhood and adolescence had combined to convince me that I was a Nobody living in world of fantasy, for whom the only reasonable future lay in aspirations to be a novelist who would capitalise on his creative imagination by writing spy stories like Bernard Newman, my favourite writer at the time. So I responded to National Service with every expectation that that the future would be no more promising than the past. As an Air Cadet and a member of the RAF Volunteer Reserve I had, in fact, been selected to train for air crew, but this exciting prospect was scuppered by the success of the Allied advance in Germany, the expectation that the war would soon be over, that not many air crew would now be required and if I was still keen I would have to wait at least two years. Eager to don a uniform of some sort before it was too late, I seized the tempting opportunity to volunteer for the army with the promise that I could go into the corps or regiment of my choice. Baloney! I had opted for the Tank Corps, for no better reason than that I fancied myself in one of their little black berets. But when my call-up papers arrived I was despatched with a rail warrant to the DCLI Barracks in Bodmin, Cornwall on February 1st, 1945.

Trains being somewhat chaotic, I missed my connection in Bristol, was directed by the RTO to Plymouth and spent a sleepless night there in a hostel with a naked bulb blazing and a bearded sailor snoring loudly on the top bunk across from mine. Even so, I ate a good breakfast next morning and was put on a train for Bodmin. On the train I fell asleep from sheer exhaustion and slept soundly right through the stop at Bodmin. I woke up in a panic as the train was pulling into Lostwithiel, a few miles further on. There was a bus, someone said, that would drop me off at the very gates of the barracks. But I was sick with apprehension at being late on my very first day in the army, fantasised dire consequences and emptied my breakfast between my legs just as the bus was pulling up at the dreaded place. 'Oh, hell' exclaimed the blonde clippie and called for newspapers to clean up my mess. I got out of the bus with a confusion of feelings, of embarrassment and fear, exacerbated by the sight of the forbidding entrance to the barracks right across the road. It seemed to my fevered imagination like the Castle of Doom, complete with portcullis and, no doubt, with dungeons as well!

But the sergeant on duty at the gate was a thoroughly nice chap who welcomed me and told me not to worry about reporting late. In fact, he said, there were several others still to turn up. He directed me round the parade ground to Hut C where I was greeted by a roomful of other ex-RAF Volunteers types. Apparently we made up the whole intake.

Six weeks basic training is not much to equip an eighteen year old to fight a war but we did square bashing and route marches, learned to fire a Lee Enfield rifle and to use the nine inch bayonet on the end of it, shouting 'Kill, kill kill!' as we plunged it into a dangling sack full of straw. And we were interviewed at length, by a variety of officers and NCOs, to establish where we would be most useful to the army. To my delight and astonishment, I was recommended for the Intelligence Corps and was sent off to the War Office for further interviews whilst German V2 rockets were exploding all around. One interview was by an I Corps major who, somebody told us, spoke forty one languages fluently! It was probably an exaggeration but he tested me on my schoolboy German and although my conversational skills were severely limited, I was accepted nevertheless.

Why? What was going on? My train had suddenly started going in an entirely new direction. Possibly my School Certificate, though third rate and obtained only at the second attempt, had something to do with it. But there must have been more. What was it about me that the army could identify as somehow rather special, despite my lack of any significant achievement during my first eighteen years? Was there a 'guiding hand' at work?

At the age of eighteen I doubt if I had seriously considered such a possibility. God was, if anything, only a vague notion at the back of my mind, no matter what I had learned in Sunday School, and even taught others. I have no recollection of being confirmed – or 'coming into membership', as Methodists usually say – but Betty, now my wife, assures me that we were all 'done' together when we were about sixteen! Anyway, at Bodmin, with the encouragement of a lad called Peacock who said he might become an Anglican priest, I joined the padre's confirmation class and was eventually confirmed by the Bishop of Truro in the church hut on the 6th of March. Anyway, I was at least now qualified for Church Parade, which was preferable to the alternative of spud bashing in the cookhouse!

Six weeks at Bodmin was followed by a couple of months in Rhosneiger,

Anglesey, for further training and then on to the Intelligence Corps Depot, then at Wentworth Woodhouse, near Rotherham, the beautiful Palladian mansion of Earl Fitzwilliam. Only the officers lived in the house itself, however; the rest of us were accommodated in the stable block, which had been converted into barrack rooms. But we were free to use the 'cube room' – the vast entrance hall to the mansion, which was used for concerts. It housed two grand pianos, a Bechstein and a Blüthner, on which my friend Jared Armstrong and I occasionally entertained our educated colleagues with duets as well as solos. Needless to say, I played my party piece, the *Warsaw Concerto*, all through from memory!

At Wentworth, we all did training on motorcycles and 15 cwt trucks. By this time the war was over, both in Europe and in the Far East, so we would be in an army of occupation committed to what was, effectively, oversight of local government, with special attention to matters of security. So we were despatched from Wentworth to the School of Military Intelligence, then located at Smedley's Hydro in Matlock, Derbyshire. The three weeks course there was aimed at giving us a general background understanding of intelligence work. We were, we were told, the military wing of MI5, which is concerned with security and counter-intelligence. We had no expectation of doing anything undercover although there was always the possibility that we might be seconded for such work if we were particularly well qualified, especially if fluent in some foreign language. I was not, of course, but I was proud actually to be a student at the School of Military Intelligence and my youthful imagination was fuelled by this low key introduction to 'the real thing', in addition to the exciting fiction of Bernard Newman.

When we got back to the Intelligence Corps Depot at Wentworth an ATS girlfriend called Joan, who worked in the Docs Office, said she had had a peep at my documents and had seen that I was recommended for a commission. I was delighted, of course, but heard the news with mixed feelings because being even a private in the Intelligence Corps seemed more prestigious than having a commission in anything else. Anyway, that was not to happen yet. I learned I was to go to India, which was exciting; and also that I would be promoted to Lance Corporal and put in charge of a draft of ten men. So maybe my proposed status was being tested out. It was all actually happening – for real. And I was only nineteen!

A spell of embarkation leave gave me an opportunity to brag about my achievements and gave my father an opportunity to remind me that I was still a Nobody and should not get too big for my boots. I also had chance to show off to Betty in the hope that she would be impressed by what the army thought of me. But Betty was not impressed with any kind of showing off or with anything the least bit pretentious; in any event, she was still interested in my friend Kenneth Wilcockson – another 'top notcher' according to my perceptive father. He was in the Navy and destined to become, in due course, a Judge Advocate. So I made no progress but we did correspond a bit whilst I was abroad.

India was an adventure indeed and deserves a whole chapter, or even a book, to itself! But this is not that book. However, on arrival at the Intelligence Corps Depot in Karachi I was promoted to Corporal and all the Privates in my draft became Lance Corporals. That was the way of things in the I. Corps. When I took up my first appointment with 572 Field Security Section in Ranchi, Bihar – five days train journey away at the other side of the sub-continent – I became a sergeant. And six months later, when I was posted to the North West Frontier Province in charge of a small security detachment in Razmak, on the boarder of Afghanistan, I became a Staff Sergeant. After another few months I was sent off to a War Office Selection Board at Dehra Duhn, a beautiful hill station in the foothills of the Himalayas. This was a four days event at the Indian Army Staff College – the Indian version of Sandhurst – where we were all carefully appraised for fitness, personality, powers of leadership, sociability and the ability to speak in public. Again I passed. I was on my way 'up' and enjoying it enormously. So back to Karachi I came to await shipment back to England, again in charge of the draft. On the face of it, my Indian adventure made no significant contribution to my spiritual growth though it must have done something for my self esteem. There was, of course, the opportunity to learn something at first hand about Hinduism and Islam and I have since regretted that I took no advantage of it. At that stage I was not yet tuned in to it.

Disembarkation leave was another chance to woo Betty but there was still no sign of romance, although we were still good friends and went around with the same crowd from church, except those who were still in the forces. And then to Mons Barracks, the Officer Cadet Training School at Aldershot for those who were unsuitable candidates for Sandhurst. Amongst them, in my squad, was Billy Cotton Junior, later to become Head of BBC Light Entertainments. I played the *Warsaw Concerto* for him and other showy pieces but it got me nowhere! At the end of the two month course we had a passing out ball for which a section of the Billy Cotton Band came to play for us. The newly commissioned officers all invited their sisters or their fiancées but I could not yet have invited Betty.

However, there was Enid. Mons Barracks stood at the other side of the road, more or less opposite to Oudenarde Barracks, the new location of the Intelligence Corps Depot, following Wentworth Woodhouse. Private Enid Cobb of the ATS came on stage quite briefly in the story of my life, changed the points on my rail track and sent me off to God alone knew where – a destination I might not otherwise have reached. We met at the bus stop which served both our barracks and she, noticing my white cadet flashes and my Intelligence Corps badges, opened up a conversation. Enid was small with dark wavy hair, bright grey eyes and rosy cheeks. She was not exactly slim, neither was she unduly overweight. She was cuddly. After that first meeting we went out together a few times to the cinema and once to a little café I had discovered just up the road in Farnborough village where we had Welsh rarebit on toast, tea and cakes. Parting from her late at night I would give her a cautious cuddle and gently brush my lips against her rosy cheek, but that's as far as it went. She had told me over our Welsh rarebit that she was going to marry a Methodist minister. Perhaps I had already revealed my own Methodist antecedents and she judged me safe, honourable and trustworthy!

Enid, as it happened (by another lucky chance, if you like) was secretary to Major Dunphy, the Mobilisation Officer for the Intelligence Corp. She told me in confidence that a vacancy had occurred for an I Corps officer and the boss had asked her, 'Do you know either of these chaps across at Mons – Humphreys and Midgley?' John Humphreys, also an I Corps man, was a friend of mine. She had said she knew us both slightly and he had asked her, 'Which one would be the best?' 'Midgley', said Enid. So, thanks to Enid, I was commissioned into the Intelligence Corps.

Enid, therefore, accompanied me to the Passing Out Ball. She looked radiantly beautiful in a blue ball gown trimmed with lace and silver shoes with peep toes. I would have preferred to have Betty on my arm but our trains had just a little further yet to travel down the line before we were both on the same track. Meanwhile, my train and Enid's went their separate ways. I have neither seen nor heard of her since. I sometimes wonder whether she did marry her Methodist minister.

* * *

Whilst on leave I was called again to the War Office in London to be seen by an I Corps major in a smart grey civilian suit, who told me I was going to be Officer in Charge of the Port Security Section, based at Harwich Transit Camp. 'There's a young chap called Ainley there at the moment,' he told me. 'But he's due for discharge. He'll stay a few days to show you the ropes. After that I'm sure you'll cope.'

I asked what the job entailed.

'Two jobs really,' he said. 'Port Security Officer for Hawrich and Field Security for East Anglian District.'

The Section, he told me, included a warrant officer and about twenty NCOs, including a Polish sergeant who could speak several languages and would be useful for interrogating European Voluntary Workers who were arriving by the boatload and had to be security vetted. Also I was responsible for checking all members of the British Army of the Rhine, regardless of rank, as they came home to the UK on leave or for discharge. If any special interrogating needed doing I could call on Lt Colonel A.P. Scotland, at the London Cage in Kensington. He was Chief Interrogator for the Nüremberg War Crimes trials. I would be promoted to Acting Lieutenant on arrival but Capt Davison, G3(I) at Colchester, was my immediate superior and he might suggest a third pip to give me a bit of extra standing.

I emerged in a daze. I had been commissioned less than a fortnight and was a captain already! Well, soon might be. I turned left up Whitehall, got saluted by the mounted guardsmen at the end of Horse Guards Parade, and took refuge in Lyons Corner House at Charing Cross, ordering a modest Welsh Rarebit on toast and a pot of tea.

A week or so later Shaun Ainley, who was due for discharge, met me in at Harwich. I noticed with a flicker of disappointment that he too was a lieutenant, not a captain. He had the Section truck waiting in the station forecourt and drove me straight to the Port Security Office in the transit camp. He introduced me to the members of the Section, and to Major Hanson, who was the camp commandant, and then we went to the officers' mess for dinner. For a few days we watched the Section at work at Parkeston Quay and on the train to Liverpool Street, and he briefed me about their individual styles and idiosyncrasies. They were a good lot of lads, he assured me, and should present no problems. I asked him about the Field Security job and he shrugged. 'Nothing much really,' he said. 'Except the POWs who keep escaping. You will be notified of any who go missing and again when they're picked up, as they always are.'

I asked Shaun, 'What's the point in escaping when they are due for repatriation anyway?'

He said, 'It's those who live in the Russian Zone. God help them if they get sent back there. So they hope to get to West Germany where 'we'll treat them very kindly as we would a valued friend', like Coward said.'

Shaun left at the weekend to claim his discharge and take up a place at Reading University.

I was on my own. My CSM was a man called Crowther, who I had known in Karachi. He was almost old enough to be my father and had once put me on a charge for going out of bounds. I would have welcomed his 'nurture', as I later came to know it, but he was respectfully detached and had nothing of that sort to offer.

After a few days I went over to Colchester to pay my respects to Capt Davison, my immediate boss at District HQ.

'Start as you mean to go on,' he advised me. 'You're pretty young to be left on your own with that lot, so you need to let them know who's boss, otherwise they'll run rings round you. I suggest you get them all out on parade and make a speech to the effect that you expect them to look and behave like proper soldiers. And have a kit inspection. Make sure they have everything right down to the housewife and bollock anyone who's neglected to darn holes in his socks. OK?'

'OK,' I grinned, relishing the prospect of being thoroughly in charge and dreading that I would not really be able to pull it off. This was simply not me. It would be easy enough for chaps educated at Uppingham and Charterhouse and brought up in homes where they had butlers and cooks and housemaids and the like. But I was not like that. I was a Nobody.

As I was about to leave, Capt Davison asked me 'Would you like another pip? Just Local, of course? Give you a bit of extra standing.'

This too, like deciding to re-sit my School Certificate, might have been a critical decision that would affect the way my train went. I reflected briefly, excited by the prospect of the status I had looked forward to, but scared of the caustic comments of fellow officers in the mess who had achieved such a rank by years of devoted service. So I said, 'Can I leave it for the moment?'

'As you like. Let me know if you change your mind. There are quite a lot of big wigs coming over from Germany to be vetted by you.'

To familiarise myself with what the Section did I arranged a birth on the troopship to the Hook of Holland back to see what happened on the other side of the North Sea. I could have gone through to Hamburg and met up with my Field Security colleagues there but I did not. There was a scared Child inside me who was play-acting the role of Officer-in-Charge and was reluctant to push it too far for fear of exposure. At the Dutch port I watched a hoard of pathetic-looking European Voluntary Workers queuing to have their documents examined. They were a miscellaneous bunch of humanity, many dressed almost in rags, others in suits and good overcoats, but many of them carrying their few belongings in a brown paper parcel. Jan Komerowski, the Polish sergeant attached to the Section as interpreter, told me that a lot of them were professional people, lawyers, doctors, dentists and the like, whose skills and qualifications might not equip them to follow their callings in Britain, at least not until they had retrained and, perhaps, learned to speak English fluently. They would probably be destined in the immediate future to mind machinery in the textile mills of Bradford and other places.

In the officers' mess at the Hook of Holland a Dutch artist was drawing cartoon portraits. I had mine done and the artist drew me at the piano, having heard me playing earlier. Noting the slightly different green of the second pip on my battledress jacket, he jokily anticipated a third and drew it descending towards my shoulder on a parachute!

As I mentioned earlier, I was notified every time a prisoner of war went missing. There was nothing I was required to do about it but, for interest, I and a couple of my sergeants got a large scale map and plotted where the prisoners escaped from and where they were re-captured. We joined these points with pencil lines and found that they all pointed towards East Anglia. I sent off Sergeants Watson and Young to investigate and they found that there was a lively trade in timber from Germany that had resumed immediately the war had come to an end. The little timber ships looked like a convenient way of crossing the North Sea for any escapee who was enterprising enough to stow away and avoid being repatriated to the Russian Zone. They never caught anyone actually doing it but the opportunity was there, especially if they could obtain forged documents. Where might they obtain such things? We went back to our map and found that there was a distinct movement of escapees in the direction of Peterborough, even when they had been picked up further east. Tony Young and I went to Peterborough and shared our information with the police who quickly suspected a butcher by the name of Henry King – originally Heinrich König – who had anglicised his name on being granted British citizenship many years before war broke out. Tony and I would have liked to be involved in the next move but the police were adamant that we should leave it to them. For some reason the butcher was not arrested, even though he was a key part of the proposed escape route, but the route was closed nevertheless.

The most memorable case I had to deal with as an intelligence officer concerned a German prison of war called Fritz Kader, though I never actually met the man. But, in connection with him, I did meet Lieutenant Colonel A.P. Scotland, a former spy, which was memorable indeed. Most prisoners enjoyed a good deal of freedom once the war was over, but their letters were censored and anything that looked a bit suspicious was sent to me. A letter to Kader from a Miss Connie Anderson in Cambridge was intercepted because it contained a puzzling reference to Jonathan Cape, the London publishers, suggesting the possibility of employment for Kader. I had the letter copied by Paterson, the Section clerk who was on loan to us from the RASC, let it go forward to Kader and alerted the camp censor to watch out for anything further. It was not long before I received another letter addressed to Kader from Miss Anderson and enclosing a letter to herself on Jonathan Cape notepaper. The publishers were evidently offering him a job with them if he could arrange for release in this country. Since this was not an option I wondered what exactly was going on. A phone call to the publisher quickly established that they knew nothing about this man and had written no such letter to Miss Anderson.

Captain Davison at Colchester suggested I have Kader interrogated at the London Cage, the Prisoner of War Interrogation Centre in Kensington Palace Gardens. Lieutenant Colonel A.P. Scotland, who was in charge of this facility was, so far as I was aware, the only officer of such high rank in the Intelligence Corps. I had heard of him because only about twelve months earlier his name had been featured in just about every newspaper throughout the world as the British master spy who had served as a member of the German General Staff! The story broke during the trial in Venice in February, 1947 of Albert Kesselring, former supreme commander of German troops in Italy on charges of war crimes against the Italian people. Prosecuting Counsel, Colonel Richard Halse, had asked Colonel Scotland, under oath, whether his intimate knowledge of the German army was due to his having been a member of it. After a very brief hesitation he gave the briefest possible answer. 'Yes.' Halse then asked, 'Was information on the organisation of the German army your function during the war?' Again he answered 'Yes'. And immediately, the press were onto it!

In fact, Colonel Scotland was an Englishman who who had left school at fourteen, worked for a year or two for Sainsbury's in London and then went to South Africa in search of adventure in the Boar War. He arrived too late to get involved but found work, on the strength of his experience in groceries and provisions with Sainsbury's, representing South African Terriitories, Ltd., a firm that supplied the German troops in German West Africa. The work required him to learn German from scratch and over the years he amassed a very detailed and intimate knowledge of the language, the German people and, in particular, the

German army. To facilitate his work he was actually recruited into the German army and was given officer status. Following the trial of Kesselring he became the subject of a popular film called *The Spy with Two Heads*, since the Germans had thought he was spying for them, and his role was played by Jack Hawkings. But this was a complete fiction so far as his function in World War Two was concerned, though he had in fact done espionage work in World War One and had actually talked with Hitler in the 1930s! So he was an intelligence officer of great consequence and it was a privilege to meet him.

I telephoned Colonel Scotland at The London Cage and arranged for Kader to be transferred there and interrogated. The colonel was most interested, especially in view of the 'Peterborough Connection', about which I also told him. 'After I've seen Kader,' he said, 'you'd better come up here and we'll have a talk about it.'

When I arrived the Colonel greeted me warmly. Anyone one less like Fleming's James Bond is difficult to imagine. He was rather thick set and an unassuming man with horn rimmed glasses. He was probably in his late fifties and wore on his service dress Intelligence Corps badges exactly like mine. This man, who had once conversed with Hitler, now conversed with me!

'Come in, David,' he said cordially, in a manner I could only call paternal.

I welcomed this and earnestly wished C.S.M. Crowther had treated me with such fatherly care and interest when I first took over at Harwich. But, then who would imagine a young intelligence officer could possibly cherish a secret wish to be parented! I sat across the big six foot by four table that served as the colonel's desk in his room on the first floor, and a middle aged lady, who might well have been Miss Moneypenny, brought in tea as he asked me about my work at Harwich. I gave him a more detailed account of closing the POWs' escape route. I thought he would laugh but he did not.

'We too were notified of all these escapes but we didn't bother to plot them on a map as you did. So, well done!'

'Why would you want them, Sir?'

'War crimes, 'he answered.

'Some of Hitler's most dangerous and despicable thugs have sat on that chair, David, where you are sitting now. Nicholas von Folkenhorst, chief of German forces in Norway, for example. He was responsible for the murder of over thirty British soldiers captured in Norway when their glider crash-landed in appalling weather conditions on a mission to destroy a heavy water plant connected with Germany's atomic weapons development. And Kesselring, poor fellow, who managed to convince the court in Venice that he had more authority than was really his! And others, like the murderers of those RAF officers who escaped from Stalag Luft 3. There is still a great deal of sickening evil to be exposed and there could be many war criminals still held in our prison camps who hope to get home without too many questions being asked. We can't be too careful. So well done, David'

'I don't think any actually got away,' I said with a touch of pride.

'Probably not. But in the circumstances it might have been kinder to let them escape. I wouldn't want to send even a German back to the Russian Zone if it could be avoided.'

I did not like the way the conversation was going so I asked, 'What about Kader?'

'Ha! Fritz Kader! Nothing much, I'm afraid. We haven't uncovered anything sinister. He met a young woman who worked in a Cambridge bookshop and had contacts with publishers. He had worked for a German publisher before the war and could probably have been useful as a translator and maybe helped with marketing in Germany. This young lady persuaded a printer friend to print some notepaper like Jonathan Cape's. What she paid him for the service I dread to think! Anyway, she herself wrote the letter offering Kader a job, addressed it to herself and she put him up to the idea of escaping . . . well, just disappearing. She posted it in London and Kader got quite excited about the idea. When I saw him a couple of days ago he was quite distressed to discover we'd rumbled it. Are you doing a report about all this?'

'Yes, I shall have to report to Major Berry.'

'What . . . Julian?'

'Yes, Sir. Everything goes to him.'

'And he gets all the credit! Rubbish! You've done the work so you should get the credit. Send it out over your own name. Confidential, of course. MI5, MI6, SIB, Scotland Yard, Naval Intelligence . . . Quite a few need to know. I'll give you a list. Send Julian one, of course. And me . . .'

Miss Moneypenny knocked and came in to announce another visitor and Colonel Scotland graciously showed me to the door, insisting that I ring him any time I needed help. Unfortunately I was due for discharge from the army in a couple of weeks so I had no further contact with 'the master spy', as the press called him.

Back at Harwich I wrote my Confidential Report, Paterson typed it onto wax skins, I signed it with the stylus and it was posted off to the impressive list of agencies Colonel Scotland had suggested. I only just had time to complete this final achievement of my career in Intelligence before I developed a heavy dose of 'flu. I was in bed in the camp hospital when Captain Reg Sessons arrived to take over from me as Officer in Charge. Poor chap! I think the first telephone call he received was from Major Julian Berry, incensed because he had received my report with such a distribution list attached to it. 'Who the hell does Midgley think he is!'

Reg fielded it skilfully and told him I had been acting under Colonel Scotland's instructions. I recovered from my dose of 'flu, packed my things, said Goodbye to the Section and to my fellow officers and boarded a train for home. I have often wondered whether, had I had to deal with Major Berry myself, I might have ended my army career being court marshalled for gross presumptuousness!

The Midgley family on David's embarkation leave, February 1946. (Arthur, Philip, David, Agnes and Patch.

Pezu Pass from India to Afghanistan, 1946; the hostile terrain in which David had intelligence responsibilities.

David and Pathan tribesmen, near Razmak, Northwest Frontier Province, 1946.

David and Shaun Ainley, Harwich Transit Camp, 1947

The Port Security Section, Harwich, at a Christmas party in 1947

Lieut. Colonel A.P. Scotland,
'The Spy with Two Heads' and Commanding
Officer of the War Crimes Investigation Unit.

The London Cage,
HQ of the War Crimes Investigation Unit,
in Kensington Palace Gardens.

3

DOWN TO EARTH

On reflection, my discharge from the army was the best opportunity I should ever have to go to university and I have regretted ever since that I did not take advantage of the government grant to ex service personnel to cover all expenses. Part of my reluctance was due, I think, to the fact that I had no considered idea of what I wanted to read if I got there, not to mention a deep seated fear that at the end of the course I might fail the exams! I had no career prospects in mind, no goal, no ambition. Except to be a writer.

So I came home to the clerical job in the Shipley Education Office that I had left when my call-up papers had arrived. I think they were obliged by law to re-employ me. Fortunately Betty was still around and our mutual friend Kenneth Wilcockson, who had had a brief romance with her earlier, was now out of the picture, pursuing a professional career in the Royal Navy. We all lost touch entirely.

I began my courtship during demobilization leave by taking Betty out to dinner one night at the Bankfield Hotel, our favourite local venue for important occasions. We had chicken – which was very up-market in those times of post-war austerity. We travelled to and from the hotel by bus because only the very well-to-do had cars. And later, walking her home from the bus stop, I tentatively told her told her that I rather fancied her. She was evidently astonished and responded as if such a thought had never crossed her mind! In all probability it hadn't. Anyway she did not reject my initiative and at the garden gate of 22, Parkwood Road we kissed with cautious passion. I was wearing my service dress and looked very handsome so perhaps that helped.

After a couple of months I began to look around for a job which was more exciting and fulfilling than the Education Office and was taken on by the Bradford office of The Polytechnic Touring Association. The travel industry suited me very well and I was soon a valued employee. I went on from strength to strength and was soon Assistant Manager. In the summer of 1950 I was entrusted with leading a party of Bradford holiday makers on a week's tour to Paris. I had never before set foot in Paris but poured over maps of the city for weeks before the trip and memorised all the main features so that I was able to impress my clients with my knowledge of the place. Only Betty, who also joined the party, knew the truth. The following year I took parties out to Switzerland and to the Italian Lakes but Betty did not accompany us. We had a holiday on our own at Morecambe and were trusted to behave ourselves at a time when self-control was expected – even assumed in good Methodists, such as we were! A decade was to pass before the liberation of the 1960s got under way.

In and amongst all this I was busy with my first novel, a family saga set in 18th century Yorkshire. Betty was an enthusiastic participant in this, helping me with the historical research as well as doing a lot of the typing. Our hope and expectation in those halcyon days was that in due course I would become a successful romantic novelist, selling film and foreign translation rights to ensure us a comfortable income and a status in the world. But I was also writing short stories. Most of my early efforts seem to have revealed a curious pre-occupation with death, even suicide, as did some of my later writing. But the story I eventually got published, whilst it did not have this feature, did reveal my profound sense of personal inferiority and expectation of failure. It was a first person story, only eleven hundred words long, which was not so much about death as about a feeling of not yet being fully alive! It was called *Maybe She Did* and was published in a popular pulp magazine called 'Answers'. They paid me ten guineas for it and Betty and I both thought I had arrived on the literary scene. But it was many years before I sold anything else. The truth is, I did not really fancy myself as a short story writer. I wanted to be a novelist – not just a run-of-the-mill novelist, but a writer of significance. So I carried on writing my novel and we pinned our hopes on it.

But one day I visited a fortune teller. I'm ashamed to admit this but do so because I believe it is relevant to my personal spiritual growth, my Life Script and what was to follow in the unknown future. The woman asked me what I wanted most in life. When I told her I wanted to be a novelist she gazed into her crystal ball and informed me, without beating about the bush, that I would never make it! I would do better to invest my energies in some other enterprise. As it turned out, she was right. Ignoring her advice, I wrote three novels, all of them publishable, I'm quite sure, but none was published! Whether this crystal gazer actually saw into my future or whether my failure as a novelist was in the nature of self-fulfilling prophecy, is something I have wondered about from time to time. But one thing is certain: despite my success in the army, my self-esteem was incredibly low. I was troubled by a deeply entrenched expectation of failure and later, in studying psychology, I became aware of the tremendous power of suggestion and, more particularly, of the Life Script I learned about in transactional analysis.

* * *

Betty and I were officially engaged at Christmas, 1950. Both our families were happy to be united by our marriage, since they all knew each other anyway and some, like our parents, were quite close friends. But everyone must have had serious misgivings about how I was going to make out as a breadwinner. What 'prospects' did I have? Even Betty, in her more sober, less romantic, moments, must have wondered whether permanent attachment to me was really a very good idea! She was a very attractive girl – and still is after more than fifty years of marriage – and could certainly have attracted the affections of bachelors who were more eligible than I. Why, then, did she settle for me, the erstwhile spotty teenager she had known all her life and never 'fancied' at all?

That is one of the big mysteries of my life. One factor, I guess, is that Betty is, at heart, a very anxious person. She does not like taking risks and has no natural disposition towards adventure. So she would be ultra-cautious about getting too close to any attractive young man she met at a dance, having no idea what he might turn out to be or what kind of family he might have. But I was different. I was attractive to women, even without my posh uniform; and I had a gentle, affectionate nature and a kindly disposition. I was not the kind of fellow an adventuress would be attracted to; but for Betty I was, perhaps, just about right.

When I say that Betty is not a risk-taker that is not to imply that she would never risk anything at all (as she was later to prove), only that she would make major changes only after the most careful consideration in which 'common sense' was the ruling factor. I am, by nature, a bit less inhibited and her natural caution has often proved a valuable attribute. In many respects we are anything but alike in temperament and outlook. Betty is more extroverted than I am and loves people. Well, I love people too, of course, but I seem to have a particular preference for those who are 'sick' in some way and in need of a physician! It enhances my deficient self-esteem to have people come to me for help! Betty prefers people who are OK. If they turn out to have any faults she will be quick to identify them! Mine, too! Personally, I prefer to look for strengths rather than weaknesses. We are both committed, church-going Christians but my interest is in ideas and theology; she is mainly interested in the people. So temperamentally we are not alike. I think we probably compensate for each other – like two sides of the same coin.

Anyway, we got engaged and started planning and saving. We had very little to start with. I was earning eight pounds a week at The Polytechnic Touring Association (later to become 'Polytours' and, eventually, 'Lunn Poly); Betty was earning something less as clerk/secretary with a small Bingley firm making and exporting knitting wool. There was no way we could afford to buy a house or even raise the deposit; so we looked around, as did many of our contemporaries, for something to rent.

As it happened an old lady at our church had some property in Shipley and a small modern semi at 41, Moorhead Crescent became available just when we wanted it. We were able to rent this for only sixteen shillings and sixpence a week, which was a modest amount even then and considerably less than some of our friends were paying. We had furniture to buy and some we got for wedding presents but somehow we got launched on what turned out to be more than fifty glorious years.

But I still did not know what I was going to do for a career. The eight pounds a week I was earning at Polytours was not really enough to get married on so I got a better paid job as a canvasser in the Bradford office of a shipping and forwarding agent. They paid me nine pounds a week, with the possibility of more when I'd learned the job! It seemed quite a substantial increase at the time!

So, on that we got married. Our wedding was on Saturday, 8th March, 1952, at Saltaire Methodist Church – the original church which was sadly demolished in the early nineteen seventies – and so many people turned out for the occasion that there was a policeman on duty to control the traffic. We had a modest four days honeymoon in London and then came home to play houses for a few days before returning to work the following Monday

We rubbed along happily, enduring the sort of economies which were the common lot of most people at the time, especially in the years immediately following the war when there was still a shortage of everything, food and clothing were still rationed and most furniture, amongst others things for the home market, was branded 'utility' or 'seconds'. All the decent stuff went for export.

Not long after we were married my Auntie Annie, who was my father's unmarried sister, died of a burst stomach ulcer and only ten days later my unmarried cousin Ella, who lived with her, died of a stroke! After this traumatic double bereavement, their house at 16, Nabwood Drive, was left to my father and as soon as the affairs were settled he and

Mother moved into it. It was a modern semi-detached house that my mother had always loved and envied and it was conveniently only a few minutes walk from ours

* * *

My two years with the shipping and forwarding agent I count as the most arid period of my working life, though it was the most fruitful domestically and in other respects. I was busy writing and was also much pre-occupied with producing an amateur performance of Shakespeare's *Twelfth Night*, for which I also wrote the incidental music and song settings. But on the 30th September, 1953, our son Jonathan Paul was born and beside that joyful event everything else paled into insignificance. Nevertheless, it was overshadowed by my concern that I still had no proper career in mind and no confidence in my ability to provide both for him and for Betty, who had, of course, to give up her job. 'Education for all' was still a political pipe dream and certainly had not filtered through to the generation that influenced me. My brother Philip, on leaving school, had been 'put' into a grocer's shop, much as I was 'put' into a Local Government office. Both jobs were considered 'safe'. We both had to make our own way as best we could without any encouragement to become anything in particular.

In this rather depressing period I began to keep a diary in a pocket notebook. Originally, there were several volumes of it, full of misery and self-pity, and I later destroyed all but the one in which I had recorded Paul's birth. But life was always busy and fruitful and by this time I was sharing leadership of a Sunday afternoon fellowship group with Eric Scott, a Bradford wool merchant, who had a profound influence on my spiritual growth. Also I was still writing my first novel, later to be called *Not From the Stars*, and had a second novel brewing that eventually became *Man in a Blue Check Shirt*. Neither of them was ever published.

But something else was happening as well. Jim Shepherd, a friend from church, was training to be a Methodist Local Preacher and was interested in the possibility of becoming a probation officer – a job I knew little about at that stage. Encouraged by Jim I began to think about both these things. Betty and I would probably have made quite close friends with Jim and his wife Eirie had they stayed in Shipley but unfortunately they moved on. They can be numbered amongst several people who briefly came 'on stage' in our lives, spoke their lines and then 'exeunted'. Jim had, in fact, been scheduled to play Orsino in Twelfth Night, but had to drop out when he got a job in Cleckheaton and my brother Philip, now back from National Service, took the part instead.

* * *

Mentioning Philip reminds me to record a strange dream I had whilst he was in the Air Force. In the dream he came to the door of 41, Moorhead Crescent and when I answered his knock he was standing on the top step with my dog Patch on a leash. He had an injury to his head. But a few yards away he was standing also, in duplicate, at the open double gates to the drive. That was all. But the next day I visited 16, Nabwood Drive and found our parents quite distressed because they had had a telephone call to say Philip had had an accident on the way home for weekend leave. He was riding pillion on someone's motorcycle and they had come off the road and been pitched on to a grass verge. Philip was in hospital but suffering only from a bit of concussion. The odd thing about it, that made the dream worth recording, was that his eyesight was affected and he had double vision, as I seemed to have had in the dream. The condition continued for some years, I believe, when he looked out of his eye corner, but eventually it cleared up.

I count this dream and its curious fulfilment as one of several experiences I have had which some might call 'psychic'. Maybe they were. But I believe they also had a spiritual dimension, if by 'spiritual' we mean 'meaning and purpose' rather than something just vaguely paranormal. The dream seems, on reflection, to say something about my relationship with Philip which, at that time, was not particularly close, though we had always got on well together. Certainly I believe that this, together with my foolish visit to a fortune-teller, and other incidents I shall mention later, all contributed in some way to my spiritual growth – my understanding, that is, of what life is all about.

* * *

On Sunday, 29th November I made a long entry in my diary. Some of it reads: 'I've gone two weeks without smoking. At the end of it I feel no better financially, physically or morally. I don't feel proud of having stopped smoking. I feel damned ashamed that at 27 years of age I have achieved so little, am earning so little and have so little prospect of earning any more. I'm thoroughly ashamed because my impoverished circumstances make it necessary for me to give up the pleasure of smoking. Instead of feeling better I feel worse.'

After a church meeting about the play I had walked with Allan Heap, my cousin-by-marriage, who was playing Malvolio, to their home to collect Margaret, who was to be Paul's godmother, and was coming to see Betty about arrangements for the christening on Sunday. From their house we completed the journey by car. It was Allan's car, of course! I just had to get a job with wheels!

4

ON THE WAY

In order to get a job with wheels, and for no better reason, I became a salesman with Thomas Hedley's, a Newcastle subsidiary of the American giant Proctor & Gamble. I sold Fairy Soap, Tide, Daz, Oxydol and several other soaps and detergents, to small private grocers and corner shops, in the days before supermarkets drove most of them out of business. I could certainly act like a salesman and to begin with it looked as though I had found my forte and I might even be considered for early promotion to sales training or even management. But it did not last.

Whilst this promising development was under way I was spending a lot of time preparing talks for the Sunday afternoon fellowship, reading religious books and suchlike things, and it soon became clear that the high pressure sales techniques I had to use if I was to achieve my sales targets, were simply not compatible with the spiritual life I was being drawn to. Oddly, this did not seem to bother Ray Benfield, one of my colleagues on the sales team, who was an enthusiastic Jehovah's Witness. From time to time Ray and I had lunch together and he took the opportunity of introducing me to the mysteries of his very demanding faith. The fundamentalist approach he took and his very literal interpretation of scripture did not appeal to me at all. Nevertheless, I was impressed by his dedication and the personal sacrifices he and his fellow Witnesses were willing to make for the sake of their Gospel. There is no doubt he contributed to the course of events.

My own Christian commitment was not to the Methodist Church as an organization, much less its theology about which I knew very little; it was simply to the people – my family and friends, from whom I would have been alienated by any meddling with Jehovah's Witnesses! My religion – my understanding, that is, of what life is all about – was, and still is, a practical matter of loving human relationships. Theology, Biblical authority, church membership and suchlike considerations I regard as quite secondary in practice, no matter how important they might be in principle.

But Ray Benfield stimulated my mind to engage with important questions about the meaning of life, the value of a belief system and whether religion really mattered. I decided that it does and began to read the kind of books that addressed such questions. The writer who helped me most (as he has helped countless thousands of others) was C.S. Lewis.

We went on holiday that year to Scarborough and on the day when 'it happened' there was a sea fret lying over the sands of North Bay and the sun, with a mischievous laugh, was brightly illuminating the hotels on the top of the cliff. Nevertheless, we hired deck chairs and sat in the cold mist like good British holidaymakers determined to 'have a good time', towels round our necks and ice creams in our hands. Paul was between us in his pushchair, screaming his head off, and refusing to be comforted, even with ice cream! Betty was reading her *Woman* magazine and I was reading C.S. Lewis's *Mere Christianity*, a small volume of broadcast talks, when God spoke to me in a decisive way. It was not an audible voice, or even a voice in my head, nor did it emerge mysteriously from the sound of the waves crashing onto the beach and the plaintive crying of the gulls. I just 'knew', quite subjectively. All the hours of Sunday afternoon fellowship discussions with Eric Scott, sermons by the Rev George Whitfield Luty, who was our minister at the time, confirmation classes by the chaplain at Bodmin Barracks and a long-forgotten address on Confirmation Day by the Bishop of Truro, Ray Benfield's lunchtime contributions – all these things came together, somewhere in the depths of my mind, mingling with the Christian example of my parents and Betty's parents and many others. I have never counted this as a 'conversion' experience, since I had been a Christian in some sense from the beginning. I was not 'born again', since I had not 'repented', or felt I had anything in particular to repent of that I had not repented of already – and there was, of course, plenty of that! I made no 'change of mind on reflection' about the kind of life I was living. But from that moment I knew for certain that I was to become a Methodist Local Preacher – though I did not know that screaming Paul would become one as well!

I said nothing about this to Betty for some time because I was anxious about what sort of a response my news would surely call forth. I did not tell her until after I had spoken with Rev George Whitfield Luty and checked out the procedures. Then I told her across the table at home after tea one day. Characteristically, she glanced at the ceiling of Heaven and muttered, with a sort of despairing resignation, 'What next!' She had thought she had married a successful romantic novelist who one day would write best sellers and have films made of them. And now, she must have feared, she was half way to becoming a minister's wife! The truth is (though she would have been outraged at the idea then, and perhaps later!) that Betty would have made a first class minister's wife. But I was simply not cut out to be a minister of religion at all. Fortunately, the Lord, in His infinite wisdom, knew this all too well and so never called me to that vocation. I am eternally grateful. But preaching and conducting services of worship was something I could do with enthusiasm. Above all else in life, I craved for attention and significance. Here I had it. If this development in my affairs is not a clear example of the love of God – no, the divine indulgence of God! – I don't know what is! Betty put up with it all with that superabundance of good humoured toleration which is characteristic of her. She has been my unfailing support along the tortuous route from where I was when we got married to where I am now!

* * *

Shortly after Scarborough, Dennis Burke, my sales manager at Hedley's who was an ex-actor, spent a day with me to ensure that I was doing the job effectively, and demonstrated with his silver Irish tongue and smiling eyes that it was possible to keep our competitors out by filling the shopkeeper's stock room with Fairy Soap. He would hold two new crinkly £1 notes beneath a vulnerable old lady's nose and say, 'If you will order forty cases of Fairy Soap, I will give you this – now!'

He could see I was uncomfortable with this sort of technique, which was fast becoming the norm, and he sounded me out over lunch to check the strength of my motivation. It was abundantly clear to him that I (who was an actor myself, of course, and could play the salesman's part when necessary) was not really suited for the job and he no doubt shared this insight with his own line manager.

At this stage Betty was again in an advanced stage of pregnancy. We were looking forward to a sister for Paul and the birth was expected on the 10th March. The baby was to be born at home and we had booked Mrs Brunt, a nurse, to live in for a week or two and look after Betty and the baby – not to mention me. We were by this time 'rich' by the modest standards of the time. I was now earning £11 a week and the prospect of my eventually being promoted to sales manager, with a 'team' of my own, were very good. But that was without taking God into account. Sometimes He clobbers people with a completely unexpected jolt, switching the points on their rail track and sending them off in a totally unexpected direction.

He clobbered me at nine o'clock on the morning of Friday, 9th March, 1956 – the day after our fourth wedding anniversary. It was also the day before our second baby was due to be born. I was to meet Dennis behind the tram shed at Saltaire so I was there in good time behind the wheel of my black Ford Popular. A few minutes later Dennis drew up behind me in his black Ford Consul. Most cars were still black and the larger Ford Consul reflected Dennis's managerial status. He climbed out of his car and climbed into mine beside me. Without beating about the bush he put his hand on my knee and said, 'David, we are parting company – and we are parting company now!'

I have to concede that Dennis was most helpful, understanding and gracious in doing what was, for him, an unpleasant job. But had he not been up to it, then he too would have been for the chop.

Our daughter was not, as it happened, born when expected the following day. Caroline arrived on March 20th, by which time I was a 'speciality salesman' selling carbon paper to offices round about. But that provided no wheels and lasted only a fortnight. Selling, with or without wheels, was simply not my scene. So I signed on at the Employment Exchange and drew £4 a week 'dole'. I decided I would now actually be a writer since there was, for the moment, nothing else to do. For about three months, whilst I searched for a job, I tried desperately – but without success – to write saleable short stories.

It was my friend Raymond, home one weekend from his school in Lancashire, who suggested I approach one of the local hospitals. So I went to see the Matron at St Luke's Hospital, Bradford who took me on as a ward orderly. In this job I was the lowest of the low, under authority to bossy-minded student nurses, who ordered me to make beds and empty bedpans. Me, an ex-officer of the Intelligence Corps, in which I still had an honorary commission! Me, emptying bed pans!

There was a small ward of twelve beds that became my special responsibility. In it were twelve men, some young, some old, and they were all terminally ill. One, aged only 37, was severely disabled with what was then called disseminated sclerosis, (now MS); another an old man in his eighties had gangrene in his right foot. Others were suffering from cancer, brain tumour, muscular dystrophy and other things from which they would shortly die. My primary job was to look after them and make their last days as easy as possible with what I now know (and enjoy) as palliative care. I loved all these dying men and I think they loved me. Being a humble ward orderly, working shifts for £9 a week, turned out to be quite the most rewarding job I had done so far. At last I was doing something really useful.

But it was not a career and it provided no wheels so after about three months I went back on the road, but this time as a medical representative with John Wyeths, an American pharmaceutical company. Wyeths, at that time, were not looking for high-powered salesmen but for educated, intelligent and attractive young men with plenty of personality who would visit doctors at their surgeries, or even in hospitals, and engage in 'medical propaganda' My sales experience would be useful, of course, because, broadly speaking, the company's products had to be 'sold' – in the best sense of the term. In fact, it was a bit like 'selling' the Gospel in Methodist pulpits. It was telling people 'good news' – but in Wyeth's case it was the good news about Penidural, Aludrox and many other products including, above all, Equanil and Sparine, the tranquillisers that were being introduced to psychiatrists in particular. Even my three months as a ward orderly was helpful experience. In fact, I was now on the fringe of the healing profession! In order to do this job I needed a medical education; not seven years of it to become a doctor, of course, but a good basis of medical knowledge so that I could talk with doctors in their own language about the company's products and the diseases they were designed to treat. This sounded much more like me.

This six or seven week training course provided about eight of us, as new trainees, with a basic knowledge of anatomy and physiology and several conditions the company's drugs were designed to treat. It included the cardiovascular system, the gastrointestinal system, the blood, and infectious diseases because we had a number of antibiotic preparations. Best of all from my point of view (though I did not realise its significance at the time) was an insight into psychiatry and the treatment of mental and emotional disorders.

At the end of the course I was sent home (with wheels) in time for Christmas. The wheels were on a Ford Prefect, still black and the first of several cars Wyeths supplied me with during the next eight years. I must have made a good impression because after about six months I was asked to join the team of about twelve 'Clinical Associates'. At last I was being recognised! I was no longer just an ordinary 'medical rep', visiting GPs but a very special one with responsibilities for representing my firm in the Leeds and Sheffield Teaching Hospitals, and with a grey Austin Cambridge to mark my new status. I got to know all the leading specialists – doctors, surgeons, anaesthetists, psychiatrists, bacteriologists, pharmacologists and many others – including professors of university departments, senior lecturers and researchers. I knew who was interested in what, especially if they were about to embark on research, and they were interested in me because my firm would sometimes give funding to doctors engaged in research projects and might finance them to attend prestigious conferences, even at the other side of the world!

But the most important and significant of my contacts in the medical profession were the psychiatrists, so I began to read extensively about mental illness. The most influential of my contacts was Dr Frank Lake. He was, at the time, a consultant psychiatrist at Scalebor Park Hospital, Burley-in-Wharfedale, Ilkley. He was, in fact, a committed Christian and an Anglican lay reader so we had quite a lot in common. He was a very remarkable man, truly charismatic and said by some to be a genius. Why he should have chosen to spend so much time with me, a drug house rep., when he undoubtedly had plenty of patients to worry about, I shall never know for certain; but I cannot help feeling in retrospect, that God must surely have had a hand in this as well. Frank Lake taught me a great deal about the meaning of mental illness, how it developed and how it might be treated, psychotherapeutically as well as with drugs Eventually, he left this appointment and moved to Nottingham where he established the Clinical Theology Association, a training resource for ministers of religion, teaching them psychodynamic counselling at a fairly advanced level. Later, I studied it myself, informally, with Rev Malcolm Sweeting who was one of our Circuit ministers and a qualified teacher of Clinical Theology.

I had, in fact, begun to explore psychology and healing a good few years before this, without any thought or expectation that I might one day pursue it professionally as a career. I had come across a little pocket-sized magazine called 'Life Science' on a station bookstall. This, too, was promoting various forms of self-esteem building but branched out into the world of spiritual healing, metaphysics, hypnosis and colour psychology. I was vulnerable to being drawn into this because Life Science seemed to be offering something that was both psychology and spirituality. But these early adventures were really into the paranormal, rather than into the meaning and purpose of life, which is what I would later understand as spirituality. Even as I began to contemplate the possibility of becoming a probation officer, it was with no conscious awareness that such a career might be counted as 'God's work'. I was in pursuit of nothing but self-esteem. Anything else was a spin-off.

However, with Wyeths I was at last earning a decent salary and we were able to think seriously about buying our own house. In late 1959 we found what we wanted. It was a large semi-detached Edwardian house at 31, Farfield Road, Shipley. It was standing empty and had earlier been a Congregationalist minister's manse. The estate agent wanted £1800 and we made an offer. The sale was not straightforward because the house, being a manse, had to be re-advertised by the Charity Commissioners who had an obligation to get the best price possible – a sort of official invitation to 'gazumping'. Others were, in fact, interested but after several weeks of anxious waiting the competitors dropped out (miraculously, perhaps) and the house was ours, at our price. We named it Westaways, after a house in one of Hugh Walpole's 'Herries' novels that we both loved. It was an expensive house to run but we loved it and felt that with our own house, me in a good job and a grey Austin Cambridge in the drive, we had at last 'arrived'.

* * *

Not long after we moved to Farfield Road, my father retired. My brother Philip and his wife Pat had two children, Nicholas and Tracey, and were living not far away. So my parents had both their children and their grandchildren nearby. This was an ideal situation for my parents, especially my mother. But my father had fantasised for years about retiring to Bridlington and he was inflexibly committed to the plan. Mother was not at all keen because she would be leaving a house she had coveted for years, and had only just got settled into, and also her friends, her close and her extended family and the church they had attended all their lives. However, they made a few day trips by bus to Bridlington in search of a suitable property. My mother was not at all enthusiastic about moving, no matter how much my father pointed out the advantages and that Philip and I both had cars and could visit easily. Eventually, he took a trip on his own and had a further look at a ground floor flat in a semi-detached house in Shaftesbury Road on the south side of Bridlington, which they had spotted earlier. It was a pleasant property, only a few minutes walk from the promenade. But it was far from ideal and was not even self-contained, so that the upstairs residents had to share the front door and the entrance hall. The short-comings were, of course, reflected in the price and my father did not have a lot of capital beyond what he could get for their house in Nabwood Drive, so when the estate agent offered him the flat at a price within his reach he agreed to it, without even discussing it further with my mother. This was, I'm afraid, typical of my father. He would sit silently for hours in his armchair, puffing his pipe and 'thinking'. Having thought out what he was going to do, he did it! I challenged him about inconsiderately buying a flat in Bridlington without Mother's agreement, but he pointed out, with some justification, that my mother could never make up her mind about anything and if he had waited for her to agree they would never have got moved at all!

* * *

Our own home in Farfield Road was a big house with big rooms and was clearly intended for entertaining. We had not been there long before we conceived the idea of inviting all the young people from church – teens and twenties – to come in after church on a Sunday evening for coffee and biscuits and a bit of relaxed, informal fellowship. So we were a large and happy group of Christian friends. I began preparing talks for them, explaining basic Christianity, hopefully a bit like C.S. Lewis, in a way they could take on board and we used to have some very stimulating discussions. The group became known as 'The Grapevine'. During the years it continued I become a sort of confidante, advisor, even informal counsellor, to several of the young people who shared their personal problems with me and talked them through in confidence. I was already beginning to feel that this was the direction I should go.

Our work with this group was probably our most important achievement at the Saltaire Methodist Church. Several of the young people married each other and many have maintained their connection with the church and even with us personally. I think it was the experience of this group that persuaded me more and more that the really essential feature of Christian life was not orthodox belief and regular church-going but good relationships. This core belief became the foundation of where my life was to go from there. Nevertheless, I became accredited as a Methodist Local Preacher in June, 1960.

* * *

My first novel, *Not from the Stars*, was revised and re-typed, mainly by Betty, several times and visited numerous publishers. But it could not find a taker. We were both deeply disappointed but I was still committed to becoming a writer so I started to write another one. *Man in a Blue Check Shirt*, as it was called, was written in my attic study at Farfield Road, mainly between six and eight in the morning before I went to work. The title of the book was the title of a picture, painted by a character called

Nicholas Burman, who was a Christian artist. It was a modern interpretation of Christ, depicting him leaning on the doorpost of his carpenter's shop and dressed in workman's trousers and a blue check shirt. Hodder & Stoughton took a serious interest in this and two of their readers recommended it for publication, to get me started. But the final office report went against it because their policy then was not to publish a book unless it could be expected to sell at least three thousand copies and they did not think mine would. So that too bit the dust and since I was preoccupied at the time with trying to get into the Probation Service I did not send it to anyone else. Had *Man in a Blue Check Shirt* been published (which I believe it would, had I persisted) I guess my life would have taken a very different course – the points would have switched me onto a railway line labelled 'I am a novelist'. But I would have been a 'run of the mill' novelist, as are the overwhelming majority. I would never have been able to make a decent living at it, I would never have been 'significant', which was what I really craved to be, and I would not have pursued the very different and much more socially useful (and personally rewarding) path of life which was to follow.

* * *

The Shipley Circuit Local Preachers met together regularly on a quarterly basis to attend to official business but also, from time to time, for fellowship, Bible study, prayer and to discuss interesting topics. One of my older colleagues, Mr John La Page, FRGS, a successful Bradford wool merchant, was a member of The Churches Society for Psychic and Spiritual Research. A dozen or so of us met at his house in Baildon to hear a speaker from this Society explain how Jesus had used certain psychic gifts that were available to all of us if we cared to develop them. During the course of the evening, this man went round the circle and spoke to each of us individually, to demonstrate what could be done. When he came to me he said, 'You will shortly receive a blue book which will be instrumental in changing the direction of your life.' He told me no more about this mysterious book but sent me home, wondering and a bit excited, to share the news with Betty.

At that stage I was ready for something new. I was doing well with Wyeths and enjoying my work but I knew it was really leading nowhere. I was good at my job but I was not 'management material'. I did not have the temperament for it. I lacked a certain kind of aggression and ruthlessness which Wyeths, under pressure from their American bosses, were beginning to call for. I was not at all happy with this development.

Since I was clearly not going to be a significant novelist, I was now asking myself those profound spiritual questions, Who am I? And What am I here for? I began to think again about joining the Probation Service. The government had come to recognise that the Probation Service would have to be expanded to cope with the work of prison after-care that was being developed. A government report on the proposals had been published and I sent for a copy. When it came it was blue and it would indeed be instrumental in pointing the way I was to go, just as the clairvoyant from The Churches Society for Spiritual and Psychic Research had prophesied!

About this time a twelvemonth Home Office course at Leeds University was advertised in the Yorkshire Observer so I wrote for details and Betty and I discussed it together. If I was accepted onto the course we would not be able to continue living at Westaways, which was a pretty expensive house to run and the Government Grant of £14 a week would not get us very far so Betty would have to go out to work. Even if I got through the course (which, with my academic track record, we could not take for granted!) I would be starting a new career on a substantially smaller salary than we were used to. And we would have no wheels! Nevertheless it seemed like the opportunity of a lifetime and we agreed I should have a go.

The selection process took several months, ending with a day at the Home Office for group interviews with other candidates. They told us all at the end of it that there had been over two thousand applicants for only twenty-one places on the Leeds course, so we were all prepared for disappointment, even though we had got so far.

But I got through. I, with my low self-esteem, was selected out of over two thousand others, to be trained at Leeds University as a probation officer! It was almost beyond belief. It is clear to me now, in retrospect and from my chosen frame of reference, that God had a hand in this. The points had been switched once again and I was sent off in a 'new direction' for which, in various ways, I had been well prepared, though I did not realise it. My friends at Wyeths, especially Peter Hurren, the Senior Clinical Asssociate, who had become a close personal friend, were genuinely sorry I was leaving, as I was sorry to be leaving them. Several managers and the Medical Director wrote to me expressing their mixed feelings of both regret and admiration that I should be taking this step. I was, in fact, leaving a job that (with bonuses, a company car renewed every two years, generous expenses and a non-contributory superannuation scheme taken into account) was worth considerably more than even a Principal Probation Officer in charge of a whole County Probation Service, was earning at that time. Everyone regarded me as a deeply committed Christian who was making enormous personal sacrifices in order to serve God. In fact, no such thought was in my mind at all. I was simply doing now, in 1964, what I ought to have embarked on when I left school over twenty years earlier. For me it was no sacrifice at all. It was an exciting adventure. All the sacrifices were being made by Betty and the children – not for God's sake but for mine!

Part Two

FINDING A NEW DIRECTION

5

SOMETHING . . . SOMEONE!

Westaways, our lovely house, had to go on the market and Betty cleaned it from top to bottom, including attics and cellars, all seventeen rooms, until the house sparkled and was most attractive to prospective buyers. Betty had to show them round, extolling its virtues. She was far better at selling than I had ever been and the house sold quickly for £3250, nearly twice what we had paid for it!

My parents, by this time, were living in Bridlington and were both puzzled and anxious that I should be giving up such a good, well-paid job to set off into the unknown in search of professional status. But they were, I know, quietly proud of me for taking this step and for having been selected. Betty's mother had sold her house following the death of her husband, and had moved to a smaller house only a few minutes walk away. She kindly invited us to move in with her whilst I was on my training course and we did so. I spent £300 on a second hand Morris 1000 so we were never without wheels. But the £14 a week Home Office grant was nothing like enough for us to live on so Betty got a job at the Ministry of Pensions in Shipley, as a temporary typist to start with but later she passed the Establishment exam which was to stand her in good stead later.

At the beginning of May, 1964, I climbed into my grey Morris 1000 – my very own car this time, and my suitcase in the boot – actually to go to university! 'Isn't it marvellous!' I remember saying to Betty through the car window. 'I'm thirty seven and at long last I'm going to university!' Well, I really was. Not as an undergraduate looking forward to a degree in three years time, but as a trainee probation officer on a twelve month crash course run by the Extra Mural Department of Leeds University at Albert Mansbridge College on behalf of the Home Office. Nevertheless, it was a tremendously exciting development for me.

One of my fellow trainees was Climie Hewitson, a Free Church Evangelical minister who had been a missionary in Nigeria and had returned to this country for his twelve year old son to be educated. Climie soon identified me as a 'searcher' and we became friends throughout the course. One day he shared with me his great distress and anxiety that his twelve year old son had been suffering severe headaches and had been diagnosed as having a brain tumour. He asked for my prayers. The boy was taken to Pinderfields Hospital in Wakefield for brain surgery by Mr Miles Gibson, who I knew well from my Wyeth days. In fact I had twice enjoyed the privilege of standing at his elbow to watch him operate. But the night before Climie's son was due to be operated on, Climie visited him on the ward. He told me over lunch afterwards that he had felt a powerful impulse to lay hands on his son's head and boldly to ask God to heal him. When the boy was X-rayed the next morning prior to the operation, Climie told me, the tumour was found to have disappeared entirely!

* * *

Soon after the first residential week's introduction the university staff were on vacation so we were all sent out on training placements in Probation Offices around the area. I was sent to the Leeds Probation Office where my supervisor was Mike Mullaney, an experienced main grade officer who had risen to the rank of Assistant Chief Probation Officer when I last heard of him. The placement was tremendously exciting. Under Mike's supervision (I called him Mr Mullanney, of course, in those still formal days) I did the work of a probation officer, carrying a small case load, spending time in court, visiting 'clients' and their families at home and even doing Office Duty, when many people called on their own initiative seeking help and advice with domestic and marital problems and with children who were a source of trouble and anxiety. Sitting behind my desk to interview people in need I found hugely satisfying and my self-esteem was enhanced no end! I felt that, at last, I was Something – well, nearly! In fact, from the point of view of my clients (who did not, of course, know that I was only a trainee) I was even Somebody. I had not felt like this since I had been Port Security Officer at Harwich!

After that we returned to college for just one day a week, for lectures and seminars, and had four days each week out on a new placement. It was a bit like an apprenticeship, with day release to go to college.

The Probation Service at that time was organised on a regional basis with a Principal Probation Officer in charge, sometimes of a relatively small number of probation officers in teams of five or six, each team supervised by a Senior Probation Officer. Some big services, however, covered the work of an entire county. The Service was funded from the Home Office but the Local Authority contributed eighty per cent of the total. The government's contribution, therefore, was effectively controlled by whatever the Local Authority could afford to pay. I was sent to the Bradford Probation Office which was in easy commuting distance from Shipley. There were about twelve main grade probation officers and two Seniors under the Principal, a Mr Hallas, of whom I saw little. The office was on the first floor of a converted wool warehouse in Vicar Lane, long since demolished to make way for city centre developments. The entire Probation Service, at that time, was run on a shoe-string, using whatever premises they could afford on very limited budgets and paying their officers a rather minimal (but strictly statutory) salary which seemed, no doubt, consistent with the vocational nature of the job. Fortunately, this was all to change but at that time Probation Officers wore threadbare corduroy trousers and old tweed jackets with leather patches on the elbows. But my wardrobe had been dictated for years by the expectations of the Methodist pulpit and by the need to dress in smart suits appropriate for a Wyeth Clinical Associate, doing business with medical consultants in teaching hospitals. Those were the days of Sir Lancelot Spratt, before jeans and tee shirts became almost universal. Doctors, even house officers, wore suits and I did not want to stand out like a sore thumb! Consequently, I had nothing but suits – most of them good quality Magees whose labels could be seen when hung over the back of an office chair. So I had an 'image' problem.

My personal supervisor, George Moore, was tolerant and understanding of this, despite his educated working class orientation and his dedication to socialist philosophy, so I was accepted by him and everyone else, even if with an amused smile at my poshness! Mr Moore(who I did not call 'George' until long afterwards!) was an Irishman from Belfast whose broad accent I often had great difficulty in understanding. Nevertheless, he was an excellent supervisor for whom I had a great deal of respect (atheist though he was!) and he taught me a great deal about my new profession, overseeing my work with all kinds of clients. Although some with serious criminal records were supervised on release from prison, borstal or detention centre, the majority were relatively minor offenders deemed by the court to be more in need of help than of punishment. Nevertheless, some of them were complex and demanding.

We were being trained, of course, not in psychoanalysis but in psychoanalytic casework, which is social work based on close study of the personal histories and circumstances of individuals and their families. As a trainee probation officer I had abundant scope for this kind of work and was required, by Home Office rules, to make a detailed written record of all my contacts with clients and to have regular consultation with my supervisor to discuss my cases and how I was handling them. Psychoanalytic theory provided the intellectual infrastructure for this process so that we had some understanding of 'what was going on' both in our clients and their families and in our own emotional involvement with them. But I quickly realised that it was of little practical help in addressing problems when face to face with the client. Transactional Analysis had scarcely been conceived in 1964 but I was ready and prepared for it when, a few years later, it came onto the therapeutic market.

As a trainee probation officer in Bradford I was in my element and as happy as Larry. But all was not well. The course members at Albert Mansbridge College were divided into two groups, one supervised by Miss Burdis, the Course Tutor and the other by Dr Laycock, the psychology lecturer. We never used their first names. I was in Miss Burdis's group and it eventually became apparent that in her view I was not really a suitable person to become a probation officer! Though I challenged her about this, she was never able to say precisely why this was. She could respond only in terms of her feelings and 'intuition'. My course work was good and I made useful contributions in seminars, which she usually led. I was getting good reports from George Moore, my fieldwork supervisor at Bradford and I was entirely comfortable with both my studies and my practical work. But Miss Burdis was clearly unhappy and made vague suggestions that perhaps I should leave the course! I shared this with Mr Moore in supervision and he declared that he would deal with the matter. He and the other fieldwork supervisors had periodic meetings with Miss Burdis and Dr Laycock to assess everyone's progress and after the next one she told me that I would in future be supervised at the college by Dr Laycock. After that there was no further problem. This strange conflict with Miss Burdis, however, was only the first of several problems I was to have with women in positions of authority.

The course ended in March, 1965, with written exams which I passed without difficulty, and we all received through the post a 'Home Office Certificate'. In preparation for the course ending, however, we all had to look for jobs. Since there were no local vacancies within easy reach of Shipley, I applied to Hull, Preston and Liverpool but in all of them other candidates were preferred to me. Maybe it had to do with my Magee suits and my posh accent! Or maybe it was the 'guiding hand' requiring me to be somewhere else.

However, I eventually landed a job in Middlesbrough. We had heard of this place but had to look on a map to discover that it was near the mouth of the River Tees and about forty miles south of Newcastle. I was interviewed by the Magistrates of the Probation Committee, as was another candidate from the course, and this time I was the one preferred – possibly, in this case, because of, rather than in spite of, my Magee suit and posh accent! The Committee, chaired by Miss Rose Gibson, a retired head teacher, seemed to be already committed to building up a team of relatively up-market probation officers but I was the first one to be recruited with 'university training', so obviously they wanted me to look and sound the part. I was appointed to start work on the 26th March, 1965 at the Probation Office in Russell Street, long since demolished (like that in Vicar Lane, Bradford) to make way for new developments. My office was in the attic of this end terrace house next to the Town Hall and a hand-painted name board was fixed to the outside of my office door: 'Mr D.G. Midgley'. At last, I was at least Something!

There were nine main grade officers, including me, in the small Middlesbrough Probation Service. We were presided over by Hugh Leslie, a Scotsman and a Senior Probation Officer – not even a Principal! They were all very friendly and quite smartly dressed. Arthur Cooper, probably the oldest member of staff, was an ex-magistrates' clerk and well into his fifties. And he wore 'court dress' – black jacket and black striped trousers. He invited me to 'sit in with him' one morning on his reporting session to observe how it should be done. Lads in their teens, or younger, would stand in front of his desk, their school caps in their hands, and address him politely as 'Sir' That was not how I intended to operate! There was a lady called Miss Smith, who had no known Christian name and who kept herself very much to herself, but she also was quite refined with an accent almost as posh as mine. So, for the matter of that, had Miss Cooper – who I did eventually call Norma; but Norma was distinguished by having obtained a Leeds University Certificate in some subject relevant to her work. So she was academically quite up-market already.

I brought a lot of professional-looking books to my office – Florence Hollis's *Casework Practice*, Felix P Biesteck's *The Casework Relationship*, J.C. Flugel's *Man, Morals and Society*, books by Mark Monger, Annette Garrett and many others and, of course, Sigmund Freud. I had no bookcase so I arranged them across the front of my desk, feeling proud and significant as I sat behind them awaiting clients. But Mr Leslie climbed the stairs to pay me a visit and see how I was settling in. He was, I believe, a 'direct entrant' to the Probation Service and had probably done a training course at Rainer House, the training centre run by the Home Office. He was not a 'university man' but he was no fool either. He looked at my impressive row of books and said, 'Ye want to get these moved, lad. They make a barrier between yourself and your clients.' He was right, of course and I got some shelves to put my books on. Later, when I was more confident and secure in my new image, I preferred to have my desk facing a wall and my clients facing me with no barrier between us.

I lived for a while in lodgings with the mother of one of my colleagues, Peter Coates, and spent a lot of time house-hunting for something affordable to buy. Eventually, we decided as a temporary measure, to rent a flat on the first floor of a big semi-detached house near the town centre. There was an enormous lounge that had once been the master bedroom and into it we moved all our lounge and dining room furniture and the piano, that we had had in storage for over a year. And there was a garage for my Morris 1000. We had our own home again and we were to live there for fifteen months.

Paul, who was eleven, had got a place at Acklam Hall Grammar School where he soon settled in and made friends. Caroline was nine and went initially to Ayresome Street Junior School, which was only five minutes walk from our flat. She too settled in well and made friends, though she was, at that time, a bit 'posh' for the local Teessiders. A tape-recording made on Betty's mother's 70th birthday party at the flat reveals, to Caroline's astonishment and ours, just how well-spoken she then was. But she gradually abandoned her relatively refined middle class West Riding accent for the local lingo because she preferred to meld in with the crowd.

We had come to Teesside with an introduction from a member of our church at Saltaire, whose cousin attended Avenue Methodist Church in Middlesbrough. Consequently we began to worship there straight away, were warmly welcomed and have worshipped there ever since. I began to preach around the Circuit, so the family was soon known to everyone and we reckoned we had fifteen hundred ready made friends, that being the approximate membership of the Circuit at the time. 'Avenue' itself then had about four hundred members, though by the end of the Millenium it had reduced to about one hundred and seventy.

Sadly, that was the trend almost everywhere. As the social scene changed, institutional religion was largely abandoned in pursuit of 'liberation' and society adopted a light-hearted indifference to old fashioned moral values and social mores. There have, of course, been many reasons for this and many welcome consequences in terms of personal freedom and opportunity; but the advantages to the individual have been accompanied, perhaps inevitably, by an alarming breakdown in the integrity of the very society those same liberated individuals were a part of. *Future Shock*, as sociologist Alvin Toffler has called it, had set in. Changes in all areas of society – religion and morality, science and technology, education, politics, industry, communications and many other fields – were happening so rapidly that people had no chance to adapt to one significant change before it was overtaken by another one, causing a worldwide sense of disorientation which is well described as 'future shock'. We might equally call it spiritual confusion.

It is, in fact, precisely this disintegration of society, especially the breakdown of the family – the basic unit of society since the beginning of civilization – that has provided expanding opportunities for such professions as social work, probation, casework, counselling and psychotherapy. It is difficult to avoid sounding cynical but, from my point of view, 'future shock' could hardly have arrived at a better time! In fact, Betty and I both found rewarding professions in consequence of society's great needs. After a few years in the Civil Service Department of Health & Social Security (sometimes visiting claimants in their own homes who were clients of mine!) she eventually became a social worker at Redcar, and was seconded onto a two year course at Sunderland Polytechnic where she gained a Diploma in Social Work and a CQSW. She finished up better qualified than I was and went on to become Senior Case Worker at Guisborough.

In November, 1966 we moved into our own house at 13, Barker Road, Linthorpe, Middlesbrough. It was an end terraced house built in 1913 just before the outbreak of the First World War, when building stopped. When building was resumed in the 1920s the occupants of No 13 bought the plot on which the next house would have been added to the terrace. So there was a double garden, a front facing garage and a drive leading up to it.

It took us many years to get everything, house and garden, as we wanted it, not restored entirely to its period elegance, of course, but comfortable and well equipped. The most important feature for me was a room I could use as a study, not imagining that one day it would be my consulting room as well. Our move to Barker Road made it possible for Caroline to attend Whinney Banks Middle School until she was old enough to join Paul at Acklam Hall Grammar School, which had become co-educational by then.

Not long after we settled in Middlesbrough, Rev Frank Crowder became the minister of our church. We already knew him well because he had earlier been a minister in the Shipley Circuit whilst I was training to become a Local Preacher. One of the delightful features of Methodism's itinerant ministry is that wherever we go, certainly in the UK, we will almost always find someone we know, or at least someone who knows someone we know! We have always thought of Frank Crowder as being as near perfect a minister as one could hope to find. He was a thoughtful preacher, a perceptive and helpful counsellor and a splendid visitor who never failed to pray with us on his pastoral visits, even going down on one knee when he did so. A lovely man. It was during Frank's ministry that a poster appeared in the church vestibule from Tyne Tees Television, inviting laymen who were interested in presenting late night 'epilogues' to apply, through their minister, to the producer of religious programme, Maxwell Deas. I told Frank (who was, of course, 'Mr Crowder' in those still formal days) that I would not mind having a go at that and he wrote to Tyne Tees recommending me. I thought no more about it until several weeks later when Maxwell Deas wrote to me inviting me to submit scripts for consideration, possibly for the Whitsuntide period. And so began a ten year career as a part-time television presenter.

After my second recording session Max came into my dressing room in great excitement and said, 'David, you look right, you sound right and you have the right material. You have a great future as an epilogian.' I glowed with pleasure to hear such unreserved praise and felt like a J. Arthur Rank starlet! But it was really true. I actually had something special to offer to the world of television and could, without question, have seriously considered yet another career change. The points had indeed changed; but it was a detour, not a change to another destination, just another step along the way to discovering who I was and what I was here for!

I am glad that my father lived long enough to see my first TV programmes. He would not, of course, have classified me as a 'top notcher'. Nor was I. Such celebrities appeared on national, not local, TV and usually at more sociably acceptable hours than last thing at night or first thing in the morning – and sometimes I did both on the same day! But he was pleased for me and, I think, even a bit proud of me. My mother certainly was. He died of a heart attack at home in their Bridlington flat on the 6th August, 1967.

My father's death was a great sadness to me. It might seem, from some of the things in the earlier chapters of this book, that I hold him responsible for my own failure to achieve anything much in the first half of my life. But we are all responsible, in the final analysis, for our own decisions and people react in very different ways to what, on the face of it, might seem to be very similar experiences All parents have a profound influence on the way their children develop but it is not a simple matter of one kind of parental behaviour or attitude causing a clearly definable response in their offspring. It is the whole quality of the parent-child relationship that matters and my relationship with my father was strong, warm, friendly and thoroughly supportive in everything that really mattered. I loved him dearly and I have never questioned his love for me. The memories I treasure most are of the many times I accompanied him at the piano as he sang the ballads, the operatic arias and tenor passages from *Messiah* and *Elijah* and other oratorios we both loved so much. I still miss him for these musical evenings together, whatever else.

Maybe, as a late night TV presenter, I was at last on the way to becoming Somebody! I never heard of any of my clients hearing my early morning Bible readings on TV or hearing Glorytime on BBC radio, which I also presented for a while. But they would watch television at night until there was nothing left but the flicker and so they were astonished to see their friendly probation officer on the box in the corner of the living room, sitting casually on a pop singer's high stool to deliver my late night epilogue. I soon got used to hearing them say, when I called, 'We saw yer on the telly'; and they got used to hearing me respond with, 'Yes, but did you listen?' Whether my late night philosophising about the human predicament and the ultimate solution, cut any ice with them perhaps no-one will ever know. But seeds are sown in this way and some, without doubt, bear fruit later – perhaps much later.

* * *

During the late 1960s and early 70s when the 'flower power' and 'Jesus People' craze was happening, young people would go off to pop concerts all over the country and would either get 'turned on' to heroin or 'turned on' to Jesus, depending on who got at them first! It was not unusual for my delinquent clients, with track records of burglary, theft and violence, to turn up at reporting sessions at the Probation Office carrying Bibles – usually quite big ones – and try to convert me! In Middlesbrough much of this activity was centred on the home of Jane and Patrick Hinton, a quite well-to-do young couple who had a big house in Roman Road. Patrick was a director of Hintons supermarkets, which then had branches all over Teesside. He and Jane were enthusiastic evangelical Christians who set aside one room in their house as a sort of coffee bar for use by the local teenagers. The kids used to ride up on Thursday evenings on their motor bikes, their birds riding pillion, park their bikes in the garden and spend the evening drinking 'Hinton's' coffee, snogging on the floor and listening to the latest pop records on a wind-up gramophone. But at nine o'clock prompt Patrick would come into the room, Bible in hand, and preach to them for a solid half hour! They would sit spell-bound until he had finished and then, at Patrick's invitation, would get on their knees in prayer. By anybody's standards this was a phenomenon, probably a miracle in itself. But I can vouch for it because somehow I got drawn in to this Thursday evening youth-club-cum-prayer-meeting. At half past nine on Thursday evenings I could be found on my knees in prayer, side by side with some of my own delinquent clients! For a probation officer this was grossly unprofessional and goodness knows what my colleagues would have thought had it come to their notice!

But other things were also happening in this remarkable house. From time to time visiting speakers or evangelists would come and address meetings in an attic 'upper room' which was big enough to seat around fifty people. One of the speakers was Edgar Trout, who addressed us each night for five nights running. Mr Trout's addresses – in fact they were sermons with a vengeance! – lasted for all of one and a half hours! But he was far from being a ranter. He spoke quietly and persuasively out of his own experience. He had been an architect and, in fact, a Methodist Local Preacher, as I was. He told us, as part of his testimony, he had suffered from cancer that had been diagnosed as terminal but he had nevertheless been completely cured by the power of prayer. In consequence of this he had decided to give up his professional work and devote the rest of his life to faith ministry.

Edgar Trout's ministry was 'charismatic' in the days before that word had become common currency. He believed passionately in the power of the Holy Spirit to heal the sick and the broken hearted and to transform lives. He believed in and demonstrated the gifts of the Holy Spirit to impart wisdom and knowledge, faith and healing, prophecy, the working of miracles, discernment, to 'speak in tongues', and to interpret what that language meant. One night Edgar Trout paid tribute to Rev George Whitfield Luty, the Methodist minister under whose influence at Plymouth Central Hall, he had begun to preach as a young man. I was deeply impressed by this further co-incidence, because it was under the influence of this very same minister that I too had begun to preach many years later in Shipley, Yorkshire.

There was opportunity for anyone who wished, to see Mr Trout privately for personal ministry and I arranged to see him myself at five o'clock after work, on Tuesday the 22nd February, 1968. I shared with him the steps in my 'journey' so far, including my television work that was already well-established. At the end of our time together he prayed with me, laid his hands on my head and asked God to baptise me in the Holy Spirit, conferring upon me the 'mantle' which he himself had worn, just as the prophet Elijah, in the Old Testament', had put his mantle on his successor, the prophet Elisha!

This was overwhelming. I only remember driving home in a dangerously ecstatic daze. I told Betty what had happened and she received the news – hardly 'good news' from her point of view – with characteristic pragmatic common sense. 'We shall just have to see', was all she said. There was not much else she could say. This sort of thing was far outside mainstream Methodist experience and I immediately realised for myself that if I made much of it in Methodist circles I should almost certainly be branded as a religious nut case and have to take refuge elsewhere. I could not believe that that was God's will for me. I must stay put among my Methodist friends, spend a lot of time in prayer and await further instructions.

But I was full of it – full of the Holy Spirit, I suppose, though I later came to regard this Person of the Holy Trinity as a holy attitude, rather than a holy spook! I began to organise Betty and the children into saying grace before meals and having prayers and Bible readings every night before Paul and Caroline went to bed. But I was not comfortable with it. This sort of thing was not only foreign to mainstream Methodism, it was also foreign to our family. After all, they had not been baptised in the Holy Spirit and I found myself wishing I hadn't either! The experience was nothing short of traumatic. Nevertheless, the family put up with it indulgently for several weeks, in fact they tried hard to enter into the spirit of it and Paul and Caroline competed for the privilege of reading the Bible passage. But it simply could not go on. It did not feel right. Eventually, Betty declared it was time to stop it – so we did, to my relief as well as hers. I can't remember how we explained it to the kids but they adjusted to being without it as they had adjusted to being with it.

I was puzzled by my own response to being 'baptised in the Holy Spirit'. I put that expression in quotation marks because it is, for mainstream Methodism, something from a foreign language. The expression might be used by certain preachers at the season of Pentecost but it has no real meaning for most Methodists – or for most Anglicans, Catholics and members of other churches for the matter of that. It is outside our experience and it is not an experience we are encouraged to seek after.

We regard such things as excessively emotional, irrational and 'over the top' In fact, any kind of ecstasy, or even enthusiasm, we tend to frown upon as getting 'carried away'. 'We', incidentally, includes me. I am, I think, a bit more tolerant and accepting of such excesses in other people than are some of my Brothers and Sisters but I would still prefer to be counted out. It is difficult to say exactly why this is. Part of it, of course, is heavy cultural programming.

It will be evident throughout this book that I have been influenced by both spiritual and secular experiences and I have been increasingly concerned, as my own understanding has grown, to distinguish the spiritual from the religious. American psychiatrist and psychotherapist M. Scott Peck in his famous best-seller *The Road Less Travelled*, has described religion as 'our understanding of what life is all about'. But the word 'religion' is generally used to mean 'institutional religion' of whatever denomination or sect. It is about creeds and doctrines, rituals, festivals and other observances, generally under the direction of a hierarchy of ministers, priests, deacons, bishops, archbishops or just 'pastors' – who are sometimes the most dogmatic and uncompromising of the lot! I do not question the value of institutionalised religion because it is what has preserved the essentials of Christianity down two thousand years of conflict and dissent, and it without it we might never have known about Jesus at all. In addition most of us would have had no fellowship to sustain our faith when the going gets rough and the world is asking in the face of tragedy, natural disasters, catastrophe and human evil, 'Where's God now?' So I value my simple and undemanding Methodism. But I am a secular person moving about in a secular world of work, politics, economics, education, sport, entertainment and many other interests and activities which, for most people, continue without any reference to the 'spiritual world'. It is imperative that I am able to communicate with them and be accepted as one of them. That is why I have chosen to be a 'secular counsellor', whose clinical work is rooted in Freud, Jung, Berne and many other eminent scientists, as opposed to a 'Christian counsellor' who counsels his (usually church-going) clients from a specifically Biblical frame of reference. I do not believe there is any rigid distinction between the two but to ignore the difference is likely to be a source of confusion to therapist and client alike. So the next chapter will focus on the discovery that effectively changed the points on my rail track and sent me off in yet another new direction.

6

CHANGES AND TRANSACTIONS

When the Probation Service was first established under the Probation Act of 1907, the first probation officers appointed were men who had already been serving the courts as 'court missioners' on a voluntary and part time basis. They were simply 'men of goodwill' who felt they wanted to help those who had got their lives into a mess through crime and antisocial behaviour and, if possible, to save them from the largely destructive effects of a prison sentence. Some of the court missioners were certainly 'religious' and could have included, for example, the local vicar or Methodist minister; but most were 'secular' people such as estate agents, retired accountants or businessman or, indeed anyone who was known to the magistrates as a person of integrity who could be trusted to respect confidentiality.

To begin with probation officers had no specialist training to equip them for their work in the courts but when the Probation Service was formed funds were made available for professional training which became a responsibility of the Home Office Inspectorate. Rainer House, already referred to, was established as the London training centre for new recruits to the Service and with the expansion which took place following the government's report on The Organization of After-Care it became the practice to run 'refresher courses', using university resources during vacation periods.

It was on one of the early courses I attended, on the theme of 'casework practice', that I first heard about transactional analysis so whilst I was there I bought Eric Berne's famous best seller *Games People Play – The Psychology of Human Relationships*. This was bang on target for the philosophy I was developing and seemed as relevant to my spiritual as to my professional inclinations. Starting from here I began seriously to think of myself as a person who ought to have something distinctive to offer – something of more practical use to my clients than the Freudian psychoanalytical theory I had been introduced to at Albert Mansbridge College and more specific than the refined common sense which seemed to characterise the practice of social casework. Unlike psychoanalysis, Eric Berne's 'transactional analysis' was not so much about the mysterious processes going on within the unconscious mind of the individual, as about the manifest realities of what was actually happening between ordinary people interacting with one another in the day to day activities of normal life.

Anyone unfamiliar with the casework/counselling/psychotherapy scene will probably be wondering what 'transactional analysis' is. It would be inappropriate to present a detailed account of it in a book like this; but since the 'secular' psychotherapeutic element is integral to what the book is all about, I will give a very brief but, I hope, adequate account of the basic features of it at this point in my story. This might, perhaps, help to explain what was going on in my own head – not to mention my relationships! If anyone wants to explore it in more detail there are plenty of books readily available.

But Berne was a psychiatrist and himself a trained psychoanalyst, who felt that the long and expensive process of psychoanalysis was unnecessary for many of his patients, most of whom could be treated successfully for their neuroses and personality disorders much more quickly and effectively. It began as a style of group psychotherapy in which about six or eight patients would be treated together and, therefore, much less expensively. However, it is now widely used as an individual, one-to-one, style of psychotherapy, even when practiced in a group setting. So it seemed to me that it might be particularly welcome for use in probation casework because it was inexpensive and easy enough to be understood by clients who were rarely very intellectual or well educated.

The first thing to know about TA is that it is founded on the recognition that we all have many different ways of being 'me', which we use in different situations. These many styles, however, can all be classified as one or another of three basic 'ego states' (as they are technically called) which Berne referred to as the Child, the Adult and the Parent. However, I can use my Child ego state even when I am a grown up. One of the many ways the Child can be seen to think, feel and behave is clearly demonstrated on the football field when somebody scores a goal. Grown men in their twenties and thirties react with great excitement, jump into each other's arms and run about waving their hands in the air and shouting joyfully. So do their supporters in the stands! That kind of thinking, feeling and behaviour is what we call 'Free Child' – the Child in us acting freely in a spontaneous and uninhibited sort of way, as it used to do in early childhood. In different circumstances the Child in us might be equally uninhibited in expressing sadness (with tears, perhaps) or anger (with a raised voice or even violence) or perhaps in expressing much more complex emotions. The important thing is that the person is 're-playing' the kind of thinking, feeling and behaviour that was first learned in childhood. So if you think my fantasies of becoming 'Someone', and my pursuit of status and significance, was all a bit childlike – like chanting 'I'm the king of the castle and you're the dirty rascal' – then by all means ascribe it to my Child ego state. But please bear in mind that I have others ego states, or ways of being me, as well! Many Child ways of thinking, feeling and behaviour are not, of course so free or natural as those described above. We refer to these as 'Adapted Child' ego states because they are the Child in us adapting in ways which take into account the needs and desires of mothers, fathers and other parent-like figures who might have been unwilling to put up with children behaving freely, naturally and spontaneously. However, that can get a bit complex so I am not going to say more about Adapted Child ego states here.

The Adult ego state is the one that deals with the realities of here and now. It is often thought of as the 'thinking' part of the personality but, like the Child, it not only thinks but also feels and behaves, but it does so in a ways which are appropriate to what is actually going on in the present, uninfluenced by childhood experiences and expectations. Even a small child can use an Adult ego state – for example by going to the toy cupboard for a box of bricks when he can see it is too wet outside to play in the garden. It is often regarded as just 'common sense', but there's more to it than that.

The Parent ego state is a way of thinking, feeling and behaving which has been copied from parents and parent-type people such as teachers. It can be seen in a little girl of three nursing a dolly or in an orchestral conductor teaching his string section how to interpret a passage in a Beethoven symphony. But there are two distinct aspects to the Parent ego state characterised by Care – nursing a dolly, perhaps – and Control, maybe giving the string section a good telling off for playing too loudly! But both Care and Control are equally aspects of good Nurturing – a reality which many 'liberal' thinkers (and some transactional analysts!) fail to recognise.

Another important thing to know about is what we call 'Stroking'. This simply means giving recognition to someone or acknowledging that they are around. If we do that in a way the person welcomes and enjoys we call it a Positive Stroke, that is one that is encouraging and life enhancing. In fact the term 'stroking' has become part of the normal vocabulary of many people who know nothing about transactional analysis. But there can also be Negative Strokes that are unwelcome and the opposite of life enhancing. Insults and snide remarks are Negative Strokes but they can be much more subtle and less obvious that that. Receiving Negative Strokes is likely to provoke bad feelings and a desire to respond in a similar way. Both positive and negative Strokes give recognition that someone is around and worth noticing but there are many ways Strokes can be given without actually speaking. A glance might be sufficient, or a present or being selected from a number of others.

We also speak of Time Structuring. There are six basic ways of doing this: Withdrawal, Rituals, Pastiming, Activity, Games and Intimacy. Withdrawal is 'switching off' from engagement with other people and usually involves no exchange of Strokes at all. Rituals, like shaking hands (or sometimes ceremonies that can be quite complex, as in church or a court of law) involve some limited exchange of Strokes. Pastiming is a way of passing time with people but without any real emotional involvement. Nevertheless, this is a bit more rewarding in terms of recognition or Strokes than mere rituals. Activity is when people do something together – a crossword puzzle, a game of football or a joint effort at changing a car wheel, for example – and this is usually much more rewarding in terms of Strokes. Games are psychological Games, usually played to get Negative Strokes when Positive, life enhancing, Strokes are in short supply. I will describe them in the next paragraph. And, finally, Intimacy – this is altogether the best way of engaging with other people, because all the barriers are down, there is complete mutual trust, as in a good marriage, and all ego states can be used as appropriate.

So, if the question is 'What do you do with your time?', the answer is probably 'I collect Strokes – positive, life-enhancing Strokes for preference; but if not, then I will have Negative Strokes rather than be ignored altogether!'

Eric Berne used the word 'Games' to refer to transactions that are basically dishonest. They seem, on the face of it, to mean one thing whilst, at a psychological level, they actually mean something else. A Game usually begins when one person fails to take into account the thoughts, feelings or behaviour of another person; or else does not take account of what is going on in reality. For example, Kathie (who is quite capable of solving her own problem) might play the Victim role, having noted Monica's inclination to play the Rescuer role by always offering advice. But, when Kathie persistently rejects Monica's suggestions, Monica eventually realises that she is no longer a Rescuer; instead she feels more like a Victim, and Kathie seems like a Persecutor. So the two have switched roles, which neither intended in the first place. It is this switching roles that proves it was all a manipulative psychological Game. At the end of the Game, both will experience a familiar bad feeling, called a Racket Feeling, which seems to reinforce a life-long feeling that 'life's like that and there's no way out of it.'

This sort of thing is going on all the time, not only in coffee-time chat but in marital situations, business conferences, anywhere where people apparently try to communicate but secretly are jockeying for position and are really trying to win some sort of battle instead of trying to solve the problem in an Adult way.

The deep down feeling that 'life's like that' is a feature of what we call the Life Script, as in this book. It is founded on the observation that we all have a tendency to do the same kind of thing over and over again, perhaps throughout life if nothing is done about it. This is why some people get married and divorced several times, perhaps choosing the same kind of partner each time, so that a detached observer might well say, 'Here we go again' and anticipate yet another divorce. A classic example of this sort of Script is that of actress Elizabeth Taylor who has, I believe, had no less than eight marriages! This kind of behaviour is called a Script because it is like the script of a play. The players learn their lines and perform them on stage. When the tragic climax comes and the final curtain falls, all the actors go back home until the following evening when they are back on stage doing the same thing all over again, perhaps (though not necessarily) with someone else playing one of the leading roles. Many people's lives seem to follow this kind of repetitive pattern. It was an important discovery for me as a Probation Officer because so many of my clients played a Game called, in TA, 'Cops and Robbers'! They showed a repetitive pattern of offending, being arrested and sentenced and then before long doing the same thing all over again! In certain ways it was, I realised, actually happening in my own life, though without involving either divorce or imprisonment, I'm pleased to say! Readers familiar with game playing theory will no doubt track this sort of thing in my own 'case story'! A goal of therapy, then, is to explore what is really going on and what is the 'pay-off' (usually the bad 'Racket' Feeling) for the client when it happens.

Obviously there is much more to TA than I have briefly described above but, hopefully, readers new to the subject will find this introduction useful. Clients usually start by learning to recognise which of the three ego states is being used, either by themselves or by someone else, and changing the one they themselves are using (they can't change the other person!) if it seems it might result in better communication. I soon found that, say, a ten year old child whose parents were in conflict and threatening divorce, could actually influence what was happening at home simply by using a different ego state and maybe aborting a dangerous Game. Although the basic ideas behind TA are very simple and can be learned by anyone, new theory has, of course, developed over the years and TA has become much more sophisticated. It is now a very comprehensive system of psychotherapy and the 'treatment of choice' for many psychiatrists, psychotherapists and counsellors throughout the world.

But social casework was my recognised professional skill and my first concern was to enhance my competence in this. When my colleague Norma Cooper was promoted to be Senior Probation Officer in South Bank, I had the opportunity to transfer to her team. Undoubtedly Norma had the kind of professional training and expertise I was seeking and I looked forward to helpful casework supervision from her.

About this time Betty decided she could be more usefully employed as a social worker. She had learned to drive and, with her DHSS experience to build on and her natural way with people, she had little difficulty in getting appointed as an untrained social worker in Redcar. She was good at it, professionally better than I was as a probation officer in some respects because, whilst having abundant resources of 'Parent' sympathy, she could be a bit more emotionally detached than I was and could, therefore, use her Adult ego state more readily. Social casework, with its commitment to enlightened common sense, was exactly the right job for Betty.

* * *

For many years after joining the Probation Service I was so pre-occupied with doing the job and with entertaining fantasies of advancing my professional image, that I did virtually no writing at all, apart from the numerous scripts I wrote for talks on television. I had had very limited success in writing short stories but had already written two novels, albeit unpublished. And being a novelist was a much more likely to encourage people to think I was Somebody! So surely, it was time for me to write another novel. I had ideas, which had been gestating for many years, for a novel set in Wharfedale, so I set about writing it in an unused page-to-a-day hardback diary. It would be called *A View Across the Valley* but the 'valley' in my mind, believe it or not, was 'the valley of the shadow of death' – a sombre theme that has crept into so much of my writing. Writing that book was largely a secret enterprise pursued in the study in the early hours of the morning and all my other activities – probation work, church and preaching, TV and radio and everything to do with home and the family – continued at the same time!

In the summer of 1972 Paul left Acklam High School with some good A Levels and in the October started a four year course at the University of Keele, reading history and sociology. In his first year, of course, he was exploiting his freedom from parental control and was being far from 'religious'. In his second year, however, a team of evangelists moved in on the Students' Union and Paul (or rather Max, as everyone called him), though perhaps not entirely sober at the time, was nevertheless moved to respond and subsequently began attending their rather charismatic church in Silverdale nearby. Later (although baptised, of course, as a baby) he chose to be baptised by immersion in the sea at Redcar. It was the 2nd July, I remember. Betty did not attend the event but I did. Looking out to sea there is nothing between Redcar and the North Pole so it was perishing cold just standing on the beach to watch. If salvation had been 'by works' Paul would, I am certain, have been eligible for immediate entry into the Kingdom of Heaven as a just reward for his fortitude! Fortunately, it isn't, otherwise I – and many others – would never stand a chance!

When he joined the Christian Union he encountered Mary Martin, who had just arrived to do sociology and qualify as a social worker, and she evidently marked him out for further attention. Mary was one of seven children of a very religious family whose mother had strict Brethren antecedents. Her father, a Bachelor of Divinity amongst other things, was an Anglican lay preacher and principal of a Sixth Form College. Paul was warned by friends that Mary had her eye on him so one evening he visited her in her rooms on the campus to sort things out. He confessed in his wedding speech a few years later that when he got back to his own rooms he and Mary were practically engaged! He graduated on a blistering hot day in 1976, Princess Margaret, as Chancellor of the University, conferring the degrees.

Paul was unsure what sort of a career he was heading for, but social work seemed an obvious choice since his mum was a social worker already, his fiancée was to become one and his dad was a probation officer. So Paul was taken on as a temporary probation officer on a twelve months contract with Cleveland County Probation Service, as it had become by then. He was able to live at home whilst working at the Thornaby Probation Office and during that year, after spending a lot of time in court and seeing what happened, he decided that he wanted to train to be a solicitor. He got articles locally, went on to Law School at Leeds and was in due course admitted to the Law Society..

Paul and Mary's wedding in Nottingham where Mary's family lived, was the third one in our family in as many years. The first was my brother Philip's second marriage, to Margaret (Maggie) Thomas, in 1976. After Philip's marriage to Maggie came Caroline's wedding to Peter Phillips in 1977.

Caroline completed her education at Acklam High School, which had become co-educational, and then went into nursing training at Harrogate District Hospital. It was in Knaresbrough, nearby, that she met Peter, an electrician with the Yorkshire Electricity Board, and they were attracted to each other. Late one night, after leaving a nightclub, Peter took her home to meet his parents, Kath and Fred, and his sister. They were still up watching television – and there was I, on the screen, presenting the late night Epilogue! 'Gosh, it's my Dad!' cried Caroline. It must have been a bit alarming for Peter to have his first sight of his prospective father-in-law on the television screen, especially presenting a religious programme! The Phillips family were not churchgoers. Peter's father was in some kind of engineering job and his mother a Nursing Auxiliary so there was a cultural divide between our families in two areas. However, that did not bother Caroline who (whilst, perhaps, quite 'spiritual' in her own quiet way) was not committed to institutional religion and church-going and was not much interested in academic things either. Anyway, her relationship with Peter flourished. They got engaged and were married in due course, in September, 1977, at Avenue Methodist Church in Middlesbrough.

*　*　*

Throughout all these events I was writing *A View Across the Valley*. But the writing became, from Betty's point of view at least, quite obsessive and she was concerned for my personal well-being. Knowing I was an inveterate dog lover, and with memories of Patch, she decided that the best possible way to give me something else to think about was to give me a puppy for my 52nd birthday in 1978. She and Mary arrived one day with the furry brown and white pup, about six weeks old by then. As recorded in my 'journal', I held her in my hands with mixed feelings of sheer delight and a slightly heavy heart. I said to her, 'You are going to change the whole pattern of my life!' And so she was. That was Betty's intention! We christened her Sally. She was one of a litter of five born on a farm in Moorsholme, the fruit of an illicit liaison between her mother, a springer spaniel, and a Welsh border collie. She had the brown and white colours of her mother and the short hair and pointed nose of her father, though smaller than most border collies. She was loaded with personality, even if we sometimes doubted her intelligence, and became our replacement child of the family. Daily walks and weekend runs on the beach at Redcar or Saltburn became obligatory.

The writing of my third novel continued in spite of Sally and she would lie at my feet in the study whilst I scribbled away, usually with music playing quietly in the background. This was long before the days of computers and I invested an enormous amount of time and effort in writing, typing, revising and re-typing *A View Across the Valley* and, as usual, Betty helped with the typing. But she was disappointed with the book. It was a bit depressing, she thought. That was hardly surprising since the 'valley' of the title was, in my mind, 'the valley of the shadow of death' and it was not 'racy' enough for Betty! But, then, I was not a 'racy' person. Nevertheless, I had put a great deal of myself into it, identifying with the different characters in various ways and I was disappointed by Betty's disappointment.

But she was right, of course and her opinion was re-enforced by several later readers. I was at the time a member of the Middlesbrough Writers Group and three of our members read the MS. All assured me the book was 'a good read' but also noted its shortcomings, as did a professional reader to whom I paid a fee to get a totally unbiased opinion. Essentially, the book was quite simply old-fashioned and would, I was told, almost certainly have found a publisher in the days of D.H. Lawrence and H.E. Bates! I was flattered to be compared with such illustrious writers though, in all probability, they themselves would not have found a ready publisher in the 1970s, when John Braine, Alan Sillitoe and Andrea Newman were selling their film and TV rights.

At last, I admitted to myself that I was not cut out to be a successful novelist. When I was unable to find a publisher for *A View Across the Valley*, even after further revisions and the introduction of some fairly explicit sexy stuff designed to spice it up a bit, I gave up the ghost and invested in transactional analysis.

7

NEW DIRECTIONS

Well-integrated, well-adjusted people might keep diaries, like Pepys, but they have no need whatever to write journals in which they indulge in introspective self-analysis. If I had not had this need I doubt if I would ever have taken Christianity seriously, beyond the merely institutional. I would have been 'whole and in no need of a physician'. Neither would I have had any need to pursue transactional analysis as an alternative means of sorting myself out when the simple institutional Methodism I'd been brought up to failed to help me out of the spiritual mess I was in. The journal eventually became a book of prayers, written down to help me keep my wandering mind on the spiritual exercise in hand.

So I was pursuing two different approaches to solving the problem of being truly myself – one religious and the other secular. Had my Methodism been of the 'spiritual' kind taught by Wesley I might never have needed TA – not for myself, at any rate. But it wasn't. I do not mean to imply that my Methodism had no spiritual value. It had for me, and has still, a very real value exemplified by the warmth of its fellowship, which is truly spiritual without being, for many of us, particularly religious. In addition to regular weekly services of worship, our spirituality manifests in coffee mornings, bring and buy sales, drama productions, choir concerts and other social events of various kinds. Some of these might begin with a hymn and a prayer and end with a benediction but much of what happens in between could just as well happen, and probably does, at meetings of the Towns Women's Guild or the Round Table. Whether these 'secular' events might also have a 'spiritual' dimension I don't know. But I think they probably do. Fellowship of any kind is tremendously important but I don't think Methodist fellowship is distinctively different from Anglican, Baptist or any other kind.

But it was neither Methodism nor transactional analysis that led me to give up my television work in the late 1970s. It was writing; in particular, my third novel *A View Across the Valley*. I put everything I'd got into that book. In some ways it is deeply spiritual without being even marginally religious. It was, I suppose, about people who were as confused as I was about the meaning of life and just as unsure about what direction they were taking. That, no doubt, is why it was so depressing, and why I could not find a publisher to take it on. My disappointment was intense because (as my journal reveals) I was so confident that this time I had got it right and had written something really worthwhile which some publisher would surely want. Indeed, one professional reader did, as I have said, identify it as a 'literary novel' but felt it was not quite literary enough! With hindsight I realise now that I had not been sufficiently persistent in seeking a publisher and had not known the right way to go about it.

Nowadays, publisher do not seem to want a complete MS; they just want a 'project', in the form of an outline and, perhaps, a specimen chapter or two. But if *A View Across the Valley* had been published, I would yet again have thought I was at last 'a writer', just as I had always wanted to be. I would, thereafter, have invested all my energy in writing further novels, always hoping that one day I would hit the jackpot with a bestseller. I would have abandoned my struggle for 'significance' in striving for advancement to Senior Probation Officer status because, as a writer, I would have had all the significance I had ever wanted. And I would never have become a transactional analyst.

However, my prayers for success as I writer did not go unanswered. They were answered by a God who said, 'No. You are indeed a writer, but right now I have something more important in mind for you. Trust me.' TA was not yet a major interest. All I wanted was that I might become a more effective caseworker and, in due course, a Senior Probation Officer.

After reading *Games People Play* my next step in the direction of transactional analysis was attending a one-day course in it at a local college. Through that, my belief was confirmed that TA had real potential as a casework tool in dealing with offenders. Not long after this I attended a '101' Introductory course in TA held in Birmingham. The 101 course, which is presented over two days, is the official introduction to transactional analysis and a pre-requisite for anyone wanting to proceed to advanced training and Membership of the International Transactional Analysis Association or, nowadays, EATA – The European Association for Transactional Analysis. There were about thirty people on the course, held at Winterbourne, an extra-mural college belonging to Birmingham University, and it was led by Dr Michael Reddy, a Teaching Member of ITAA. Michael was an ex-monk and only the first of many practitioners I met who had abandoned religion for TA. He was an excellent presenter and I came away from the course feeling well-equipped to go further. In fact, I was with Michael again only a few months later on a four day 'Intermediate Course' held in London.

Training to become a transactional analyst does not involve going to university or a specialised college for several years, after which the trainee might be considered fit to be let loose on an unsuspecting public! The entire training process, like my training to become a probation officer, is, again, a kind of 'on the job' apprenticeship, under the supervision of a qualified practitioner, although the supervisor does not normally sit in on therapy sessions. So after getting myself launched on professional training I attended numerous courses at my own expense, held in different parts of the country and led by a variety of experienced and qualified practitioners, frequently from Europe or America. In due course, I approached Michael Reddy at a conference we were both attending, to see if he would take me on as a contracted trainee. This was the next essential step after the 101 Introductory Course. However, he regretted that he could not sponsor me as a clinical trainee because he was about to make an important change himself. Although transactional analysis began as a form of psychotherapy for people suffering from a variety of mental illnesses, emotional distress or relationship problems, it soon became clear that the theories Eric Berne had developed could be beneficial in other areas as well. The first of these was Organisational work in which TA was used as an approach to staff training in industry and so became of interest to personnel managers. Later, special applications were developed in the field of education and in counselling. This latter is, of course, a form of psychotherapy but it is generally recognised as the treatment of choice in cases where there is no mental pathology, in marital work, for example, or bereavement counselling. But Michael had decided to go in for Organisational work which, from a purely commercial point of view, is much more rewarding than clinical work.

However, he suggested that Dr Margaret Turpin, at whose home in Muswell Hill we were meeting for a Conference, might be willing to consider sponsoring me. Margaret hardly knew me at all so was unable to agree contract terms there and then. She invited me to visit her again in the near future to discuss things and, perhaps, to bring some work for supervision. Margaret had given up general medical practice in order to concentrate on TA psychotherapy, so sponsorship by her was an attractive option. I began to visit her about once a month, taking a day's leave and travelling by train on a Day Return ticket to London. The Probation Service knew nothing about it at this stage and only the generosity of the annual leave arrangements made it possible, as with my earlier television work. The very minimal leave granted by the Middlesbrough Probation Service had been much improved after the Service had expanded under Chief

Probation Officer Alec Nuttall, who now directed work in the whole of the newly formed Cleveland County. So I had a regular and experienced supervisor in Margaret Turpin, although she herself, whilst a Clinical Member of ITAA, was still only a Provisional Teaching Member. However, I was now a professional trainee and going in the right direction.

Around this time changes were taking place, many of which proved to be significant for me. I was becoming well known for my use of transactional analysis in case work, and various interested agencies, such as Marriage Guidance, The Alcohol Council, the local Nurses Training School and the Young People's Unit in the psychiatric hospital all invited me to run courses for them.

Whilst all this was going on I continued my work with probation clients, some of whom made important life changes in consequence. One of these was David Brodie, a man in his early forties, who had a long criminal history. I first met him on a visit to another client in HM Prison Haverigg, in Cumbria. Hearing that a Cleveland probation officer was around David asked to see me and became a voluntary prison after-care client on his release. He was not in prison for the first time, he actually wanted to change the criminal life he was leading, and since he had the right attitude to achieve something I took him on. He was married, with a teenage son and daughter and his wife was amazingly supportive of such a delinquent husband. David had, in fact, already benefited from a year at a Methodist-sponsored probation hostel in Bradford, during which time he had attended a free church mission and been converted. This ought to have meant that he never again put a foot wrong but rarely is a religious conversion as tidy as that! Even where there is a memorable 'event' (which there never was in my case) there is always a period of spiritual growth and conflict and falls from grace. For most of us – and probably for all of us to some extent – this growth is a life-long process. David's subsequent history involved many ups and downs, including his wife eventually losing patience and divorcing him. After a while I lost touch with him until I met him 'by chance' in Darlington one day. He had an attractive lady on his arm who was now his partner and he told me that he was an official Volunteer with a probation Service in the North East. He was also doing an Open University degree in criminology! A few years after that I learned from a mutual friend that he actually passed the exams and qualified for the degree but, sadly, died of cancer before he could receive it.

Another success story was a young man called Billy. He had a list of over two hundred convictions on his record, mainly for petty theft, and the governor of a local remand prison once told me that, in his opinion, Billy was 'damaged beyond repair'. At that stage he was not yet twenty years old. When I last saw him he was living with an ex-prostitute twice his age who had five children by various fathers. Nevertheless, it seemed to be a very stable relationship in which he had a much-needed mother-figure for himself whilst somehow providing an acceptable father figure for her offspring. Best of all, he had a regular job with the corporation and seemed to have abandoned crime.

But not all my probation clients did so well. My most spectacular failure was Brian Charrington. I can identify him without breaching professional confidentiality since his name, his face and his story have appeared numerous times in the press. When I first met him he was sixteen years old and on Aftercare Licence from a Detention Centre where he had experienced a few months of doing everything at the double. He was a smooth, self-confident, secretive and cynical lad even then, and the revealing half smile I knew so well then, still figured in his press photographs thirty or more years later. He is now a notorious international drugs baron with a fortified villa in Spain, though at the time of writing he is in prison in Germany. Only recently the Teesside Evening Gazette reported that the police had raided his Middlesbrough home and found over a million pounds stashed away there in used bank notes! I often wonder whether he remembers me.

Eventually, I moved from the South Bank Probation Office to a Team in Baker Street, Middlesbrough, whose Senior Probation Officer was Peter Sugden, an ex-policeman and twenty years younger than I, with whom I had competed for this senior post. Peter and I were good friends and he gave me a lot of support and encouragement as I developed my TA work. I was already running a therapy group in the office for probation clients, some of whom were referred by colleagues on the team. During this period, whilst Betty was on secondment to the CQSW course at Sunderland Polytechnic, one of her fellow social work students, Joyce Arkless, had a training placement in the Probation Office and she, too, became interested in my work in transactional analysis. Our friendship had a most important spin-off later on.

Whilst there was some cautious interest in my TA work amongst the management of the Cleveland Probation Service it was never whole-hearted and there seemed to be no likelihood that the Probation Committee would sponsor me for full clinical training. The position was made clear by Norma Cooper, by now an ACPO, when she attended a team meeting at which I was doing a case presentation. As I talked to my colleagues about a certain client's 'scripty behaviour' and the psychological Games he was undoubtedly playing with both me and the police, Norma broke in to say in her fine and authoritative contralto voice, 'David, you really must remember that you are a probation officer, not a psychiatrist!' Her observation was apt enough because I was indeed beginning to experience a certain amount of role confusion!

My interest in TA spread into the Durham County Probation Service, just to the north, and I was invited by Tony Walker, a Senior Probation Officer in Darlington, to do a series of talks on TA to his team. About six or seven officers attended regularly and, from time to time, the Chief Probation Officer himself, Peter Warburton, also came, as did his Assistant Chief, Charles Hocking, who was a marriage guidance counsellor with 'Relate', as it came to be called. This course also ran for several weeks.

Many would say, of course, that I was just 'lucky'. But I don't think it was just a matter of luck. I am quite committed to the belief that God had a hand in it. However, I am not at all sure I use the word 'God' to mean what other people might mean. God, I have decided, is a 'Humpty Dumpty' word, as in *Alice Through the Looking Glass*; it means whatever the speaker wants it to mean! For me, however, it has come to mean more than 'a guiding force' which influences – but does not necessarily control – everything that goes on in the universe. For me, 'God is love' (as in the First Letter of John, Chapter 4) and I see this love perfectly exemplified in the person of Jesus, the carpenter of Nazareth, who declared that he would draw all people to himself.

I have elsewhere used, as an analogy for the attractive power of love, the experiment most school children do in the physics lab. The monitor distributes to everyone a bar magnet with a North and South pole; then sheets of paper are handed out which are laid on top of the bar magnet. Finally, a small tube of iron filings is given to everyone. The iron filings are sprinkled evenly over the paper. The magnetic field from the bar magnet draws the iron filings into a predictable pattern, following the lines of magnetic force. God, as I know Him in Jesus, I now say, draws human beings to Himself and into harmonious relationship with one another, not by the power of magnetism, but by the power of Love. Unlike the iron filings, however, we can choose whether or not to respond to the power of love. We have 'free will'. No-one can prove this, of course. and some people think free will is an illusion. That is too big an issue to discuss here, though I might have a bit more to say about it in a later chapter. For myself, I have decided to believe that I do have free will and that I am responsible for the choices I make which influence not only the direction my life is going, but other people's lives as well. God, I believe, is drawing me in the direction He wants me to go, and the spiritual element in my human nature makes me sensitive and responsive to His leading.

* * *

Eventually an opportunity came for me to apply for a Senior Probation Officer post in County Durham. In fact it was in Darlington because Tony Walker, who had been instrumental in inviting me to run the TA course there, was making a horizontal transfer to another Senior post in Durham City. I visited Peter Warburton, the CPO, to discuss what the appointment would entail. The team at Darlington included ten main grade probation officers and Bea Walker, who was responsible for organising Community Service as a alternative sentence to imprisonment; and another officer, Arnold Robinson, was developing a Day Centre. Most teams had five or six officers, which was enough for one SPO to supervise; but Darlington had ten, so two SPOs were necessary. The other one, Tom Peacock, was another ex-police officer who had had many years in the Probation Service and it would be important for me to work harmoniously with him. What the Chief had in mind was that Tom should manage the whole team because such management was where his main strength lay; but the new SPO would be a specialist casework supervisor, an area in which Tom had less expertise. I could not have asked for anything more to my liking.

My application was accepted and I was short-listed along with three or four others who were already in the Durham County Probation Service. Almost the first thing the Chairman, Mrs Denham, said to me was, 'Mr Midgley, tell us about transactional analysis.' Peter Warburton had warned me this might happen and had suggested I respond in no more than five minutes. So I delivered my well-prepared exposition. But I was at pains to assure the Committee, as the interview proceeded, that TA was only one of the strings to my bow. I had also taken an active interest in youth work and was on the management committee of a community centre on my patch, as well as being involved with a Prisoners' Wives Group. I had explored Durham County's own Community Service facilities, was Deputy Chairman of the Middlesbrough Branch of the National Association of Probation Offices and Convenor of the Branch Training Committee and had had quite extensive experience in supervising trainees on secondment for various counselling, probation and social work training courses. I left them in no doubt that I was eminently well equipped for the post they wanted to fill!

I got the job and took up my appointment as Senior Probation Officer responsible for casework supervision at Darlington in September, 1979. My Senior colleague, Tom Peacock, who was responsible for management and administration, was a tall, quite handsome man with horn-rimmed glasses who was good-humoured enough but rarely smiled unless there was some special occasion for it and I never heard him give a whole-hearted belly laugh. He was just not that kind of man. At heart, I think, he was still a policeman. He discussed office business with me and we met once a week for that specific purpose but otherwise he kept me at arm's length. I was not at all comfortable with this very detached business relationship and was sad that Tom clearly had no desire at all for the kind of friendship I would have liked. When, after a few weeks in my new post, I tried to get to know him better by inviting him and his wife Pat to come over to Middlesbrough for dinner with me and Betty, he declined without much explanation. I guess I discovered some years later what might have been the explanation for Tom's attitude towards me, when I made important discoveries about myself!

Senior Probation Officers, unlike many Senior Social Workers, usually carry a small caseload of clients and prepare social enquiry reports for the courts. So I was never cut off from the grass roots of probation work and usually had ten or a dozen clients with whom I was working closely. They included burglars and ship lifters, sex offenders, people convicted of violence and some murderers released from prison on Life Licence. These latter were, by and large, the least troublesome and those I supervised were men who had committed only one serious offence and might never have offended again even had they not been convicted. My clients were both men and women and represented all ages from young teenagers to people in their seventies.

It was not at all unusual for close dependency relationships to develop in probation casework and I must admit to being vulnerable in this area. It happened with men as well as with women; but, of course, there is always an extra risk with a client of the opposite sex. I once had a prisoner's wife tell me quite frankly that she would like to go to bed with me! Fortunately, she was bigger than I was and my preference has always been the shorter woman!

But I supervised old people too. One was Reg, a man of seventy two, about twenty years older that I was. He did not have a serious criminal track record but, mysteriously, he had started shoplifting. His style was to enter a toy shop – rarely any other kind – select an attractively boxed electric toy of some kind, maybe a 'Scalextric', and simply walk out with it under his arm, to be secreted away in the loft at home. I visited the home and found it clean, comfortable and welcoming, with plenty of family photographs on display. But there was a curiously tense atmosphere in the house that I could not account for. Hilda, Reg's wife, had arthritis in her right arm and it was protected by a moulded plastic splint that she fastened on with buckles. She was a pleasant enough lady, welcomed me to the home and made a cup of tea for me and Reg. But she would not have one with us. She had 'things to do' upstairs and left me and Reg to talk alone together. So one day I called unexpectedly when I knew Reg would be out. She admitted that things were not happy between them but would not say why. I asked her if she would call alone to see me at the office and, to my surprise, she did. Gradually, it all came out. She and Reg, had not slept in the same room for several years. He had taken the initiative to go into another room and, in consequence, she felt rejected and unloved. She wondered whether this had anything to do with his offending. I took it up with Reg alone and discovered that he was unhappy with Hilda because she was always wanting a cuddle in bed but would go no further. He himself still had sexual needs and he found it easier to sleep alone than to be continually frustrated. He assured me he had never been with another woman, though he had often wanted to.

I began to see them both together and we quickly established communication about the problem. They learned to understand each other and found ways to meet each other's needs in the same bed. The atmosphere in the home changed. They were happier than they had been for years. After a while I noticed that Hilda was no longer wearing her plastic splint and remarked about it. She told me with obvious delight that the arthritic pain had simply disappeared. In addition, Reg was never in trouble again for stealing from shops and when I applied to the court, the magistrates were pleased to discharge the Probation Order early.

What had happened? Both the stealing and the splint, it seemed, had been attention-seeking strategies. This sort of thing happened several times in the course of my counselling and psychotherapeutic work, when puzzling physical ailments simply 'got better'. Of course, the psychosomatic dimension of illness generally is well-known to the medical profession but very rarely do doctors regard psychotherapy as an appropriate treatment in itself, beyond the observation that the patient is 'under stress' and perhaps in need of a holiday. In fact, a Working Party set up in the North East in the late 1980s to study this matter concluded that as many as fifty percent of patients seen by GPs in a deprived area were 'emotionally disturbed'. Other research has found that of every thousand persons in a research population, 250 had emotional problems; twenty of these would not consult their family doctor and of the 230 who did, 90 were not recognised as emotionally disturbed. Of the 140 who were recognised only 23 would be referred to a psychiatrist.

The Working Party was concerned specifically with the treatment of 'emotional problems', many of which did not amount to 'mental illness'. Nevertheless, in many cases they 'found it reasonable to suppose that an absence of psychotherapy sometimes leads to patients substituting physical or mental illness for personal problems, leading to greater morbidity and greater demands for medication or other physical treatments.' I was invited by the Clinical Tutor of the South Cleveland General Hospital to deliver the postgraduate lecture on this subject. The audience of nearly a hundred was made up mainly of GPs but a lot of hospital doctors attended as well. They all recognised the importance of the subject (though those attending were no doubt attracted by one of the best buffet lunches I have ever had!) but nothing, so far as I could see, came out of it. There is a curious reluctance in the medical establishment to take practical account of a reality that has been known for thousands of years. The writer of the Book of Proverbs, for example, declared that 'A tranquil mind gives life to the flesh, but passion makes the bones rot.'

Of particular interest to me in the Working Party's report was that 'consultant psychiatrists were very concerned about a group of patients with severe personality disorders . . . which were refractory to traditional psychiatric treatments and caused considerable management difficulty.' Traditional treatments, of course, relied heavily on drugs because few NHS psychiatrists had time to offer psychotherapy, even if they had undertaken the necessary training. Psychotherapy, the Report proposed, 'could offer a specific treatment service for this group of patients.'

This was the client group I was specifically concerned with as a probation officer. My clients were not, for the most part, neurotic, neither were they psychotic; they were character disordered. Unfortunately, I had discovered, the term 'character disorder' was often used interchangeably with 'personality disorder'. So I had to distinguish my special group as 'antisocial'. Both character disorder and neurosis were described by some writers as 'disorders of responsibility'. Neurotics, it was said, were over responsible and thought they were responsible for everything; character disorders were not responsible enough and thought everything that went wrong was someone else's responsibility. This dichotomy was, of course, grossly over-simplified but I found it very useful as a starting point nevertheless. Most of my probation clients were more or less character disordered, antisocial or 'sociopathic', as the Americans would say.

A factor I had to take into account, however, was that the character disorders I was dealing with were not necessarily 'severe'. By this time, only very severe character disorders were being classified as 'psychopathic', especially when their behaviour involved violence. But earlier there had been a tendency to use 'psychopathic' as a blanket term for anyone whose antisocial behaviour did not respond to medication. One psychiatrist from whom I learned much in my early days in Middlesbrough, was Dr Jack Blackburn, Physician Superintendent of St Luke's Psychiatric Hospital. He said to me one day when we were discussing this, 'I'll name three well-known psychopaths: Sir Winston Churchill, Sir John Betjeman and Mr John Stonehouse.' Few to-day would refer to Churchill as psychopathic, much less John Betjeman, whatever their idiosyncratic behaviour. Perhaps John Stonehouse was, even by my criteria. He was a minister in Harold Wilson's government who engineered his own disappearance in the sea off Miami beach, later turned up in Australia and was imprisoned for offences of fraud! The common feature in these three disparate people was evidently their tendency to ignore normal social expectations and do their own thing. Perhaps they all had their own understanding about what was 'right' and what was 'wrong' and to what extent it mattered. But apart from Stonehouse, their behaviour was not criminal even if it was sometimes insensitive and distressing for people, especially for those close to them. The term 'character disorder' suits them much better. Because of that they were unable to form stable and enduring personal relationships, in which a primary requirement is a common set of moral values. Many counsellors and psychotherapists (including me) would prefer to be regarded as 'a bit character disordered', rather than 'a bit neurotic'! In due course I explored this matter in my book *New Directions in Transactional Analysis Counselling*, which was published by Free Association Books in 1999; but at this stage, in the 1970s, I was just beginning to find out what made people 'tick' and to find out why we behave as we do.

The problem of medicine paying only lip-service to patient needs that were not obviously physical, extends also to the spiritual arena. This is not exclusively a religious concern, as some suppose, but has to do with meaning and purpose in life. Nevertheless, the spiritual life is the professional concern of ministers of religion and the NHS invests a lot of public money in employing them, some full-time, as hospital chaplains. And yet there is no general expectation that these professionals will be seen as part of the 'therapeutic team' with any input about treatment plans. A government paper in the nineteen nineties talked about holistic 'care' but not holistic 'treatment'. All these issues were swilling about in my mind at this stage as I wondered what particular contribution I could make to the world of 'healing'.

To begin with, my training in transactional analysis was quite informal, with attendance at training conferences and workshops. Dr Margaret Turpin agreed to monthly sessions of supervision to which I took tape-recorded segments of my work with probation clients. To begin with things looked quite promising and we got along well together. It was not long, however, before I had a major opportunity that changed my direction significantly and changed my relationship with Margaret. I had a phone call one day from Joyce Arkless, the social worker mentioned earlier who had been on the same CQSW course as Betty at Sunderland Polytechnic and had done a practice placement in the Cleveland Probation Service. She was now working in the Department of Psychiatry at North Tees General Hospital and the Senior Consultant, Dr John Hawkings, had suggested on a ward round that they could do with facilities for group treatment. But who was equipped to practice group therapy? Joyce herself did not feel that she had either the experience or the training so she had suggested that I might be interested. Dr Hawkings and I knew each other quite well already because certain of my clients had been his patients in the past, so he was quite enthusiastic. He was a very impressive figure of a man, over six feet tall, a bit over-weight and with a splendid head of curly white hair. His personality was very out-going, even charismatic, and he had an impatience with medical conservatism that must have been rather like Eric Berne, the American psychiatrist who had developed transactional analysis a decade or two earlier. He saw no reason why a layman should not be used if he could help patients to get better. Joyce asked me, would I like to think about working with him? The matter hardly needed any thinking about so far as I was concerned. It was exactly the opportunity I wanted and never expected to get! My contribution would have to be entirely voluntary because the hospital had no provision to pay me but I wasn't bothered about that. Joyce and Dr Hawkings would suggest likely candidates for group treatment and I would then see them individually in the Out Patients Clinic on a Monday evening and make the final selection. Ideally, we needed five or six to start with and probably not more than about eight in total at any one time. Joyce would take part in the group in the role of co-therapist whilst she was, at the same time, learning from me.

* * *

Whilst all this was happening I was still busy being a Senior Probation Officer in Darlington. At the Chief's invitation I set up a TA training course for probation staff throughout the County, including several members of my own team, that ran weekly for several months. I provided detailed type-written notes for every session and these formed the basis for a good deal of writing I did subsequently. I produced a book I called *The Winner's Handbook – A Beginner's Introduction to the Theory and Practice of Transactional Analysis*. Betty, as usual, helped with the typing and she liked the book. We both thought it was a 'hot property' and that I should not have much trouble in finding a publisher. But we were wrong. There were, it seemed, more than enough do-it-yourself TA books on the market. So it went into a bottom drawer along with my three unpublished novels. Instead, I wrote a little twelve page booklet called *Taking Charge of Your Own Life – A Brief Introduction to Transactional Analysis*. I established my own publishing imprint as 'New Directions Publishing', contacted Whitakers for an ISBN number for it and published it myself. It was an instant success – not a multi-million best seller, of course, but it was well-received by the TA community, well-reviewed in the ITA NEWSLETTER and was bought in quantity by quite a number of colleagues who distributed it to clients and trainees. I contacted scores of branches of Waterstones throughout the UK and almost all of them agreed to take half a dozen copies on a sale or return basis. And not one of them returned any. All were paid for and many shops re-ordered. Later I revised it and published a Second Edition, taking into account *Physis*, the growth force of nature, which I see as having spiritual implications. I still get occasional orders from one wholesaler twenty years after the booklet was first published, and colleagues still occasionally ask for it. It has sold several thousand copies and now I have an unexpected income from the Publisher's Licensing Society and the Authors' Licensing and Collecting Society, both of which collect fees for photocopying from several educational establishments all over the country.

8

SERIOUS TRAINING

So here I was, called to be a therapist, a healer, for people who actually wanted to be made 'whole'. They would not be sent by the courts in the hope that a probation officer would 'do them good'. They were all in search of love, hope, healing, peace of mind and a sense of spiritual security that many had never known before. I was to be the channel that would provide what they would be coming for. But my need was, of course, at least as great as theirs. Being further along the road, perhaps, you might think my feeling of need would be less. But that is not true. People deprived of love (or of Positive Strokes) sometimes learn to live without it. They 'adapt'. They might even develop a kind of spiritual anorexia and shun the whole idea of love. But once those with some appetite left have discovered a source of love their appetite is likely to grow; they might even become ravenous, hooked on love as if addicted to a drug.

Patients for the group were referred to me at the Monday evening clinic at the hospital. They were all quite young and mostly, though not entirely, out-patients who had been in the wards earlier. For confidentiality their names and other details in the following account have been changed, of course. Adrian was twenty, a tall, good-looking lad with an engaging personality and a tee shirt bearing the bright, smiling face of Thomas the Tank Engine! He was diagnosed with an anxiety state that had kept him off his laboratory job at ICI for over six months. He was clearly intelligent and had good A Levels and he lived with his widowed mother, his dad having died when Adrian was only eleven. It was immediately clear that he and his mother were all-in-all to each other and that this smothering relationship was a big part of the problem. Adrian warmed to the idea of joining a therapy group because he did not get out much and he had not many friends.

Next came Joanne. She was twenty four and diagnosed with simple schizophrenia, though she was now quite functional on medication and able to look after herself. She did not hear voices or suffer from bizarre delusions or paranoid episodes but she was curiously detached from the rest of the world and failed to make close relationships. She had no job and lived in a bed-sitter in the home of a lady who was a kind of adopted aunt, since Jo had no relations nearby and the ones she knew found her difficult to relate to.

Chris, an able young graduate aged twenty six, was the younger of two sons, his thirty year old brother being happily married with a family. Chris was unemployed and, like Alistair, lived with his widowed mother. But there was something curiously unhappy about his memories of his deceased father. Chris was diagnosed manic-depressive, but it was 'monopolar' – that is there was no 'manic' phase; the depression alternated with periods of normality. He was pretty normal now.

Gillian, the oldest of the group, was about forty, divorced, as thin as a lath and still on the ward. She was severely anorexic, had been down to only four stones but was now built up to six stones. She was not keen on the group but, in her despair, was reluctantly willing to give it a go. Janice was also still on the ward, an attractive lass whose paranoid feelings seemed to be associated with a personality disorder rather than schizophrenia. She was nervous about the group but agreed to 'think about it'. Then came Elaine. She was twenty two and had had two spells on the ward with depression but now was at home on medication and back at her job working in a supermarket. But she was far from well. Her older sister was married and there was a younger brother who was an apprentice joiner. Elaine felt totally unloved by both parents. She was clearly intelligent and articulate but she had truanted her way through school, often kept at home to help her mother, and left without even a CSE to her name. Like Janice she was far from enthusiastic about the group but agreed to try it out. She arrived on time for the first meeting but, seeing the rest of the group, assembled ready to go in, she took fright and ran away! I went to see her at home after the session and persuaded her to try again. The next time the group were primed and greeted her warmly on arrival so she stayed.

It took several weeks to see them all at the clinic, and some others who were not suitable for the group for one reason or another. However, when there were five Joyce and I decided to start sessions at six o'clock on Thursday evenings. It was a big commitment for me, at the end of a full day at the Probation Office, especially when, after the group had dispersed, I would frequently go upstairs to the clinic to grab a few minutes with Dr Hawkings between patients to discuss progress.

However, my main supervisor was still Dr Margaret Turpin and I continued to visit her once a month at her home in Muswell Hill. I had hoped she would be delighted to know I was now recognised by the psychiatrists and employed, even though on a voluntary basis, to treat their patients. In fact a period of attachment to a psychiatric unit was later to become a requirement of clinical training in transactional analysis. With this development, surely, Margaret would be willing now to agree to a training contract with me. But to my disappointment, not to say chagrin, she was not. She had been evasive from the start when I had mentioned a formal contract but seemed to have no real reason why we should not go ahead. I was reminded very much of my problems with Dorothy Burdis, my course tutor at Leeds University who, for no clear reason, would have had me off the course altogether, had not George Moore, my fieldwork supervisor, not intervened on my behalf. Also, I again experienced feelings I had had with Norma Cooper, my line manager in Middlesbrough, who had declined, at one stage, to endorse my applications for a senior post despite my effectiveness as a main grade probation officer and a supervisor of trainees. There was 'just something', she said to my SPO and to a visiting Home Office Inspector. She could not say what it was but she was clearly uncomfortable with me for reasons that, I concluded, must have been within herself. Now Margaret Turpin was doing the same thing. What had these women in common? They were all in positions of authority, and all unmarried so I even wondered whether there was something 'Freudian' going on! Whatever the reason it was blocking my progress. Anyway, I button-holed Margaret over coffee one day at the annual ITA training conference.

The Conference, always held in April, during the Easter vacation, was held at various universities around the country to give everyone an opportunity to attend. That year it was at Warwick. From the beginning of my membership of the Institute of Transactional Analysis I had presented a workshop at each conference, despite my humble status as a trainee, and this time it was on the theme of 'Treating the Reluctant Client', a subject in which, as a probation officer, I was certainly experienced even if not exactly expert! The workshop was well-attended by other trainees and by some qualified practitioners. Margaret herself actually looked in for half an hour or so to see how I was making out and since I was quite good at that sort of thing I thought she would have been impressed. Maybe she was but, of course, I was not asking her to train me to run workshops!

Over coffee I asked Margaret, 'Can we go ahead with a clinical training contract now?'

'No, David, I'm afraid not,' she said without beating about the bush.

I had the same feeling I had had nearly twenty years earlier when Dennis Burke had sacked me from Thomas Hedley's with the words, 'David, we are parting company – and we're parting company now!'

'But, why, Margaret?' I asked in distress and frustration. 'What's the problem?'

She hesitated and then said, 'These psychiatric patients you are working with are far too difficult for a trainee.'

They were difficult cases, of course. But had they been simple, straight-forward people with minor problems they would not have been candidates for psychotherapy in the first place. They would probably have responded to a brief course of tranquillisers or anti-depressants or to a chat with the GP. But Margaret was adamant. I was certain that this could not be the real reason. It was just an impressive excuse. If I wanted to pursue advanced training, she said, I would have to look elsewhere.

At that time there were in the UK very few practitioners of transactional analysis who were qualified to teach. Trainees sometimes had to go to Germany, Italy or even the USA to find a sponsor. And then someone put me in touch with Gordon Law, a South African, who was a social worker with Hereford and Worcestershire Social Services. Gordon was a 'Provisional Teaching Member', as they were then called. He was already an experienced 'Clinical Member' of the International Transaction Analysis Association (ITAA) and under training himself for a higher qualification. We spoke on the phone and he invited me to go down to a training weekend at Worcester. There were about nine trainees in Gordon's group, including Jenny Robinson whom I had got to know already because she was a prison psychologist; so we had something in common. She was actually a clinical trainee under contract to Dr Michael Reddy who had got me started a year or two before. But trainees attended workshops led by a wide variety of trainers and Jenny, who lived and worked nearby, was using a convenient opportunity. Anyway, Michael, by this time, was developing his interest in organizational work and was not running groups for clinical trainees.

From this point my training started in earnest, although I still had to prove myself competent before Gordon was willing to enter into a clinical training contract with me. The training session would usually begin with some theoretical in-put by Gordon and then he would illustrate the theory by using one of the group as a 'client'. This was not role play. We always worked on real issues. For example, Jenny might have been having problems getting enough attention from Michael Reddy in view of his new interest, though he was still her sponsor and still had overall responsibility for her training. She felt neglected, victimised or persecuted by him because of this and wondered if they had some sort of psychological Game going on. In the therapy, Gordon would put an empty chair in front of Jenny, ask her to imagine that Michael was sitting on it and tell him what her problem was. She would then change chairs, 'become' Michael and respond, as if she were Michael, to the complaints she had put to him. This dialogue might go on for several exchanges as she moved from one chair to the other. Through identifying with Michael she would gain insight and understanding into what he was experiencing in their relationship and at the end of the exercise would be better equipped to take some constructive initiative to solve the problem.

Two Chair Work like this had become a standard technique, used for all sorts of therapeutic purposes to enable the client to identify with different elements in their experience. This could be individuals (dead or alive), ego states, dream symbols or other fantasies. This technique was not one much used, if at all, by Eric Berne, the originator of TA, but is drawn from the Gestalt therapy pioneered by German psychoanalyst Frederick S. Perls and developed in transactional analysis by Robert and Mary Goulding. The Gouldings established the 'Redecision School' of TA that became a favourite approach among many therapists. They influenced me deeply, both through their writing and through a five-day workshop I attended with them near Stratford-on-Avon in May 1984. This technique I also used with my group at the hospital.

Gordon was, as I mentioned earlier, himself in training to become a Teaching Member of ITAA. His sponsor was Graham Barnes, an American practitioner and writer on TA. In particular he was the editor of a book of important papers on the theory and practice of TA called *Transactional Analysis After Eric Berne*. Graham came over to England regularly to see his trainees, including Gordon, to sit in on weekend training workshops, to watch Gordon at work and to contribute quite a lot of the teaching for the benefit of all of us. So I saw a lot of Graham and we got on well together. I soon discovered that he, too – along with Michael Reddy, Raymond Hostie, a Belgian Dominican priest, Ken Hills, an Anglican priest, and many others – was a minister who had given up the church in favour of transactional analysis, which he found to be a much more effective way of bringing healing and happiness to those with enough insight to be aware of their need.

I travelled to Worcester once a month for weekend training workshops. In the context of these events I began to work on my own issues, particularly my lack of self-esteem, despite my several achievements and successes, and especially my relationship with my parents which, although superficially very good, had nevertheless served to undermine my sense of personal worth. Just as a psychoanalyst undergoes a personal analysis during the course of his training, so a transactional analyst must undergo extensive personal work. The reason, in both cases, is to ensure that the trainee becomes aware of his or her own personal needs and the way that these can affect the therapeutic work with a client. We need to be able to stand back from the relationship, to see, objectively, what exactly is going on and to make appropriate adjustments for the sake of the client. This might sometimes involve terminating work with that client altogether. Perhaps Margaret Turpin discussed with her sponsor her relationship with me and decided, in the light of it, that we should not continue.

In the training group, not only was I doing my own personal work, with one of the other trainees being my therapist under Gordon's supervision, but I would be acting as therapist myself with one of the others as my client. In the context of group work others can also intervene and contribute, sometimes at the specific invitation of the person acting as therapist. The point at issue is that this is not role-play; it is one trainee being authentically himself, presenting a real problem, and another trainee actually being the therapist. At any time Gordon could intervene and either make a suggestion as to what might happen next or he might take over as therapist himself, demonstrating whatever approach or technique was appropriate.

After several months of training workshops like this both Gordon and Graham had seen me in action a good deal and were able to make an assessment of my potential as a therapist. When they were satisfied that I would 'make it', and eventually pass the very exacting Final Exam Board, they agreed that Gordon and I should enter into a proper clinical training contract. This is a formal written document that was signed by both of us and, in Gordon's case, by Graham as well. It provided, at that time, for a minimum of nine months contractual training before I would be eligible to go before the board and could extend for three years. If I was not ready after three years a further contract could be agreed, possibly with a different sponsor. By the Spring of 1982 I had my contract and felt that the rest was just a matter of time; and, of course, a lot of hard work.

* * *

But plans for moving the Darlington Probation Office to new premises, where the whole team could be consolidated into one building, were under way and Tom Peacock and I spent some time together inspecting various possibilities. Eventually, we agreed that vacant offices in Gladstone

Street would meet our requirements. The premises had been used earlier by the Inland Revenue but had been standing empty for a few years. There was a reception office and waiting area on the ground floor but the main offices were on the first floor, including a large open area that had to be divided up with movable partitions. Tom had a semi-open office there and seemed to be quite happy with it. I had a large front office at the right hand end of a long corridor at the top of the stairs. I furnished it with a small settee and two easy chairs and a bookcase for all my books. I sat back in my swivel chair and relaxed.

But all was not well. Tom and I had radically different ideas about how the team ought to function. A particular bone of contention was about the staffing of the Magistrates Court. Tom already had a well established system by which the same two experienced probation officers were on court duty every day and prepared all the Social Enquiry Reports on defendants who were not currently under supervision. The system had much to commend it because the magistrates knew these probation officers well and this made for good communications. But I, with my developing 'therapeutic' ideas, felt strongly that a Social Enquiry Report should be prepared by an officer who would supervise the defendant later if a Probation Order was made or if the defendant was given a custodial sentence to be followed by a period of after-care. My argument was that the preparation of a Social Enquiry Report was an important diagnostic opportunity, when the client – having a court appearances to look forward to – was best prepared to be cooperative. Furthermore, at this stage, a therapeutic relationship could usually be established between an anxious defendant wanting help and the probation officer who would be providing it. Tom's scheme, whilst easier to operate, wasted both these opportunities. He put the interests of the court first (with abundant management justification) whilst I was more interested in the benefits to the client.

This dispute, together with Tom's disinclination to allow a closer relationship with me, and other staff considerations to do with office duty responsibilities, led to the whole team becoming unsettled. Almost certainly, a psychological Game was being played that Berne, with his predilection for folksy language, called 'Let's you and him fight'.

A transactional analyst, of all people, whose skills equipped him to help other people resolve their relationship problems, ought, surely, to be able to deal more constructively with this sort of thing. It was the only time in my life when I needed to take tranquillisers. I felt so depressed and ashamed that the idea even crossed my mind that I could even take the whole bottle of tablets at one go! I did not actually contemplate doing it but I did briefly consider it an option!

It was a salutary experience and I count it now as one I needed to have, both as a part of my training as a psychotherapist and also as an important element in my own spiritual growth. Whether we see the unpleasant experiences of life as being, on later reflection, fortunate or unfortunate probably depends on what we have decided to believe life is all about. Certainly, in this crisis I was dependent on my relationship with God as never before; I felt His closeness and I spent a lot of time in prayer.

9

UNDER CONTRACT

In due course the Chief Probation Officer 'shuffled his cabinet'. This happened about once every couple of years, when Senior Probation Officers were moved from one appointment to another. We had about six 'field teams' serving the courts in various parts of Durham County; plus a number of teams, or individual senior probation officers, on secondment to the Prison Department. There were also some specialist appointments including Training Officer, Community Service Officer and Warden of Fir Tree Grange Probation Hostel. The system ensured that we all had the opportunity to broaden our experience, and those who had their sights on further advancement to Assistant Chief Probation Officer posts around the country, would have something extra to offer on their CVs. At the next shuffle, then, I was redeployed to a team based in Sedgefield, where there was a Magistrates' Court. However, a fortnight before I was due to take over the job, an arsonist burnt the office down! Fortunately, the steel filing cabinets with all the records in them, survived the conflagration but the office Mike Creedon, my predecessor, had had was gutted along with practically everything else.

There were five probation officers in the team, three men and two women. In addition we had a Community Service Organiser who was not qualified as a probation officer but who nevertheless did an excellent job finding work for offenders to do in the local community and appointing someone 'on site' to make sure they did it. All the probation officers were experienced and I found them a friendly and congenial group to work with. For the first couple of weeks we had to work without proper offices and the Clerk to the Court kindly let us use his office first thing in the morning until I had got work allocated.

My first task, therefore, on taking over as SPO of the Sedgefield team, was to find some office accommodation. There was nothing suitable in Sedgefield itself but there were plans to build a new court building with an integrated Probation Office at Newton Aycliffe, a few miles away, so we found premises there and, after several weeks in temporary offices whilst refurbishing was under way, we eventually settled in.

Whilst the team was getting established in its new premises, I was busy working with psychiatric clients at North Tees General Hospital and preparing for my final examination to qualify as a clinical transactional analyst. I was attending monthly training events and supervisory sessions in Worcester with Gordon Law and also undertaking as much additional training, supervision and personal therapy as I could afford, with a variety of qualified teachers. Training to be a transactional analyst is an expensive business in terms of fees, travel and, sometimes, accommodation, though many trainers suggested we take a sleeping bag and sleep on their floors.

Although I was becoming known amongst the TA community for my work with character disordered 'reluctant clients', and although they were not good training material from my own point of view I sought particular opportunities to work with trainers who specialised in this client population. Of these the main ones were Jacqui Schiff and her 'adopted' son Shea. Jacqui was an American social worker who had been one of Eric Berne's early associates in the San Francisco Social Psychiatry Seminars, where a lot of the seminal developmental work had been done on transactional analysis. She was especially interested in the psychotherapeutic treatment of young schizophrenics, which most people regarded as impossible, since schizophrenia had already been well-established as a biochemical condition which could be treated only with suitable drugs, mainly the phenothiazines such as chlorpromazine hydrochloride (Largactyl) promazine hydrochloride (Sparine) that I had introduced on behalf of Wyeths, or possibly radical brain surgery in certain cases. So I was fairly well-informed in this area. But, as with many conditions, the aetiology was not so simple. Undoubtedly, there was a biochemical predisposition to schizophrenia in many, perhaps all, cases but no-one seemed to be interested in finding out what caused the biochemical predisposition or, if it was simply genetic, what precipitated the actual disease. Generally speaking the medical profession chose a biochemical approach as the most appropriate and scientific and the least expensive in terms of treatment time. But frequently, drugs alone were not sufficient and Jacqui Schiff, as a social worker, began to explore the social and developmental factors present in cases she saw. She recognised that, in many cases, a significant factor was deficient – or even down-right toxic – parenting!

So Jacqui and her husband began to take young schizophrenics into their own home and, effectively, bring them up all over again. Her book *All My Children*, written with Beth Day, provides a dramatic account of their method. It involved a radical treatment programme called 're-parenting'. The subject, who might be in his or her teens or early twenties, would agree to be regressed into an early childhood state – to 'become little', as it was said. This was found to be remarkably easy once the client had decided to do it. The therapist would then become 'mother' or 'father' and would exercise, under contract, parental rights and responsibilities over the client for a period of several weeks, re-educating them in the disciplines of communal living and social responsibilities. The entire process (which was not, of course, appropriate for everyone) could take as long as three or even four years in some cases but the results were encouraging. A colleague of mine 'adopted' a teenage girl who took his name and he even saw her through university. Such treatment demands a huge amount of commitment from both client and therapist.

Shea Schiff, as a young man, had been successfully treated for schizophrenia by this method, with Jacqui as his adoptive mother. Subsequently he became an outstanding practitioner and teacher of transactional analysis himself and I had the opportunity of working with him on several occasions. One in particular was a three day workshop in Walsall in which he taught and demonstrated regression techniques. This was in November, 1982, when I was 56 and probably the oldest trainee present. Nevertheless, I agreed to experience being regressed to the age of four and one of the women trainees was appointed to be my 'parent'. I gave her a hard time! I turned out to be an extremely naughty four year old. I do not recall having been a particularly naughty child, though my mother often described me as having been 'wick', which seemed to imply that I did mischievous things when her back was turned! I have always imagined myself to have been reasonably biddable as a child; but I had evidently been very heavily adapted at the time, concealing my real nature for the sake of domestic harmony and parental affection. In the regression, the 'real' four year old manifested! I was 'little' in the workshop for about four hours and was so difficult over lunch that I had to be spoonfed. Later, Shea took over my parenting and made me stand in a corner with my face to the wall (where I stamped my feet angrily) until I calmed down and decided to behave myself. This practice was later abandoned for political reasons, as was Jacqui Schiff's practice of spanking the bottoms of naughty 18-year old 'kids' – as they were known in the early days.

Jacqui was eventually struck off the ITAA membership because her techniques were publicised in the American press and brought the entire transactional analysis community into disrepute! The fact that the system 'worked' was neither here nor there. It was regarded as unethical and eventually became illegal, as did the caning of school children, not to mention the smacking of children by their parents at home! But it could be that Jacqui Schiff had got it right. So had Susannah Wesley, the mother of John Wesley, founder of the Methodist Church, who also practiced loving discipline and, when necessary, chastisement of her many children.

A client of mine, some years later, told me of a book she had read by James C. Dobson a Christian child psychiatrist who advocated the Old Testament principle of 'Spare the rod and spoil the child'. But, the book said, 'rod' means 'rod' and not a hand; hands were made for loving, not striking. And 'child' meant 'little child' of pre-school age, not a stroppy teenager! My client had a naughty three year old and she threatened him with a wooden spoon when he was disobedient. He persisted in his bad behaviour so she gave him two sharp taps with the wooden spoon on the back of his legs. It stung him and made him cry but it did no damage. After a couple of applications of this treatment, the child gave in, improved his behaviour and even took to fetching the wooden spoon from the kitchen himself when he knew he deserved it! Later generations will pass their own judgment on the 'enlightened' child-rearing philosophies of the twenty first century!

The principle of establishing clear boundaries was one of several strands in what is called the Cathexis School of TA psychotherapy. It is of value not only in the treatment of schizophrenics but also in the management, and sometimes treatment, of character disordered clients. Preferring the term 'antisocial personality' for this category of subject helps to avoid confusion with 'personality disorder', but with the introduction of ASBOs (Antisocial Behaviour Orders) as a sentence for noisy and disruptive youths whose behaviour might not be frankly 'criminal', there is even more confusion. I do not propose to explore the issue in detail in this chapter because I have dealt with it more fully elsewhere but it is important to say something about it because antisocial behaviour is relevant to my understanding of human spirituality and personal spiritual growth.

M. Scott Peck, in *The Road Less Travelled*, has defined both neurosis and character disorder as disorders of responsibility: 'the neurotic', he suggests, 'assumes too much responsibility; the person with a character disorder not enough.' It is fair to say that all of us fall into one category or the other and most of us probably display features of both in different situations. For most of us, however, the emphasis on one or the other is no more than a tendency, or a 'personality adaptation', and is not so serious as to be either personally or socially disabling, though it might be relevant to the development of other conditions that are.

Another teacher to whom I owed much was Petrüska Clarkson, a South African and a clinical psychologist of some distinction. She is a qualified teacher not only of Transactional Analysis but also of the Gestalt therapy pioneered by Frederick S. Perls, mentioned earlier in the context of two-chair work. Gestalt is a German word that has no exact English equivalent but which implies a wholeness that cannot be described as merely a sum of its parts. Gestalt therapy, therefore, emphasises the wholeness of the personal relationship between practitioner and client, over and above the specific techniques the therapist might employ, on the one hand, and the client's symptomatic needs on the other. A central feature of gestalt therapy is the bringing of memories of the past into an experience of present reality. As well as two-chair work, or multiple chair work in which the client 'becomes' various figures in order to experience 'self' from different perspectives, the client might also identify with, for example, the various elements in a dream or a fantasy. I benefited from scores of hours of teaching, supervision and personal therapy with Petrüska that certainly contributed to my understanding of what it means to be truly human and a being for whom the experience of relationship provides the matrix of spirituality.

Robert Goulding, a psychiatrist, and his wife Mary, a social worker, together developed the Re-decision School of transactional analysis. This approach draws very largely on Gestalt therapy, pointing to 'early decisions', made in childhood when the youngster had only limited information and understanding of what was going on around him, and facilitates the making of new decisions, or redecisions, made with the benefit of insight and adult wisdom. In my own case, for example, I had grown up with the belief that I was of no great significance or importance and was expected to take a back seat; so I decided, effectively, that I would be better loved for doing my best and failing than for succeeding, with the attendant risk that I might begin to feel that I was 'somebody'. My father, I believed, was the only one allowed to be 'somebody'. He would have been appalled (as would my mother) had he known the kind of 'redeciding' it became necessary for me to do in order to escape from the negative effects of parental programming. What happened to me in my developmental years was far from being what they would have consciously intended; but a crucial factor, I am certain, was my becoming my father's accompanist from a very early age, as he sang, either to a live audience or just to his own reflection in the lounge mirror over the fireplace! He was 'somebody', in my perception probably even more than his own, for I guess he suffered from the same problem I had! It was transactional analyst Fanita English who introduced the idea of the 'hot potato' into TA in the early days when folksy language was much in vogue. The idea was that the parent (or other person) would get rid of his own problem by unloading it onto someone else. My father, I believe, unloaded his own sense of inferiority onto me; and also, I suspect, his anger at his mother, who loved her children so possessively that she refused to attend the weddings of all those, including my father, who married! But he can have had no idea what he was doing.

I had the benefit of a five day training workshop with Bob and Mary Goulding in May, 1984, held at an hotel near Stratford-on-Avon. Most of us on the course, including Bob and Mary, went to the Royal Shakespeare Theatre one evening to see Kenneth Branagh in Henry V. It was a memorable occasion before Branagh had become widely known. On our last night together at the hotel we had a party at which those who could sing, play something or 'recite' entertained the rest. I got up on my feet, with my liberated 'Free Child' cathected, (as opposed to my 'Adapted Child') and recited, first the Prologue to Act One of Henry V ('O, for a muse of fire . . .') and then Henry's speech before Harfleur ('Once more, unto the breach, dear friends . . .') I got heartily applauded and everyone agreed that my performance was every bit as good as Branagh's! Before we all went home Bob and Mary kindly signed my copy of their book *Changing Lives Through Re-decision Therapy*, which I treasure.

The following year Gordon Law, my sponsor, agreed that I was ready to take the final oral examination which, if I passed it, would now qualify me as a certified transactional analyst specialising in clinical applications. Exams were held from time to time in various locations, often during a training conference when both candidates and examiners would be there anyway. On that occasion, however, in November, 1985, the exams were held on a separate occasion at Heidelberg, when there was no training conference happening. A few weeks before I was due to go, I attended a weekend Marathon workshop led by Ian Stewart at his home near Kegworth, Nottingham. This workshop was probably going to be my last opportunity to resolve any personal problems that might sabotage my plan to secure professional qualification before setting up in private practice after retirement from the Probation Service, to which I was looking forward.

The marathon started on a Friday evening and continued until the Sunday afternoon. There were ten or a dozen trainees present, of whom I, at almost 60, was by far the oldest. Many practitioners have their clients sit in a circle on the floor because that encourages experiencing a Child ego state, which is often therapeutically important – and it certainly was for me on this occasion. But until it was my turn to do some work, I sat in a chair because I was already beginning to suffer the ravages of old age and found the floor a most uncomfortable place to sit, quite apart from a strong inclination to avoid getting into my Child ego state – my Free Child, at any rate – which was the object of the exercise. Ian had a large mattress on the floor on which we were required to sit when we were actually doing a piece of personal work.

It was the practice, as I mentioned earlier, to tape record therapeutic work with clients for review either during the therapy session or for use in supervision. I also tape-recorded much of my own personal therapy, so the account following was transcribed from the tape recording and edited for ease of reading and to clarify the content where necessary.

As we prepared for the personal work I was going to do, Ian said to me, following up on some previous exchanges, 'I agree that you have lots of Adult reasons why passing the CM exam is crucial and I think that, at the same time, when you first said it you were saying that partly out of Script . . . the Adult reasons why it's crucial are alongside the Script reason, which is that you believe your worth – your significance – depends on your passing the CM. When you're in Script, and believing that, you are also very likely to set yourself up not to pass, because you also believe, in Script, that if you pass it you will hurt Dad. But passing the CM is, in many ways, of extremely little importance. Another point is that I hear you Discounting, that is you seem to be indicating that 'If I don't pass this time, then that's it!' You then added an Adult bit that you're getting a bit of pressure from your wife to pass and that you've actually told her you will discontinue training if you don't pass this time. So it may be you want to consider whether you are getting into a high old Game with her . . .'

I was aware of this and acknowledged it.

'OK, so I'm glad to have that feedback from you that you think it's a Game. Well, the thing about gamey contracts is that you can step out of any contract. If I were you, I would take time to review that situation with my wife because it seems you've got enough pressures on you already without getting into a Game with your wife whereby she's supposed to feel guilty if you discontinue and you're supposed to feel guilty if you don't! . . . Now I'm all for positive thinking and for positive visualisation and, if you like, we could run through some techniques of that for you. Do you use this already – positive visualisation type exercises when you're going to do exams, and so on?'

'Have I used them? No.'

'Well, I can give you a tool bag of self image techniques which are all really good to get you into an exam to pass. And at the same time, I think that part of your work here would be to really look at this issue, that you feel humiliated if you don't pass. And the reason for that is that you have this Racket going on – this humiliation Racket around not passing. So you're increasing the chances that you actually set up not to pass. The Winner knows what he's going to do if he loses but he doesn't talk about it, whereas the Loser does talk about what he's going to do if he loses. And I experience you as a Winner, much more than you're a Loser; so what I invite you to do is really take a look at the possibility you might be going to lose this time round and find out what size that really is.'

I said, 'That's reasonable'.

'So, if you go from this workshop having got what you wanted, what will you have got?'

I paused for thought before answering, 'A sense of ease about going into the exam.'

'How will you experience your sense of ease?'

'By . . . er . . .' (A long pause.) 'I'll feel less hassle, less pressured to do absolutely everything and cover every little eventuality before I go. . . . And . . . er . . . above all, I think I'll be sufficiently relaxed to do better work with my group and take some better work with me. I think that's probably, at this late stage, the most important thing of all.'

Ian said, 'I agree with you. And the central point, crucial in an Adult sense, is that whether you pass or get deferred will depend mainly on the tapes you take along. And this is a fairly late stage in the day for you to be thinking what tapes you take. So I think there is a reasonable chance that you might get deferred at this exam. And if you get deferred it will be because the tapes you take along are going to be zapped by the examiners. I don't think it's necessarily going to happen but I really want to up-front with you that the possibility is real you might get deferred; and if you do it won't be any reflection on you as a therapist, it will be because, in the time scale available, you are still looking for the tapes. And that's a practical Adult supervisory point. So I quite agree with you that you maximise the chances of getting an examinable tape if you work well between now and then. But it just might not be practicable to do that.'

'OK.'

'So, I agree with you that if you go more relaxed than when you did the mock exam there's much more chance that you'll pass. In fact, I think at the mock exam, there was a chance you could have passed with the tape you'd got, even though it had one or two holes in it. And one of the things you did was that some of the holes you could have defended more from an Adult position.'

I said, 'I know I could. I've been through it with a toothcomb. I've done a transcript of the whole tape.'

'The other point I'll tell you about while we speak, is your Script Decision, 'I'm acting'. And whether you are acting or not, I don't know – but acting goes with tension. And I think it could be quite appropriate for you to go into that exam being you, instead of acting. Get used to the fact that . . . you've got enough going for you without acting.'

I said, 'That's not quite what I mean by acting. Maybe it's a bit of that but it has more to do with my way of presenting the real me than . . . I don't really imagine that when I'm doing things in the public eye I'm being inauthentic, and I'm glad you said that. But it isn't the kind of inauthenticity that's designed to mislead anybody. It's as if . . . I believe I'm a much more low key person than I present myself as. I think that's more like it.'

Ian said, 'Suppose you presented yourself as the low key person you really are, then it would be different?'

I paused a long time before saying, 'I imagine that the other people would feel I was being more authentic. Yes, that's it.'

'That's how you imagine they would perceive you but how would you really be?'

After another long pause, I said, 'I would think I was being inauthentic.'

'Right now,' Ian commented, 'I'm doing a double take on what you just said.'

'I've never thought of it that way until right now. I do have a natural disposition to present myself fairly dramatically. But I'm not supposed to do that because that's what Dad did . . . and I'm taking the limelight off him.'

'And if you take the limelight off Dad?'

'He might die . . . in some sense.'

'And that's what you really believe, isn't it? So you've got to keep the limelight on Dad in order to keep the guy from dying. What happens, if you then get significant?'

'Well, he'd die.'

'That's what you believe, yes. But it's not actually true.'

'No, of course not.'

'So that's one thing you don't need to take with you to Heidelberg.'

After a pause lasting nearly half a minute, I said, 'I'm very pleased about that.'

'About what?'

'That I can present myself as I want to present myself and it's OK.'

'Yes. You are OK. Whatever you do with that insight, just keep on doing it.'

'OK.

'What's the positive opposite of that negative self image you used? How would you describe it?'

'Promoting myself.'

'Do you believe it's OK to promote yourself?'

'Yes . . . Well, yes, it must be.'

'Do you want to promote yourself in the work you are going to do now?

'Yes, I want to do it now.'

'OK. I suggest you get on the mattress. . . . I suggest as a starting point that you close the three Escape Hatches to your father, will you?'

I said, as to my father, 'No matter what happens, no matter what you do and no matter what you want, I'm not going to kill myself or anybody else, either deliberately or by accident, and I will not go crazy.'

'How's he taking it . . . ?'

I moved over to the other side of the mattress, 'became' my father and spoke as I believed he would. As Dad, I said, 'Yer what, lad? Kill yourself? Nay . . . Don't talk so daft! Course you're not going to kill yourself . . . and you're not to talk about killing people and going crazy. That's daft talk, that is.'

I moved and, as myself, asked him, 'Do you believe me, Dad?'

I moved again and as Dad, answered, 'No, I don't believe you . . . I believe you're not going to do it. Nay, you're not going to kill yourself . . .'

I said, as myself, 'I know I wouldn't . . . but I've thought about it often enough . . . had fantasies about it . . . but . . .'

Ian prompted me to be explicit.

I said, 'I will never do it, kill myself or anyone else . . . And I'll never go crazy.'

Ian, now satisfied that my Escape Hatches were securely closed, said, 'OK. Tell Dad what you were talking to me about before you came on the mattress . . . about being his accompanist. What do you want to do now?'

Me as myself: 'The one thing I liked best about life then was . . . I liked best of all being your accompanist and playing for you. I would enjoy it. But I like to play on my own as well sometimes. But you liked me to be your accompanist best so . . . I enjoy that most of all.'

Ian, prompting me: 'So I don't play . . .'

Me as myself: 'So I don't play very much on my own. You always complain it's too noisy . . . and there's a shout from the kitchen . . .'

Ian: 'Of course, I can apologise.'

Me as myself: 'I'm sorry, I didn't mean to play so loud. I know it drowns your singing.'

Ian: 'Maybe you should tell him how you're feeling now. . . What is that your hands are wanting to do? . . . Do you want to do some squeezing . . . pushing . . . ?'

Me, to Dad: 'I don't think I want to kill you because I love you. I can't want to kill you.'

Ian: 'Let your hands do what they want to do . . .'

Me: (I burst into tears and sob loudly throughout the next speech) Let me be myself! Just let me do what I want to do. . . . I'm always doing what you want me to do. You just want me to be . . . ordinary . . . but I want to do my best! I want to achieve things. I want to be significant and I want to be important. You seem to think that's daft! . . . Just let me be. (I am crying, shouting and sobbing incoherently) I've . . . just got . . . used to it. I'm sick of this . . . Get off the stage! Will . . . you . . . just . . . get . . . off . . . the stage!'

Ian presented me with a big cushion to represent Dad and indicated that I should attack it physically, which I did, pushing against it (and against Ian who held it) as I cried out (still weeping and angry): 'Get out of the way . . . Get out of the bloody way! Get out of the bloody way! I'm flaming well sick of you getting in my way all the time! You won't let me do anything! Get out of my way! Get . . . out . . . of . . . my . . . way!'

I am gasping breathlessly as I shout and struggle and cry and the other people in the workshop, all sitting around the mattress and witnessing this, begin to laugh. Soon they are all laughing loudly and bring the episode to an end as I gasp for breath and very gradually stop shouting until I am silent but for my heavy breathing. The laughter also stops. There is silence. I blow my nose loudly and the silence continues for several minutes as I recover, everyone clearly anticipating some dramatic conclusion to this extremely emotional piece of work. I muttered, 'I'll have to wait until my breathing's settled . . . I can still feel my heart pounding . . . You will just have to wait.'

Ian asked, 'What did you say then?'

I answered, loud and clear, 'You will just have to wait.'

After a full six minutes of silence, I stood up and recited the prologue to Act One of Henry the Fifth, just as I had done at the end of the five day Goulding workshop a year or two earlier. Again, I got a great round of applause and shouts of Well done! And Ian, much impressed, said, 'Well, you're a fantastic actor.' There was lots of laughter then and everyone, especially me, relaxed now that the tension was over. I said to them all, 'Thanks for helping me to do that because it really was worthwhile. I needed an audience!'

After I had recovered we had a debrief. I said, 'First of all, I've done it before – not in such a concise way as this but I did some work on this issue with the Gouldings. It wasn't precisely the same because I don't think I had quite this issue with Father. No, I haven't done that bit before. But it was a matter of giving my Free Child some outlet. We had a party at the end of the workshop on the last night and I delivered that speech from Henry the Fifth that I've just done again. But the important part of this to-day was pushing Dad out of the way . . . and so the acting bit at the end was more significant to-day, more important. But even whilst I was in the midst of that terribly emotional stuff just now – and I was really crying – I was really feeling and experiencing everything that you saw and heard. It was totally genuine and totally authentic – but at the same time I was standing back from myself and watching it happen and I was aware of acting.'

Ian said, 'That's OK, I'm really glad you were, because the whole point of this work is that you can experience the real Child in you again and also that you can sit back and re-appraise what's happening. If you really get into the Child ego state, what you're doing is regression, not re-decision. And I agree with you that the impact of what you did was in the physical action of pushing Dad out of the way. First the Adapted Child was begging; but it was the Free Child doing the pushing.'

Ian then added, 'I was aware also that when you were standing up to declaim the Shakespeare you were breathing in a completely different pattern from what you'd been breathing in before, when you said several times 'I need to get my breath' – and he demonstrated my loud exhaling gasps – 'almost as if you were experiencing your own right to breathe without having to ask Dad's permission.'

I said, 'Yes. No way was I going to start until I was ready.'

'And, in line with all re-decision work, the next step of continually reinforcing that, is to find ways to be centre stage again quite often and anchor onto that feeling of enjoying it – and the anchor for you will be the applause. So any time you want to look into the pleasant sensation of being an actor, and a good actor enjoying it, move back into how you felt when you heard us applauding. And then go ahead and do the behaviour. Get centre stage. And you can do that several times again during this workshop if you want to.'

At that point we all took a natural break and had a cup of tea.

* * *

Another trainee, Andrew Gage, was also to be examined at the same time, early in November, so we arranged to travel together. The exam was to be held at Heidelberg, West Germany, so I spent the night with Andrew's family in Stockport and next morning his wife took us to Manchester Airport. We flew from there to Frankfurt and then took a train to Heidelberg, which was, I felt, a very prestigious seat of learning at which to take one's finals and, hopefully, graduate. However, the European Association for Transactional Analysis, which had arranged the event, had not taken over the university for the occasion. Andrew and I had rooms booked at the Schwarzer Adler Hotel, overlooking the River Necker and a few miles out of the town. The exams were held in another hotel near the centre of Heidelberg and the arrangements were anything but satisfactory since there were 86 candidates from all over Europe and the facilities for so many were grossly inadequate.

The candidate faces a board of four experienced transactional analysts, perhaps with an observer present. The room should be appropriate and quiet and properly equipped with a blackboard and chalk or, ideally, a wipe-off board, because diagramming is an important feature of the process. The candidate was expected to take two cassette recorders – one to record the entire exam and one on which to play the recorded segments of clinical work he wished to present. The room in which I was examined was a hotel bedroom and the examiners and I faced each other in the available space at the foot of the bed! There was no wipe-off board provided but fortunately I had brought a small one myself and was able to use this.

The exam began with the four examiners first introducing themselves, telling me of their background and qualifications. Arlene Moore, the Chair, was an American psychologist, Berthold Christoph and Ute Hagehülsman were both German psychologists and Alan Byron was an English psychiatrist working in Germany with the British Army of the Rhine. Bertholt and Ute both spoke good English but their accents occasionally presented problems, as did their understanding of some of the ideas and language I used. I asked the examiners various questions about themselves, particularly their 'orientation' – that is, which of the various schools of transactional analysis they favoured.

The next stage was the presentation of my very carefully prepared documentation. This included Training Contract details, sponsor's evaluation of the written exam completed earlier (this was, at the time, an 'open book' exam requiring 3 5 essays on various aspects of TA theory and its practical application. It was later changed to a long case study), a very detailed curriculum vitae with an account of professional practice, a list of published books and papers, a list of Conference presentations; a detailed record of supervision and the names of supervisors, and a record of Advanced Workshops, all covered by signed slips by the supervisors or workshop presenters; an account of my 121 hours of personal therapy, both individually and in groups, (this was in addition to the personal work done in training sessions), a detailed account of TA teaching and presentations in hospitals, colleges etc., and a summary of hours of my treatment of clients, both individually and in groups.

In addition to all this the documentation included personal recommendations from several Teachers. Gordon Law, my sponsor, declared in his Endorsement to my candidature that I was 'a competent therapist of high ethical standards and a strong commitment to the welfare of his clients . . . successfully introduced TA as a viable method of working with difficult and unmotivated clients who desperately needed therapeutic help rather than . . . the strictures of the criminal law.' And Dr Petrüska Clarkson wrote, 'I know him to be a conscientious, solid and capable clinician who is creative in his own gentle way with a client population whose psychological problems are exacerbated by social deprivation and unemployment.' Jenny Robinson testified to having supervised my work over three years, had visited my group and had seen my work and its results at first hand. 'He is a conscientious therapist who thinks carefully about his patients and their needs'. I could not have wanted for better support from highly respected colleagues who knew my work personally.

The members of the Board each had a copy of this material in neat folders and they spent the first twenty minutes or so perusing it whilst I sat in silence or answered their occasional questions. After this the Board members asked me about myself and the kind of work I did and I talked about my special interest as a probation officer in working with offenders and other character disordered or antisocial clients. However, I explained that the cases I was presenting for examination were private clients with more conventional diagnoses, referred to me by a psychiatrist.

The Chair, Arlene Moore, asked me to present my first case. I first outlined the background. Marcia was a 3 2 years old Rumanian lady who had been diagnosed by the psychiatrist as suffering from reactive depression that was related to stress within her marriage. She spoke very good

English and had, in fact, married her husband Martin, an engineer, at a civil ceremony in Rumania where he was working at the time. She had returned with him to England and they now had two small sons aged 5 and 2½. But Martin still had to travel abroad from time to time, leaving Marcia with the children, and she was often very frightened to the extent that she took the children into her own bed in order not to feel alone.

The five minutes segment of tape I was presenting was of a piece of 'permission work' and each examiner had a type-written transcript to follow. Marcia was oppressed with Script messages from her parents, saying, in effect, that she must not be independent and self-sufficient - or 'Don't be you', as it is often expressed in TA textbooks. The contract was for me to give Marcia my permission from my own Parent ego state, and to do it with sufficient potency to overcome the original parental Injunction. This was exactly in line with TA philosophy and should have been entirely acceptable to the exam Board.

But before they listened to the tape, Arlene said, 'That was your contract for this piece of work; but what was your overall contract?'

As already explained, contracting is fundamental to TA psychotherapy so that both client and therapist know what they are aiming to achieve; so I had anticipated such questions and prepared the answers with Gordon, my sponsor. I said, 'The overall contract was to resolve the domestic problem in order to stabilise the marriage.'

This produced an immediate interruption from Ute Hagehülsman. She wanted to stop the exam there and then because, she said, the contract itself constituted a 'harmful intervention.' Bertholt and Arlene both expressed agreement with this.

I was asked, 'How could such a contract be harmful to the client?'

After a moment's pause for thought I admitted frankly that I did not know. I explained again that she had been referred by the psychiatrist with this goal in mind and it was what Marcia herself declared she wanted. On reflection, after reviewing the tape later with Gordon, I realised that it would have been perfectly in order for me to ask the examiners why they thought it would be harmful to the client if we set out to stabilise her distressed marriage. But I did not.

Alan then asked, 'So for whose benefit was the contract made?'

'For Marcia's benefit,' I said.

'Why,' asked Alan, 'was the marriage unstable in the first place?'

'Because Marcia was a rather demanding and histrionic personality who complained loudly when Martin came home tired from work and wanted to relax in front of the TV and watch rugby.'

Bertholt asked, 'So what change did Marcia want to make?'

'She wanted to become a person who would be kind to Martin.'

'Why kind?'

'In order that she would be a better wife for Martin and a better parent for the children. She wanted to change her attitude so that she would not provoke Martin.'

'I am still not sure,' said Ute, 'that this contract was not a harmful intervention.'

However, I was eventually allowed to play the tape I had brought and the examiners seemed to listen and to follow the transcript without much interest.

Ute, Bertholt and Arleen all had their minds so focussed on this overall contract about stabilising the marriage that they seemed unable to attend to the work I was actually presenting. They kept on asking me questions that seemed to me to be rooted in an understanding of the nature of marriage that was quite different from mine – if, indeed, they acknowledged the sanctity of marriage at all! Perhaps they did not. The social attitude to marriage in the western world was being subject to a great deal of questioning.

The probing continued for quite a long time, question after question, so that I felt less like a candidate being examined, than a defendant in court being cross-examined! And my answers, on hearing them again on the tape recording, seem to me to have been confident, relaxed, thoughtful, well informed and entirely appropriate. After a lot of further questioning, Arlene said to me, 'We seem to have a problem, David. Would you like to call the Rover?'

'Yes, please,' I said.

I ought, of course, to have called him myself long before we reached this stage. The Rover was an experienced examiner who could be called in by any candidate or Board of examiners to act as adjudicator where there was a dispute. Alan left the room in search of him and returned a few minutes later to say he would be with us shortly but was presently tied up with another candidate. We all sat in stony silence for about fifteen minutes, all of us leafing through my documentation for want of something better to do. Normal conversation was impossible and any further reference to the exam was out of the question now that the Rover had been called.

Eventually, he came. A tall, dark German called Bernd Schmid, of whom I had never heard before. He listened to Ute's complaint, my explanation and the comments of the others. He pointed out that his concern was with the process of the exam, not the content. I declared that my contract had been misinterpreted by three of the Board members. 'They are not hearing what I have actually been doing with this client.'

Alan said he felt the problems of language and interpretation had been part of the difficulty. 'On the whole,' he said, 'I felt that their reaction was unfair.'

Bertholt said, 'I did not get satisfactory answers to my questions.'

Arleen said, 'I'm not satisfied.'

Bernd Schmid listened to everyone and then said, 'I hear nothing problematic, only different conclusions. ' He asked Alan, 'How do you think it was unfair?'

'To want to stop without hearing the tape or exploring. I was quite surprised that they could react that way. It was a prejudicial response and when they eventually heard the tape they were still looking for evidence to confirm the conclusion they had already come to and were giving more weight to that than I thought was necessary.'

Bernd said, 'There is an atmosphere here. Even if there was a harmful intervention it is not a good reason to stop the exam. It is clear now that there was a mistake. You are open to have another check, hear another tape. It is up to you.'

He left us and the examiners were silent for a moment, smarting a bit, I should think, from the Rover's rebuke. Then Arleen asked the Board, 'Would you like to hear another tape?'

They agreed, without much enthusiasm, to do so.

My second tape was of Adrian, now twenty five, the young man described earlier, who had turned up to see me at the clinic wearing a tee shirt that bore the smiling face of Thomas the Tank Engine. By this time he had a First Class honours degree in sociology and was a trained Youth Leader, but was still having problems being grown up. The tape was of a piece of two chair work in which he was telling his very possessive mother to 'Get lost' and displaying the new Parent ego state he had incorporated from me in the course of re-parenting. The Board asked very few questions, not even what the contract was! But the recording was, in fact, of a very sound piece of clinical work. Since they had already spent the best part of two hours with me they went on to make their individual assessments before declaring whether I should pass or be deferred.

The assessment was made under ten headings: Theory, Various TA approaches, Treatment direction, Awareness of discounts and incongruities, Clarity of client assessment, Potency, Effectiveness, Professionalism, Intuition & Creativity and, finally, an Overall Rating. Each area was rated from 5, if very impressive, down to 1 if very unimpressive. Some of the worst ratings seemed to come from Arleen, the American Chair, rather than Ute, as I would have expected. Overall, I scored a total of 29, which could have been a bare pass had the Board felt so inclined. In the event, only Alan Byron voted for me to pass so I was 'deferred'. No-one in TA is ever deemed to have failed. If you were not ready to pass at this stage accreditation was simply deferred and you could, if you wished, have another go later.

I received this rejection with mixed feelings – even more mixed when I reflected on it later. The simple fact of the matter is that I had never expected to pass in the first place. I was not a person who passed exams – at least, not at the first attempt. I had failed my County Minor exam at the age of eleven; I passed my School Certificate exam at sixteen only at the second attempt; and I had twice failed to pass 'O' Level Greek in my early thirties whilst trying to qualify to do a London University External degree. I had, fortunately, passed my Probation training course at Leeds University – but only after George Moore had intervened on my behalf and got me Dr Laycock for tutor instead of Dorothy Burdis. Here I was again facing yet another woman in a position of authority – Ute Hagehülsman, who seemed able to impose her authority even on two other members of the exam Board, including the Chair, to ensure my deferment!

That evening there was a party at which all the successful candidates, including Andrew Gage with whom I had travelled from Manchester, were able to celebrate, and a group of musicians came in to entertain us. I did not feel like being entertained and certainly not like dancing. I 'sat out' and told my sorry tale to anyone who would listen. There were, in fact, several English practitioners present who knew my work well and who fully expected that I would pass the final exam Board. Amongst them was Alice Stevenson – who, for some reason, always addressed me, though quite affectionately, as 'Midgley'. She was, of course, a TA Teacher and a woman in a position of authority so maybe that was her way of keeping me at arm's length! Nevertheless, Alice and I had always got on well together and it was she who had assessed my written exam and spoken well of it. Over a drink, whilst the others danced, Alice heard my tale of woe and said, very positively, 'You must appeal.'

10

THE THREAT

The next day there was nothing in particular to do because our plane from Frankfurt did not leave until the following afternoon so Andrew and I visited the castle of Heidelberg and had a look round the city. We were tremendously impressed by its cleanliness and the orderliness and courtesy of the people. We travelled into Heidelberg by bus from our out-of-town hotel and were amazed to have German schoolchildren stand up so that we could sit down! I had, of course, been brought up to practice such old world courtesy myself but had seen nothing of it at home in the post war years.

When I got home I immediately contacted Gordon to discuss the Appeal procedure. There was, of course, documentation to be completed and I had to provide four copies of the tape-recording of the exam to be sent to members of the Appeals Board. Gordon had to support my appeal in a letter of his own, after we had met and listened to the tape together. And since Graham Barnes, Gordon's sponsor, had moved on, he had to seek support from his new sponsor. Unfortunately, this was now Margaret Turpin who, predictably, withheld her support! Nevertheless, my appeal was allowed to go ahead and it would be the best part of a year before we heard the result. However, even if the appeal was upheld, I still would not have passed the exam. It would be acknowledged that the exam process had been unsatisfactory and I would be allowed to take the exam again without paying another exam fee. Nevertheless, I would still have to travel to wherever the exam was held and pay for accommodation.

In the meantime, Gordon suggested that it might be a good idea if I changed sponsors at this stage. Someone else might enable me to identify an area of personal need that had so far been overlooked. He had already spoken to Ian Stewart about this possibility and Ian had agreed, in principal, to take me on. We already knew each other quite well from various workshop contacts, not least the dramatic and somewhat theatrical piece of therapeutic work I did at the 'marathon' detailed in the previous chapter. So I began to make monthly visits to Ian at his bachelor home, The Old School House, in the village of Kingston-on-Soar, near Nottingham.

Ian was, at that time, a single man in his forties who had graduated at Oxford and then gone on to Nottingham University to do a PhD in the Department of Agriculture. He too had had his personal problems, associated in part at least, with a rather fragile physique. Whilst at Nottingham he came into touch with Professor Alaway, who had discovered transactional analysis in the USA and had set up a therapy group for students. Ian had joined it and became one of many others who started out as clients, not only solving their own problems but going on to become practitioners and sometimes teachers of TA themselves. One of the rooms in Ian's home was equipped as a gymnasium, where he made good whatever deficiencies there were in his physique. He had a keen interest in music and there was a harpsichord in his lounge. His hobby was Morris dancing.

Few people were probably aware that Ian's PhD was not in psychology or anything remotely connected with transactional analysis. He had gained it with a thesis on brewing! Nevertheless, he was one of the most knowledgeable practitioners in the country and when I began to work with him he had just published, jointly with Vann Joines, an American practitioner, a book called *TA Today*, which quickly became the standard text for trainees throughout the world. It has been published in at least eleven languages, including Japanese and Chinese.

Ian's first requirement was to hear the tape recording of the Heidelberg exam himself. He gave me some detailed feedback, much of which did not support my own earlier conclusions and he declared, frankly, that on the basis of my performance in the examination room, he too would have deferred me had he been on the Board! This was a shock but Ian was quite clear about why he would have done that and his perception of what had been going on was extremely helpful in more ways than one.

My first mistake, he said, was to emphasise my interest and experience in working with character disordered clients. This would immediately put the examiners on the defensive because CDs were the most difficult category for anyone to treat and it was likely that the examiners themselves would hesitate to take on such clients! They would wonder what sort of a whiz kid they had before them and would be on the defensive. In TA terms that meant they would be in their Adapted Child ego state, feeling threatened by a 'Critical Parent', and they would be all set up for Game-playing. One would suppose that experienced and qualified TA practitioners, of all people, would be able to avoid getting into psychological Games in the examination room! But it happens all too frequently because Games are played out of awareness and the examiners themselves are vulnerable human beings. They would, no doubt, eventually realise what was happening and take steps to abort the Game and get into 'Adult', but by that time the damage could have been done. I had inadvertently set myself up to be Persecuted and they might even have decided, in their own heads, in the first ten minutes that this candidate was going to be deferred! I did not even present a tape of one of my CD clients so they had no opportunity to judge whether I was all I cracked myself up to be. If I talked at a future exam about my work with character disordered clients, Ian said, I would do well to speak only in terms of management, not treatment.

Having created this gamey situation it was, Ian pointed out, now my own responsibility to take charge of things, watch out for Games and abort them straight away. He noticed that in describing my own practice I was over-detailing and advised me to answer a Board's questions in no more than three sentences. It was important, Ian said, to 'clear out your anger at the Board'. This shook me because I was not aware of being angry. But, on reflection, I was. I was anticipating from the start that they were going to defer me – after I'd done all that work and gone all that way to the exam and spent all that money! It was enough to make anyone angry!

Ian agreed with the Rover that my overall contract did not constitute a 'harmful intervention' but it was, nevertheless, 'an Adapted Child contract', unhelpful, ineffective and insufficiently precise and explicit. It was not clear what 'stabilising the marriage' would involve and what we could expect to see objectively at the end of the exercise that would signal that the contract had been completed.

Effectively, Ian said, my deferment had already happened before I played the tape of the work I was presenting. After more than an hour, the Board members were all tired and there was really no point in presenting another tape. This was unfortunate, because the second piece of work I presented was good, based on a simple and straight-forward contract (which, as it happened, I was not asked to declare) and had I presented it first I would probably have passed. It would, in any event, have accounted for the relatively high marks I got when it came to scoring. But afterwards Ian and I agreed that it was as well I did not pass, because there was more work I needed to do – not so much on therapeutic technique (though I still needed to sharpen up on contract making) as on myself. 'You are a good therapist', Ian said. 'The problem is with how you handle the Board. You must learn to be more relaxed. They want to see self-confidence, of course, but not quite so much self-assurance! The Board felt threatened!'

I could not believe this to begin with. I had never knowingly threatened anyone in my life. But the more I reflected on this the more I realised that Ian was right. It had always puzzled me that I seemed to generate some kind of defensive hostility in certain women 'in positions of authority' – Dorothy Burdis, Norma Cooper, Margaret Turpin – and then Ute Hagehülsman and Arleen Moore on the exam Board. And why did Alice Stephenson always keep me at arm's length by calling me 'Midgley'. I had wondered whether there was some ulterior, out-of-awareness sexual explanation for this.

But now I began to realise that that was probably not the explanation at all. It was my posh accent and my Magee suits and my general air of being somehow a bit superior! Lack of self-esteem and feelings of inferiority and inadequacy were undoubtedly my perception of myself, a deeply entrenched Script I had established in response to the well-meaning but unhelpful way my father had dealt with me. Now I began to wonder whether he had felt threatened as well! This gentle, self-effacing, understanding fellow was not how some other people saw me at all! Maybe I had over-compensated? People saw me as someone to be reckoned with, even a threat to their own self-esteem. And not only unmarried women in positions of authority either. Vanity must have suggested that explanation. There had been many others, regardless of gender.

Not everyone was fazed by this, of course. Betty certainly wasn't! And, on reflection, I realised that there were others too who had reacted more positively to qualities I was unable to see in myself. Why was I, at eleven years old and with no scientific connections whatsoever, selected to be the form's science society representative? Why was I immediately appointed Patrol Leader's Second when I joined the Scouts and some other lad demoted to make way for me? Why was I selected for prestigious aircrew training in the RAF Volunteer Reserve? Why was I selected for the Intelligence Corps, promoted to lance corporal and put in charge of the draft to India; then later promoted to Staff Sergeant in charge of a Field Security Detachment on the North West Frontier, selected for officer training and finally commissioned in the Intelligence Corps? Why was I selected out of over two thousand applicants for the Probation Service and in due course made a Senior Probation Officer? What had been happening throughout my life whilst I continued to see myself as a non-starter?

The insight I gained through Ian's appraisal of my Heidelberg exam set the course for some of the personal work I would now have to do. Our work together went well. To-day trainees are required to find

120

different practitioners from their sponsor to provide supervision and personal therapy, since 'dual relationships' are to be avoided if possible. However, these were early days in the development of TA and Ian was not only my sponsor but also my primary supervisor and my main therapist as well, as Gordon Law had been.

Whilst all this was going on I was still Senior Probation Officer at our new offices in Newton Aycliffe, using TA with my clients, teaching it to others and working with the group in the Psychiatric Department of North Tees General Hospital. It was Petrüska Clarkson who eventually suggested I change this arrangement at the hospital, valuable though the opportunity had been. She said to me one day at a private session at her home in Ealing Common, 'David, you will never make it to clinical membership until you get yourself some clients who are sufficiently well-motivated to be willing to pay.'

Undoubtedly, she was right. I shared this with Dr Hawkings, who entirely understood, and thereafter he and some of his colleagues began to refer cases to me for treatment privately. I saw my first private client at Dr Hawkings' own rooms in Darlington, not far from my office in Newton Aycliffe, so that the client, who lived in Darlington, could avoid a trip to Middlesbrough every week. I saw most of my clients in Middlesbrough but the problem with my study at home was that our dog Sally greeted all clients with noisy enthusiasm and continued to bark in the kitchen as long as they were with me unless Betty was there also to keep her quiet! So I arranged with Relate and with the Alcohol Counselling Service in Middlesbrough to use rooms in their premises for clients who lived conveniently nearby. However, I eventually began, with Betty's oversight of the dog, to have group therapy sessions in the study at home in the evening and the hospital therapy group was phased out.

Chris and Elaine had both been members of the hospital group. I had had a contract with all the members on joining the group that they would not attend under the influence of alcohol, would not be physically violent to either persons or property and they would not engage in sexual relationships with other group members. After the group ended one evening, Chris and Elaine came to me and shyly told me that they were 'seeing each other'. This presented me with a problem because they were both making excellent progress in the group and I was most reluctant to ask either of them to leave. I tentatively established that on one occasion at least their love making had become frankly sexual, though far from successful and a disappointment to them both. Also, it was abundantly clear that their relationship was much deeper and more meaningful than being merely an excuse for sex. I discussed the situation with Dr Hawkings and we agreed that we allow them to continue in the group together if they would agree to 'cool it'. On the face of it this was really asking too much but they both saw the point of it and agreed that they would exercise self-control, until at least one of them had terminated therapy, because the sexual dimension was bound to introduce an imponderable element into the therapeutic process and was best avoided. In addition, both of them turned out to be church-going Christians, particularly Elaine who was a convert to Roman Catholicism, and were feeling guilty and inhibited in the first place. But guilt about sexual matters was regarded by many of my TA colleagues as pathological in itself; in fact Bob Goulding, to whom I owed much, declared in one of his books that he would urge certain clients to 'Go out and get some sex' as a necessary 'home-work' contract! My own traditional Methodist morality was quite prohibitive, even if, in practice we could secretly indulge ourselves with some 'heavy petting' so long as we did not 'go all the way'. So this was another area of conflict between my 'spiritual', or possibly religious, orientation and my secular psychotherapy. Anyway, Chris and Elaine both joined the private group that met weekly in my study at home. Neither of them could afford to pay the fee I was charging so I agreed to a small, token fee to meet the needs of the situation. Their relationship flourished and in due course they got married. Betty and I were both invited to the wedding. In fact, the Catholic priest who officiated, hearing from them that their therapist was a Methodist Local Preacher, kindly invited me, at the couple's request, to take part by leading a responsive part of the service. I told no-one in the TA community about this! Elaine, a very intelligent young lady who had been referred to me with severe depression, had left school without any kind of qualification but during and following therapy she had passed O and A Level GCSEs, been accepted into Teesside Polytechnic (now University) and completed an honours degree in English Literature, despite having to take a year off due to a miscarriage. One of my real success stories! She and Chris now have two growing sons.

Another client referred to me by Dr Hawkings I will call 'Jack', a young man in his late teens who was diagnosed as pre-schizophrenic. Jack's mother, also one of Dr Hawkings' patients was, in fact, more psychiatrically disturbed than her son and this was undoubtedly a factor in Jack's problem. I regarded him as more personality disordered than schizophrenic and to-day would probably diagnose him as 'borderline'. However, he was firmly committed to the treatment process. A swift, and sometimes unhelpful, symbiotic relationship is common in clients with Jack's personality structure but it meant that re-parenting was facilitated and was clearly indicated in his case, although the symbiosis would, of course, need to be resolved before he would be free to live his life independently of me. This is not always easy. In fact one client who I had effectively re-parented became so dependent on me that his perceptive GP realised we had an unresolved transference relationship and suggested he have no further contact with me at all and he did not. But I have never been entirely satisfied that this 'cold turkey' response to the situation was in the client's best long term interests.

Returning to 'Jack': during the course of his treatment, before he joined a group, Jack did some fantasy work in which he took himself off on a visit to the planet Mars! There he encountered a 'wise old man' (for which Alec Guiness in *Star Wars* was probably a model!) and engaged with him in profound dialogue which took him into some kind of spiritual realm. In the subsequent 'debriefing' I asked Jack who the 'wise old man' represented for him, expecting that he would say his father – a real but rather shadowy figure in Jack's life. But he declared that the 'wise old man' was God. Jack, like most of my clients, had no religious background at all but, like many, if not most, he had a real hunger for a spiritual dimension to life that would give him a sense of meaning and purpose. This is not necessarily the same as a desire for religion but institutional religion is, nevertheless, the most readily available access route to the world of the spirit and (in one form or another) the one most likely to offer opportunity for genuine spiritual growth in community. Later, when he was an undergraduate reading Information Technology, Jack was influenced by a fellow student and became a Christian. He telephoned me one evening in great excitement to tell me that he was being baptised shortly and could I be there? I said, 'Wild horses wouldn't stop me.'

The baptism was in a disused Methodist church that had been taken over by an evangelical group. There were three candidates and the place was heaving with several hundred enthusiastic supporters of all ages. The small children were all placed strategically around the baptistry in which the baptisms would take place and each candidate, including Jack, gave his testimony. I was interested to see two attractive young women translating all that was said into sign language for the benefit of a group of deaf worshippers. Someone told me the girls had undertaken training specially in order to do this. It was a most impressive occasion and a great joy to me to see Jack make his commitment. In doing so he adopted the baptismal name of Timothy. But becoming a Christian is not some kind of divine magic, guaranteed to solve all our problems, and Jack called Timothy still had far to go. He was on a journey of discovery.

As a further step in that journey Jack spent a few months at the Cathexis residential treatment centre, then in Shropshire, set up by my friend and colleague Jenny Robinson. This is an intensive, disciplined and highly structured treatment programme in which all the residents are actively involved in the domestic work of the establishment and all take part in daily group treatment sessions. They function as a large family in which Jenny, as director and principal therapist, is known to everyone as 'Mum'. This facility is now a very well established resource for the treatment of young people suffering from serious mental disorders, but has been relocated in Birmingham. During and following this experience I continued to be Jack's 'home' therapist to help consolidate his re-integration into normal society and I visited him in Shropshire. Subsequently, he kept loosely in touch with me. He visited America where he met Tracey, who was also a Christian, and in due course they got married. He brought her to see me before they both settled in the USA where his IT skills were much in demand. After that we lost touch.

Although there are several committed Christian transactional analysts, I do not know how many of them deal with spiritual, and even religious, issues quite as frankly as I do, treating religious belief as a possible resource rather than as part of the pathology. Certainly, the use of any kind of secular counselling or psychotherapy as an opportunity for proselytism would be quite unethical and I have carefully avoided any suggestion of that. My clients themselves have introduced the subject, as Jack did in identifying his Martian fantasy 'old man' as God. I responded to his initiative by inviting him to explore exactly what he meant by the word 'God'. As a Christian myself, and a qualified Methodist Local Preacher, I believe I was particularly well-equipped to deal with this kind of issue; but it undoubtedly presented me with problems from time to time, in balancing my rights against my responsibilities, both as a Christian and as a professional counsellor and psychotherapist.

During the course of my work with Ian Stewart, I had a letter from Vann Joines, Chairperson of the Appeals Committee, saying 'After reviewing the tape of your exam the Appeals Committee has decided to allow you to retake your exam without further cost. I regret that you had a bad experience the first time and hope that your second exam will be more pleasant.'

11

PRISONS

Round about this time Peter Warburton, the Chief Probation Officer, again 'shuffled his cabinet' and I agreed, without much enthusiasm, to leave the Aycliffe team and take up the post of Senior Liaison Probation Officer, on secondment to the Prison Department, at Deerbolt Youth Custody Centre (as it was then called) at Barnard Castle. I took up my new appointment on the 20th October, 1986. Bert Satchwell, my predecessor and an ex-army major who was also approaching retirement, stayed on for a few days to show me round and explain how he had done the job, and then he left to become SPO of one of the field teams – a job he was not enthusiastic about either!

Deerbolt had once been an army camp but after the war it became a Borstal. Borstals, however, were abolished. They had been structured on a public school system in the hope (not widely fulfilled) that young offenders would gain the same sort of character-building benefits attributed to a public school education. The Youth Custody Centres catered for offenders from 17 to 21 who were either too old for a Detention Centre sentence or for whom fairly long-term training, as well as punishment, was seen as desirable. The Detention Centres were patterned on the army 'glass house', where the inmates were made to do everything at the double under the bawling authority of a prison officer who was expected to behave like a ruthless army drill sergeant. It was designed to be thoroughly unpleasant and to teach the miscreants 'a lesson'. The idea carried much public favour but few prison officers had joined the Prison Service to play at drill sergeants and were, by and large, men and women of compassion. However, sentences were usually limited to three months (six in more serious cases), with remission for good behaviour, because the inmates quickly got used to even a harsh regime and showed little improvement in subsequent behaviour if subjected to it for longer. The Youth Custody Centres, however, were designed with training in mind.

Deerbolt had been entirely re-built since its army days. There was an Education Centre staffed by well-qualified teachers where inmates could study a variety of subjects, from reading and writing to information technology. There was also a trade training centre, for which the architect had taken his inspiration from the old 'prison hulk'. There, the trainees could learn brick-laying, plastering, joinery, painting and decorating and many other useful skills, possibly up to City & Guilds standard. The kitchens and the laundry were also useful training venues and there was an Assistant Governor who had special responsibility for keeping the gardens and greenhouses in good order and training lads to be gardeners. Deerbolt must be the prettiest prison the Prison Department has to offer! The trainees, lived in seven residential blocks, in one of which specially selected lads even had keys to their own rooms. They would set off each morning to go to work or school or the training centre, returning 'home' for lunch and tea. Some of the more mature trainees, who could be trusted not to abscond, worked at various jobs in Barnard Castle, which was within walking distance. At Deerbolt there was a well-equipped gymnasium staffed by trained physical education instructors, and extensive sports fields which, in Borstal days, had been mainly farmland. The prison chapel was a modern, hexagonal building where a full-time chaplain held regular services, including a Thursday morning communion for all denominations that was often attended by the Governor, Assistant Governors, Prison Officers, me, of course, as well as trainees and we would all sit together and receive the elements side by side at the communion rail.

Each Tuesday morning I would attend the Governor's Meeting with his Assistant Governors and other staff members and contribute to discussions about the running of the establishment. I had an office on the Reception Unit, to which all trainees were allocated initially, and there I would see individuals to deal with personal matters, either at their request or mine. I saw all the new admissions collectively soon after their arrival, to brief them on what they might expect of the regime and what the staff would expect of them. Within a few days of arrival each would attend individually an assessment meeting with an Assistant Governor, myself and their Personal Officers who had a special, almost paternal, responsibility for the welfare of individual trainees. Generally speaking, the prison experience is one in which the prisoner learns to do whatever he is told and for the length of the sentence he has no decisions to make. Many prisoners find this relaxing, and sometimes even congenial, and the same kind of organisational discipline necessarily applied at Deerbolt as well. But personal responsibility was emphasised nevertheless and every trainee was encouraged to choose what he wanted to do with his 'time' that would best equip him to live a responsible, law-abiding life on release.

I had some responsibility for liaison with families and with each trainee's 'home' probation officer who would be responsible for after-care supervision on release. Most trainees and their families already knew their home probation officers, at least from the preparation of a Social Enquiry Report to assist the court in sentencing, and frequently from previous supervision, perhaps under a Probation Order. Probation Officer and trainee would usually correspond during the sentence and the Probation Officer would, ideally, visit the trainee at least once, especially when release was imminent. This relationship between Probation Officer and trainee was an integral feature of the entire probation system and one that provided me with the foundations for my later style of work as counsellor and psychotherapist. Most such professionals would, I think, hesitate to visit their clients – much less their clients' families – in their homes but I sometimes did so.

One of the reasons why the Chief Probation Officer wanted me to go to Deerbolt was because he felt it would provide opportunities for me to practice group therapy, a development that was being favoured by the Prison Department. I was not enthusiastic about this because I could not be optimistic about the benefits that could be achieved in a prison setting, even under the relatively enlightened regime at Deerbolt. An American transactional analyst, Dr Martin Groder, had established, in an Illinois penitentiary, a Total Learning Environment, called Asklepieion, for a community of prisoners with severe character disorders. This wing of the prison functioned independently of the rest of the institution. Inmates chose to join it and knew that they were committing themselves to a highly unconventional prison regime in which decision-making was what life was all about. The regime was educational rather than medical, was highly disciplined and structured in such a way that 'residents' were made to face the reality and consequences of their own behaviour and to make adjustments accordingly. In a criminal community of men whose essential purpose as individuals was to win battles, to make fools of people and to corrupt the system, whatever it was, the goal to which they committed themselves was that of solving problems. One of the features of the programme was called 'The Synanon Game', which had been developed elsewhere. This was a highly confrontational event in which participants were invited to attack one another verbally (but not physically) in order to get feelings and prejudices 'out into the open' where they could be addressed and resolved. Whilst the process was hostile and abusive the goal was good will and harmony between those taking part, and this was usually achieved. I once took part in a workshop in which The Synanon Game was set up for trainee transactional analysts. I found it extremely challenging, since my natural disposition is the very opposite of this, but the experience was enough to convince me of its usefulness. Similar provision for overt hostility towards other participants is also a feature of the community building programme developed by Scott Peck, which I shall write about in a later chapter.

The Asklepiein approach was successful for a significant number of prisoners but it was, of course, expensive and called for such exceptional commitment from specially trained staff that it was not practicable to extend it into the penal system as a whole. In any event, I myself had not nearly enough experience and expertise to promote such a development and sentences at Deerbolt were not long enough.

Most transactional analysts, Groder believed, practiced some kind of religion, philosophy or ethical system, no matter how secretly, and this dimension he called the 'Suprapersonal'. The term most widely used now is 'transpersonal', which I shall refer to again in a later chapter. It refers to what Alcoholics Anonymous and derivative groups, call 'a power beyond ourselves' – a resource for change and healing that is somehow outside and beyond the individual but perhaps present within a therapeutic group, even a group of only two, and available to those who want it. Berne's concept of *Physis*, the 'growth force of nature which makes things grow and makes growing things more perfect' is, in my view, another manifestation of this, as is 'God'. It is interesting how many offenders in prison 'turn to God'. The Alpha' movement – an on-going and now world-wide evangelical initiative aimed very specifically at 'bringing people to Christ' – now operates very successfully at almost all prisons in the UK and has undoubtedly led to many changed lives. The point at issue for me now, in the context of my own personal spiritual journey, is that this 'power', whether we call it God or something else, is universally available. It manifests as Love in personal relationships between individuals or in groups and can be seen, I believe, as the ultimate source of all creativity.

* * *

My early retirement from the Probation Service was a prospect to which both I and the CPO were looking forward – I because I wanted to set up in full time private practice, and Peter (who always had balancing the budget at the back of his mind) because I was at the top of my pay scale and the job I was doing could be done by a younger, less experienced SPO on a lower salary! But I was anxious to pass my clinical membership exam in transactional analysis before I retired and also to be eligible for accreditation with the British Association for Counselling, so I had plenty to do in preparation. So far as TA group work was concerned I did not actually do very much of it at Deerbolt, though I did do some. The trainees who took part seemed to think it was worth while but I had no opportunity to follow up their progress or find out what happened to them subsequently. Most of my psychotherapeutic and counselling work was, by this time, private at my home in the evening.

My two and a half years at Deerbolt were not very satisfying professionally though I enjoyed my time there. The most rewarding thing I did was the preparation of a report the CPO had asked for on the treatment of sexual abusers of children. This had nothing at all to do with my actual role as Senior Liaison Probation Officer but the Deerbolt job was far less stressful than managing a field team, and not very demanding so I had time to do it. The issue of child sexual abuse had become a major social outrage during the years before I took up my post at Deerbolt. It had, no doubt, been going on throughout human history and had simply not been acknowledged. In modern times it had been 'kept quiet' by everyone concerned from the abused children and their abusers to the police, solicitors, probation officers and even some social workers because what was happening could not *possibly* be happening! Everyone went into denial so that the matter was never addressed. My wife Betty, as a Senior Case Worker with Social Services, all too frequently found herself faced with domestic situations where she knew intuitively that something of the sort was going on within the family but was unable to provide concrete evidence to justify proceedings of any kind.

Sexual abuse was, and is, extremely difficult to establish unless the child complains and very rarely did they do so. Frequently the abuse had taken place in the context of an affectionate relationship and might even have been taken for granted, at least by the abuser. If a child was old enough to complain, and did so, it would to be to their mother, and she would often dismiss such an allegation as preposterous. With older children it was frequently schoolteachers who were the first to raise the alarm, when behaviour at school clearly indicated that a child was emotionally distressed and was, perhaps, unwilling or unable to talk about it. Sometimes a social worker felt certain that a father was having an incestuous sexual relationship with his daughter of, perhaps, only twelve years old or even younger. In fact, the abused children were sometimes only babies! It was this latter fact that precipitated what came to be known as 'The Cleveland Crisis' because it first manifested as a significant matter in what was then Cleveland County, centred on Middlesbrough, where Betty and I lived. A consultant paediatrician, Dr Marietta Higgs, learned from a colleague in Leeds that anal dilatation in small children was a sign that the child was being abused. The theory was that the child's anus would dilate spontaneously to admit anything being introduced into it and, if this reaction had been established, it would occur when the child's buttocks were drawn apart on medical examination. In consequence a large number of cases were referred to the police and social services. Betty and I were never involved in the same case but we were both concerned professionally for different reasons. The social worker's essential concern was with the welfare of the abused children and this frequently meant that, after police investigation, a child's father appeared before the courts and would probably be sent to prison, often causing further emotional trauma for everyone involved. My concern, as a probation officer, was essentially with the welfare of the offender. This did not mean, of course, that I would defend his behaviour in any way but it did mean that I was inclined to see it as a problem needing a solution and not just an offence demanding punishment. There was general recognition that breaking up families was not an ideal response to the problem of sexual abuse but society had no established alternative as a means of ensuring that it stopped and did not happen again. Even when the father was released from prison he could not return to the family and if he did so the children would promptly be taken into the care of the Local Authority. If his wife would not have him back he would soon form another relationship and if there were children involved the offender might well find some new victims unless they too were taken into Care.

It was this situation that prompted me, as a transactional analyst, to think carefully about what society might do that was more constructive. An article had appeared in the *Transactional Analysis Journal* of April, 1984, under the title *Sexual Abusers of Children – The Lonely Kids*. The 'lonely kids', however, were not the abused children but the abusers! The writers recognised that men who abused children in this way frequently did so because they were themselves emotionally immature; they were locked into a Child ego state and were unable to make mature relationships with adult women. Their marriages would be more a relationship of mother and child rather than husband and wife. Several workers in the UK, as well as in America, had begun to explore this, notably Tilman Furniss and Arnon Bentovin, child psychiatrists, working at the Great Ormond Street Hospital for Sick Children.

In July, 1987, therefore, I was asked by the Chief Probation Officer to ascertain what treatment options were available for sexual abusers of children because this was clearly a Probation Service responsibility. Many individuals and agencies responded to my enquiries including Probation Service colleagues, Social Services, the NSPCC, psychiatrists, paediatricians, clinical psychologists and academics. I did a great deal of reading of books, and articles in professional journals, and visited significant people all over the country in the course of my research, including the Psychiatric Prison at Grendon Underwood, near Aylesbury. In particular I received a lot of help and guidance from the eminent criminologist Professor D.J. West. We had already met at a conference on the treatment of mentally disordered offenders held at Park Lane Hospital, Liverpool, where such notorious killers as 'moors murderer' Ian Brady, were confined. Dr West remembered me and when I wrote to tell him what I was doing he kindly invited me to Cambridge, where I stayed at his own college and had the use of both his own private library and of the extensive Radzinovicz library at the Institute of Criminology.

Eventually, I amassed a considerable quantity of books, papers, notes and personal communications and started to draft my report, describing a variety of treatment approaches – individual psychotherapy, group treatment, family therapy, marital work, behaviour therapy and even such physical treatments as surgical castration and hormone therapy. My report was called *Who are the Lonely Kids? – Treatment Options for Sexual Abusers of Children within the Family*. It was a catchy title and should have been of interest to anyone thinking of setting up a treatment programme. The Chief Probation Officer allowed me to retain the copyright myself but I was unable to find a commercial publisher, evidently because my subject was too narrowly focussed. So I was asked to produce a fully referenced abstract and the Durham County Probation Service published this but I have no idea to what extent it might have influenced future treatment programmes. The most widely used treatment, I believe, has been a behavioural model pioneered by another probation officer, Ray Wyre. This model is favoured because objective results can be seen fairly quickly although benefit is not always maintained after treatment stops. Nevertheless, twenty years later, Ray Wyre is still a valued resource.

The most significant and comprehensive model that I discovered during my research was The Network Approach developed in Seattle, Washington. This approach called on a wide range of community resources but the focus of interest was the offender himself. Family therapy was one of several contributions within a comprehensive network. The community acted in order to protect the child victim, to protect itself from further exploitation, to hold the abuser responsible, to help him control his sexual arousal, to alter those factors in the environment which facilitated the deviance and to monitor the offender's future behaviour.

This comprehensive programme required the participation of psychiatrists, social workers, community nurses, police, probation officers, courts and sometimes prisons. It was highly structured and disciplined and depended for its effectiveness on the use of authority and sanctions if the offender failed to comply with the rules. Detailed evaluation eliminated those who were unlikely to carry out the programme so that resources were not wasted and the success rate was high. An essential feature of the evaluation process was an 'offender group' whose members themselves contributed to the decision as to whether a new 'candidate' was sufficiently well-motivated to justify accepting him into membership of the treatment programme. Once the candidate was accepted a support system would be mobilised that included friends, family, supervisors and others. Individual work would proceed with the offender, using cognitive-behavioural, aversion and other techniques and work would go ahead with the family. Provision was also made for sex education and alcohol counselling, since alcohol was found to be a major disinhibitor. Throughout a three year probation order the offender's behaviour would be carefully monitored and the possibility of his being taken back to court was a major incentive to keep him in the treatment programme. The need for long-term follow up was seen as essential because there was evidence that some would revert to offending behaviour if they lost contact with the therapist. Obviously, such a programme as this was so demanding on resources that most authorities would dismiss it as economically impracticable. The significant feature of it, however, was that it had a high success rate.

I have described The Network Approach in some detail because it has both secular and spiritual dimensions. It seems to me to provide a model that could be applied, with modification, to many other social problems besides the sexual abuse of children within the family. Several features of The Network Approach are reflected in both Martin Groder's Asklepieion regime for treating character disordered offenders in prison and in the Cathexis approach to treating young people with schizophrenia and other serious mental disorders.

There are two features in particular which I regard as crucially important for the success of any approach to treating people whose behaviour deviates from the socially acceptable 'norm'. The first is that the deviant behaviour is addressed directly – rather than hoping that punishment, social intervention, counselling, psychotherapy or skills training alone will make a significant difference, even though they might be helpful in addition. The second feature is the use of authority. The current cultural emphasis on human rights and universal freedom is an ideal well worth aiming for and any community that can achieve this will indeed have established a sort of heaven on earth. I have decided to believe that such an idyllic state could, in principle, be achieved, even if only within some sort of 'total learning environment', as in Groder's Asklepieion, and we must keep aiming for it. But the catch is that human beings are programmed with an insatiable, and necessary, desire to 'fill the earth and subdue it' and in order to fulfil this basic function (either Biblical or evolutionary) we need powerful instincts for both sex and aggression, like the rest of animal creation. All the other animals, however, also have programmed into them – genetically or in some other way – controls that limit the exercise of these impulses. Human beings have no such controls. We have 'free will'.

'Free will' is generally held to mean that we are somehow free from the deterministic cause and effect 'prison' that accounts for the behaviour of the rest of creation and which, in principle at least, is scientifically predictable. But the concept of human free will cannot mean that we alone are free to do as we like. Dogs, cats, camels and centipedes can do as they like – in fact they can do no other! The distinctive thing about human free will (shared by no other species, so far as we know) is that we are free to do what we do *not* like. We alone are free to do as we believe we ought!

The prevailing scientific philosophy of determinism, of course, insists that such freedom is an illusion. The universe, they say, is a closed, mechanical system of cause and effect. The notion of morality, whilst useful as a means of social control, is nonsense, scientifically speaking. Whatever happens to us, whatever we do, think or even feel is pre-determined, they say, by an infinitely complex web of things that have happened before and we cannot escape. We are in a 'prison' that is both psychological and spiritual. Life has no meaning and no purpose. There is no 'power beyond ourselves', no matter how helpful it might be to believe that there is, especially if we are trying to escape from an addiction to alcohol or gambling. The one thing that this philosophy of determinism fails to take into account is that – if it is true – the philosopher himself is not free to embrace any other philosophy than that of determinism. He is 'hoist with his own petard'! In the very nature of the case, no-one can 'know', in the absolute, mathematical, scientific sense, whether absolute determinism is true or not. Determinism itself is a matter of choice! Each one of us must decide for ourselves whether we will live with the assumption that we are morally free – and, therefore, morally responsible – or not. Of course, if absolute determinism is true then our choice is not a free choice at all – we only imagine it is!

But human beings are not free from 'laws' altogether. Countless generations have learned from experience what behaviours are socially constructive and what behaviours tend to cause society to disintegrate. The Ten Commandments are consistent with the codes of law in cultures everywhere and stable social life depends on them. And all the rules, whatever one's religion or lack of it, are summed up in the simple, all-embracing commandment to love one another. These laws of love are ideally passed on from parents to children and whilst they might seem, on the face of it, to limit our freedom, the reality is that without them we should have no freedom at all! A community without laws is a community without freedom.

Love, unfortunately, is often confused with indulgence. Countless mothers have said to me, when I called on them to prepare a social inquiry report for the magistrates before whom their delinquent children would shortly appear, 'I can't think why he should steal. He gets everything he wants'! Love, as the Chinese philosopher said, is a many splendoured thing! But the most useful definition of the kind of love I am talking about, is having the disposition and the will to give a bit more than usual, to make some sacrifice, in order to nurture someone's spiritual growth – including your own or society's. Eric Berne, who was not a religious man, saw this same principle in terms of *Physis*, the growth force of Nature, 'which we see evidence of in the individual and society, (and which) if properly nourished in infancy, works along with the Superego, so that the individual has an urge to grow and to behave 'better' – that is, in accordance with the principles . . . which take the happiness of others into consideration.' Berne found this idea of *Physis* in the work of the Greek philosophers. One does not need to be a Greek philosopher or a psychoanalyst to recognise the essential truth of these statements; but such altruism it is frequently just too difficult to achieve. So this basic principle of good relationships and social cohesion is commonly set on one side in favour of some half-measure which we know from experience is unlikely to be more than partially successful. The general public demands punishment, applied by the courts; counsellors recommend counselling, politicians social engineering, doctors medication, surgeons surgery, group therapists group therapy, family therapists family therapy – and so on.

The suggestion that some deviant people might need several – even all – of these contributions if the problem of their behaviour is to be solved, is untenable because the resources are simply not available – whatever might have been achieved in Seattle, Washington.

But consideration of such a total social response to human deviance should not be dismissed out of hand. In an earlier book, *New Directions in Transactional Analysis Counselling*, I suggested that 'the total human being is a human being in relationship', rather than an individual who is independent, autonomous and self-sufficient. We are all, biologically speaking, committed to personal survival whatever happens to the rest of the world and the principle of survival of the fittest is almost universally accepted as the mechanism of evolution. But spiritually speaking, there is another option – the commitment of a whole community to the solving of problems rather than simply to the winning of battles. Sometimes, of course, winning the battle against some evil – a ruthless dictator, perhaps – is a necessary step in solving a problem but rarely, if ever, is it the only step needed. If the survival of the whole community is the goal, then the individual who is a part of the community must also participate, even though this requires the making of personal sacrifices.

If such a vision seems an impossible ideal, consider what the Brontë sisters (with whom this book started) would have thought in the early 19th century of the suggestion that medical treatment would be available, free of charge, to every British citizen and a pension for everyone on retirement And consider what they would have thought about universal suffrage, the United Nations and the European Community. Such developments might have been regarded by many as desirable, but so much in the realms of fantasy that they would have been dismissed as 'pie in the sky' But in two hundred years not only has technology created an unimaginably different world but people have changed too. Despite the risks of nuclear warfare and the evils of crime, terrorism and diseases like AIDS, there is a new surge of goodness in the world that has actually been facilitated by the advance of science and technology in many areas of life. More and more people, who would never be rated philanthropists or 'lady bountifuls' in the Victorian sense, are giving of their time in voluntary work and their money in support of those less well-off than themselves; governments and individuals give vast sums of money (though never enough!) for the relief of famine in Third World countries or help for those who have suffered from the effects of devastating natural disasters. Along with science, technology, education and communications, human beings are already developing a new vision of what life is all about and a recognition that independence, autonomy and self-sufficiency are not, in the final analysis, the most worthy goals for human beings to aim for. Although membership of the mainstream institutional church is declining rapidly in the Western world, the disposition of 'secular' human beings to love one another, regardless of colour, race and religion, is growing and this, I believe, is a spiritual phenomenon. It reflects a deep sense of authentic meaning and purpose.

In view of this present reality it is not, I think, too much to hope that a future generation will be able and willing to invest as much in the solving of the problems of human relationships as it is now willing to invest in tackling social, political and scientific problems. The Seattle approach to the treatment of some sexual abusers of children could, in reality, become a model for problem solving in many areas of life.

* * *

Whilst I was 'inside' at Deerbolt Youth Custody Centre, I was also having family problems to contend with that must have had a bearing on my own personal spiritual development. I have referred earlier to my mother having a rather depressive personality. My father's way of dealing with this was sometimes brutal and insensitive, even if superficially effective. He had no understanding of depressive illness and when Mother became depressed, for whatever reason, and was tired, withdrawn, tearful and unable to tell him what was wrong, he would get angry and shout at her, saying, 'For goodness sake, Peg, pull yourself together! I've got enough problems without all this business!' He was never physically violent but would sit in his armchair thinking about the situation and in his anger and frustration I would see him biting the stem of his pipe. So far as I am aware Mother never saw the doctor about her depression and I doubt if my father ever suggested she should, because they would both have been afraid she would finish up in 'Menston' – our local mental hospital, later called 'High Royds' – which would, at the time, have been regarded as a fate worse than death! So throughout her life Mother suffered from periodic bouts of depression that went untreated. Modern medication and psychotherapy would have helped, of course, but resources for the effective treatment of mental illness were notable for their absence at the time. I have sometimes wondered whether my father's style of angry shouting was, perhaps, a primitive form of 'shock therapy'! It is probable, I think, that my experience with Mother's depression was a factor in my becoming a psychotherapist.

My mother's first experience of treatment for this condition did not happen until she was 87, when she had a severe episode of agitated depression and had to go into St Luke's, our local psychiatric hospital in Middlesbrough. By this time her sister Anne, then aged 96, was living with her in a pleasant flat in Middlesbrough, quite near to us, where we could keep an eye on them both. Depression is often described as 'anger directed towards one's self' as a substitute for some other person (usually a parent) who would 'die' if the anger were allowed to express itself openly, and the emotional energy normally used for day to day living is used up keeping the anger in check. In my mother's case I guess her anger must have been directed at Anne, even from childhood. Certainly, when they began to live together, Mother was still the younger sister by nearly ten years and Anne still expected her to do everything, to cook and clean, wash and iron, do the shopping and 'fetch and carry', just as she had no doubt done in childhood. So it would not be surprising if the repeat of this situation around eighty year later were enough to trigger a serious depressive breakdown. She had several spells in hospital and eventually Anne, probably recognising that she herself was at least part of the problem, decided to move into a Residential Home. Mother decided later that she would do the same but, wisely, she chose a different place. Anne, who was always full of fun and interested in people, soon became everybody's favourite resident where she was, and Mother could never have competed with that! So we found another Home for her nearby. She sold her flat and most of her treasures and moved in. Even after that she had another breakdown and was unable to attend Anne's 100th birthday celebrations for which all the scattered family gathered at a local hotel. But she did recover enough to join Anne and Marge Barker, the Mayor of Middlesbrough, on a celebration flight from Teesside Airport.

After that I took her on a week's touring holiday in Northumbria and thereabouts. We visited Berwick-on-Tweed, Holy Island, Kielder Dam, Edinburgh and various other places. Betty, who did not enjoy driving around in the car just for the sake of it, did not come with us, so Mother had me all to herself for a week, which was just what she most wanted!

On the way home we stopped for a snack lunch at a pub in Craster, right opposite the kipper factory, and sat at a table outside in the sunshine. After a few minutes an elderly lady and gentleman came and sat at the next table and engaged us in friendly conversation. They were Professor Alan Guile and his wife Betty. Alan was a tall, distinguished looking man with wavy grey hair, very gracious and every inch a professor. His wife Betty was a bonny little lady, much shorter and quite chatty. I cannot recall how we progressed so quickly from the weather and the smell of kippers from across the road to the important things of life, but almost immediately, it seemed, we discovered that Alan was a converted and 'born again' Catholic. He had recently taken early retirement from the Chair of Electrical and Electronic Engineering at Leeds University in order that he and Betty (also a converted Catholic) might pursue a ministry of prayer and healing. They discovered from me that I was a Methodist preacher, a probation officer and a professional counsellor. So we established common ground over our sandwiches, exchanged addresses and telephone numbers and decided to keep in touch. Some months after this I was running an introductory one-day course in transactional analysis in Middlesbrough that I thought they might be interested in, so I told them about it and they both attended. It was a year or so later, after my retirement from the Probation Service, that I contacted them again and visited them at their home in Stockton, because I was looking for a new supervisor. I did not imagine they themselves would be suitably qualified for the job but hoped that from amongst their contacts in the counselling scene they might know someone who was. It was from them I learned of Gordon Clarke, a Methodist education psychologist who had a counselling ministry. Gordon did indeed become my clinical supervisor, a friend and confidante and effectively my spiritual director.

Again, the points had switched me onto another line.

12

SCRIPTS AND THINGS

Whilst I was busy at Deerbolt doing what a Senior Liaison Probation Officer is supposed to do and, as time permitted, researching and writing my report on treatment options for sexual abusers of children within the family, I was also working with private clients in the evenings and continuing with my TA training at weekend workshops and in individual sessions with Ian Stewart and other teachers. It was normal practice to tape record work with clients, which could sometimes be played back during the therapy session to help the client realise what he or she was saying and how they were saying it, and these tapes I might also replay later for personal reflection about what was going on in the session or I might take them for supervision as illustrations of my work. I sometimes recorded also sessions in which I myself was receiving therapy – as in the theatrical marathon at Ian's – so that I could reflect upon them later in private. Also, I was able to make notes from them that have been useful in compiling other parts of this book.

Ian was particularly interested in Process Therapy, a model developed by clinical psychologist and transactional analyst Taibi Kahler, and he used this when working with me. I described briefly in Chapter 6 some of the developmental factors that influence the formation, in early childhood, of a Script or 'life plan', which determines the general direction a person's life will take. Amongst these influences were 'Counter-Injunctions', received from the Parent Ego State of Mother or Father, that were usually positive and constructive, conveying good moral and social guidance, such as 'Always tell the truth' and 'Wear the right clothes for the right occasion'. However, there are five Counter-Injunctions (and only five have been identified!) that can be quite destructive in terms of the youngster's personal development. These are Be Perfect, Be Strong, Please Me, Try Hard and Hurry Up. These five 'messages' are called Drivers because they drive the person into a certain kind of behaviour by putting a condition on his sense of personal worth. They might also carry an Injunction, or 'Don't' message, so that the Driver 'Try Hard', which tells the youngster that he is OK only on condition that he is trying hard, might also carry with it an implicit message that the youngster is not really expected to succeed.

It might even imply 'Don't succeed – trying is quite sufficient.' Process Therapy also makes use of the 'Mini-script', a sequence of feelings, beliefs or behaviours that might be experienced in just a few seconds and in that short time reinforce the whole Life Script!

But my Script was far from straight forward! In de-briefing on a piece of work we had done together, Ian said 'What I was looking for was not only, or even mostly, how you answered my questions in terms of content but how you answered in terms of process. And what you did was to show the Be Strong Driver and then a flash of Be Perfect; and then you gave a Gallows Laugh.' (That is, laughing at something that is not funny, in order to make it seem OK). 'However, you had on your face the imprint of the Try Hard Driver, which is the two lines above the nose. So I want to pursue further what your personality adaptation might be.

'In answer to the cluster of adjectives' (an exercise we had done earlier) 'the ones you checked out most clearly were 'dramatic and dependent', which go with a Please Me (or Please Someone) Driver. And in all the Drivers I saw whilst you were answering, I hardly saw a Please You at all! But it also goes with Hurry Up – so that's a possibility. The other cluster of adjectives you checked off most fully were associated with Be Strong and indicate the shy, reclusive, loner, sensitive personality. . . . Your process pattern isn't simple'.'

In fact, this clip, from a tape recording of many years ago, clearly indicates that I was a somewhat complex personality!

My total Script Matrix, developed over a long period of work and personal reflection, is, not surprisingly, also very complex and I kept detailed notes of it that I can now share with the reader. In a book of this sort, however, it will be appropriate to provide a summary of the main features rather than attempt a detailed analysis. Happily, I have now largely overcome most of its destructive effects though there is undoubtedly a residue of 'scripty behaviour' that those who know me well will be quick to spot!

A Script is based on one of the four Life Positions referred to briefly in Chapter 6. The four positions are 'I'm OK – You're OK'; 'I'm Not OK – You're OK'; 'I'm OK – You're Not OK'; and 'I'm Not OK – You're Not OK'. Personally, I still find the folksy language a bit of an embarrassment and that itself might even be a residue of my Script; but the language is simple and understandable to anyone, and that is better than the esoteric language beloved of the medical profession that only the initiated can understand. My Basic Life Position was 'I'm Not OK – You're OK' – which will come as no surprise to some who have read so far. Its roots could well be in the incident, recorded in Chapter 1, when I was a small baby lying in my pram at home and screaming loudly – probably just for attention. My mother was out and my father, having failed to quieten me with pram rocking and comforting noises, eventually resorted to bawling 'Shut up!' at the top of his powerful voice. And I did!

An 'Early Decision' is a decision made in early childhood when the youngster has neither the wisdom nor the experience to understand what is really going on, as I clearly had not when I was probably just a few weeks old. Once made, this decision will form the basis of the Script or Life Plan that is beginning to emerge and certain later experiences will reinforce it. In my own case there were several childhood incidents, some of them described as 'Seeds and Weak Beginnings' in Chapter 1. Another child, with different Script expectations, might have taken these failures, setbacks and humiliations in his stride and not been fazed by them. But I was 'me', not someone else, and if I was to break loose from my Script and become the 'me' who reflected my real potential, then I had a lot of vitally important new decisions to make. Some of the potent Injunctions – or 'Don't' messages – received from parents and other important people, which led to my frustrating Script, included 'Don't be important' and 'Don't be you' (which, in my case, was probably 'Don't be the sex you are'). Another one was 'Don't express your real feelings'. It was all right for me to express sadness and shed tears, but anger was prohibited. The Injunction 'Don't Succeed' must have been one of the most potent in my Script. My father had failed to achieve his, and my mother's, expectations of becoming chairman and managing director of Salts (Saltaire) Ltd., so I must certainly not succeed in anything I wanted to aspire to, because that would be humiliating for Dad.

These thoughts and feelings, which I attribute to my parents, were not, of course, what they actually thought and felt; they were my own childhood interpretations as I was growing up. We all have a Script or Life Plan and it always curtails our freedom to live autonomously, even though some Scripts are better than others. Whatever the Script is, we become deeply committed to maintaining it (though out of our own awareness) because it is familiar and we grow accustomed to the expectation that 'life's like that', even though our goals and aspirations are being frustrated by it. The purpose of Script Analysis is to discover precisely what is happening, and why and how.

I was playing a lot of psychological Games to maintain my familiar, and self-destructive, Script. In order to escape from it I had to be confronted with what I was doing and become aware of it so that I could consciously stop doing it and start to think, feel and behave more constructively. This is a radical change demanding clear new decisions about the direction life is going. It demands sustained therapeutic work, not only in regular sessions with a therapist but also in 'homework' between sessions. The changes rarely come quickly although flashes of therapeutic insight can sometimes shift the work into a new and encouraging phase.

It is important that therapist and client have a clear mutual understanding about what they are aiming to achieve and this agreement is called the Contract. There needs to be an Overall Contract, which defines the aim of the whole therapeutic process, a Contract in respect of each piece of work done during the session, and Homework Contracts for the work to be done between sessions. My Overall Contract with Ian was, quite simply, to pass the oral exam, which I would re-take when we both felt I was ready, and we had a date in mind for November, 1987.

In order to maintain my Script – which included the expectation that I would be deferred yet again – I was structuring my time in such a way as to ensure an on-going supply of negative Strokes, so that my Racket feelings would be kept going as a sort of background feeling of muted misery. From time to time, as opportunity arose, I would play psychological Games in order to give the Racket Feelings a boost. My favourite Games turned out to be 'Kick Me' – in order to ensure that I kept getting put down; and 'Do Me Something' – so I didn't have to go it alone. Even now, I remember my experience at Harwich, as a newly commissioned officer in charge of a Field Security Section, with mixed feelings of pride at my achievement and fear of my own in adequacy – though I went to a lot of trouble to conceal the fear and inadequacy from both myself and others. Typical Racket Feelings associated with my Life Position of 'I'm Not OK – You're OK' include feeling scared, inferior, deprived, helpless, humiliated and inadequate, amongst other feelings.

But my favourite Game was 'Kick Me'. I hate being kicked or put down and when it happened I would feel my familiar anger but would not express it. If I expressed it, 'they' might hesitate to kick me again; but if they could be encouraged to keep on kicking me I would be reminded, as my Script required, that I was not important, not successful, not independent, autonomous and self-sufficient and not really a proper man. It is relevant, I think, that I was committed, in my Christian life, to growing the 'fruits of the Holy Spirit' – which are love, joy, peace, patience, kindness, goodness, faithfulness, gentleness and self-control. In reality, of course, these characteristics are as appropriate to men as they are to women, but they are not generally associated with a tough, macho image!

This was not, of course, mature or psychologically informed, thinking on my part. I still had to grasp Carl Gustav Jung's concept of the archetypes. These he described as coming from the Collective Unconscious, the stuff of legend, mythology and fairytales that manifest in the form of dreams and fantasies. These archetypes, Jung taught, were powerful unconscious realities that had a specific energy capable of influencing the world. Eric Berne's undeveloped concept of *Physis* seems to me now to have something in common with Jung's archetypes, both concepts being rooted in the notion that there is something transcendent in the nature of human beings which gives meaning and purpose to our existence. Two of the most influential of Jung's archetypes are the Animus – the masculine 'soul-image' of a woman's unconscious; and the Anima – the feminine 'soul-image' of a man's unconscious. Each, I had to discover, was an authentic manifestation in both men and women. In fact, having a strong, dynamic, positive Anima was, for me, clearly beneficial since it finds expression in creativity and is especially valuable in counselling.

The Script tends to have a negative and pathological connotation. In fact, I have myself described it as being over and against *Physis*, the growth force of Nature. But there are other and, perhaps, equally influential characteristics at the foundations of human personality whose roots are even deeper than the Script. Apart from their extreme manifestations these attitudes can be positive characteristics of 'the growth force of Nature' or of the 'archetypes' Jung saw as present in the collective unconscious shared by all humanity. It was Jung who conceived the idea of 'synchronicity', the notion that clusters of events which seem to be related to each other only by chance, might in fact be subject to some transcendent principle which was outside the remit of conventional science. My awareness of synchronicity is a thread running through this 'case story'.

It was Jung, again, who developed the idea of four 'temperaments' that are fundamental to each personality and which endow each of us with characteristic differences. They are Thinking, Feeling, Sensation and Intuition. These temperaments, however, unfold from within a basic tendency to be either Introverted or Extraverted. The Introvert tends to focus on the inner world of self, the Extravert to move outwards and to relate more readily to other people. But these temperaments are not mutually exclusive. We all have a bit of both but in each person there is an emphasis on one or the other, slight in many people but much more significant in others.

In the 1950s, after extensive research, Isobel Myers and Katherine

Briggs, using Jung's Psychological Types, devised what has come to be known as the Myers-Briggs Type Indicator of sixteen different behaviour patterns. The Myers-Briggs assessment is conducted ideally in an authorised workshop or individually by an authorised psychologist. Unfortunately, I never had the opportunity to undergo such an assessment and my understanding is based on the book *Please Understand Me – Character and Temperament Types* by David Keirsey and Marilyn Bates. The assessment requires us to choose between two alternative ways of reacting to a variety of situations and a score is arrived at that indicates which of the sixteen types we most nearly correspond to. The test might include the question, for example: When you go to a party do you, a) talk with a lot of people, strangers included; or b) just talk to a few people you know well? If we choose a), that would suggest we are extraverts, if b) that we are introverts. However, this preference would not necessarily imply that an extravert might never choose a few close friends, or that an introvert would never speak to someone unless they already knew them well. We can have a preference without being restricted to it. Other choices are between Sensation and Intuition, Thinking and Feeling, and Perceiving and Judging. The test result shows that the person is characterised by one of sixteen sets of choices. Sometimes a person will score equally on two functions and that is then indicated by a letter X, defining them as being a combination of two types. So there is a total of thirty two possible types.

My self-testing, showed, rather to my surprise, that I have a preference for Extraverted behaviours, rather than Introverted; that I am more likely to make decisions Intuitively than on the basis of what I can observe with my senses, on Feeling rather than Thinking and Judging rather than Perceiving. Judgers tend to prefer rules and organization and to know where they stand; Perceivers prefer to be informal and spontaneous and less bound rules. Jung's studies led him to the conclusion that a tendency to introversion in the first part of life, often evolved into extraversion later on, and vice versa. I think this must have happened in my case because I seem to be rather more extraverted now than I was when younger. The whole issue of personality types, temperaments and Life Positions is, of course quite complex and there is no need to go into more detail here. I will just outline my personality profile based on a test similar to the Myers-Briggs test.

My type is referred to as ENFJ. This means I had a preference for Extraversion, Intuition, Feeling and Judging. We seem to be quite rare, occurring in only about five per cent of the population – at least in the USA where this test was devised. We are said to have good powers of leadership and to have unusual charisma! We are willing to become involved and to communicate care and concern for others, so that people turn to us for support and nurture. We are trustworthy, tolerant and avoid being critical but friends might feel overwhelmed by us, believing that they cannot possibly live up to our expectations of them. When we find that others do not always readily understand us we might feel hurt and puzzled. (I have often been aware of this) Evenso, we have little hesitation in speaking out in groups, small or large. We are very empathetic and because of this might sometimes over-identify with others and take their burdens onto our own shoulders. Whilst the ability to empathise, or feel another person's feelings, is particularly important for a counsellor, the tendency to over-identify with a client can be seriously counter-productive. Sometimes my tendency to over-identify made it difficult for me to adopt a position of professional detachment. We tend to make important decisions intuitively and so it is important for a counsellor like me to have a supervisor who has a preference for thinking logically.

Fortunately, we make good companions and marriage partners and are deeply devoted to our children without trying to dominate them. We long for perfection, not only in relationships but also in career aspirations, so we might be a bit restless, moving from one job to another in search of something that is just right. We are best fitted for jobs involving people, such as selling, teaching, the ministry and, of course, counselling, which capitalise on our personalities.

We ENFJs are, nevertheless, planners. We like to have things properly organised in advance and can usually be relied upon to honour our commitments. Our charm and concern for others makes us popular and we value human relationships above all else. Whilst we tend to lead we can be equally comfortable as followers. We might be hurt by indifference but we are not crushed by it and will usually pursue our goals in spite of setbacks.

This personality profile emphasises the positives and a fuller account would no doubt reveal less desirable features. I have presented it this way because I have now overcome many of the negative aspects of my personality and Life Plan as revealed in the Script described above and, quite frankly, I don't want to make too much of them!

There are, however, certain other things that seem appropriate to include at this stage. Betty is quite the most important person in my life and, whilst I do not propose to try to analyse her Script, there is not much doubt that it interlocks with mine. We are not quite opposites, which Jung would regard as being particularly attractive to each other, but we do complement each other in many ways. Betty is more extroverted than I am and she is much less drawn to introspection and self-analysis. We both like to have things properly organised, rather than spontaneous and both rely a good deal on our kitchen diary, where all appointments are recorded. Betty is intuitive like I am but much more so; and whilst she can be quite empathetic, sensing other people's feelings, I believe I am even more sensitive than she is in this area. She made an outstanding caseworker in Social Services, attending to people's practical needs and giving them good advice and this, of course, involved an element of counselling

Another thing I want to mention at this point, because it comes under the general heading of 'Scripts and Things', is astrology. I must make it clear that I do not believe in astrology. But when I say that, I mean that I do not trust in it, not that I believe it is nonsense. I cannot, indeed, make any sense of it myself and see no rational basis for it whatsoever. But having said that I must confess to being puzzled by the extent to which my 'character reading' as a Scorpio, born on the 15th November, 1926, (which I once curiously read something about) seems to match aspects of my personality profile as outlined above, based on Jung's four 'temperaments'. Just to see whether anything has changed, I looked up Scorpio on the Internet and found the traits described there still saying that, as a Scorpio, I am 'Determined and forceful, emotional, intuitive, powerful and passionate, exciting and magnetic'. Well, I would hesitate to lay claim to all those fulsome attributes but I think it would be fair to say that people who know me well might detect in me at least a pale reflection of them! Since they are a pretty good set I could, I think, be excused for wanting to see myself in them; but these characteristics do not seem to loom anything like as large in other people's 'sun signs', although we Scorpios certainly do not have a monopoly of them. When it comes to the professions we are likely to enter into, there is another set of 'matches'. Analysis, research, investigation and the solving of mysteries are listed as things we might want to do; and we could find opportunities in police and detective work, espionage and counter-espionage, physics and psychology. I have done none of those things precisely, but probation officers spend a lot of time doing a kind of social detective work and whilst I was never a spy I did spend three years in military intelligence.

We Scorpios, it says on the Internet, could find outlets for our talents in the spoken and the written word; and whoever compiled the feature could not possibly have know about my preaching, teaching, lecturing, writing and television work. And they do mention 'the church' as a likely profession – one I did not follow but, as a Methodist Local Preacher, I have always been pretty close to it! And our 'inner intensity' – according to the Internet – could express itself in spiritual and mystical things. Well, it does – hence this book! There are, of course, astrological references to less desirable characteristics – 'the dark side' as the Internet puts it – and these include 'Jealous and resentful, compulsive and obsessive and secretive and obstinate'. As a writer I am, of course, a bit compulsive and obsessive, otherwise I should get no writing done. But, understandably, I repudiate all the other nasty features the Internet attributes to the likes of me!

Whilst browsing on the Internet I thought it would be interesting to see what it had to say about Betty, a Leo born on the 18th August. Traditional Leo traits include 'Generous and warm hearted, creative and enthusiastic, broad-minded and expansive, faithful and loving', all of which matches her pretty well. On the darker side, says the Internet, Leos are 'pompous and patronising, bossy and interfering, dogmatic and intolerant.' Well . . . I won't dwell too much on any of that either!

People come into counselling and psychotherapy from all sorts of professions, including astrology, tarot card reading and other occult pursuits, possibly because they find themselves counselling their clients in response to whatever is 'revealed' and are sufficiently responsible to want to learn how to do it properly. More acceptably there are, amongst us, psychiatrists and clinical psychologists, teachers, social workers, probation officers, ministers of religion, personnel managers and many others. One presenter at conferences some years ago was a prison governor; another successful therapist I knew was an ex-journalist.

I no more believe in astrology than Jung believed in flying saucers but I do recognise that there might well be 'something in it', even though I cannot understand what it is. The point at issue here is that I do not 'trust' in astrology, no matter how persuasive, or even convincing, the claims of its devotees But astrology, clairvoyance, spiritualism and various other manifestations of the paranormal, are classified by many people as 'spiritual', presumably on the grounds that they are not subject to the generally accepted laws of science. I do not argue with this. But I am conscious of the words of scripture, which I believe should be taken seriously whether we believe the Bible to be 'the word of God' or, perhaps, the distillation of thousands of years of human wisdom and experience. I refer particularly to the words of St Paul to the early Christians in Ephesus, warning them of 'the spiritual hosts of wickedness in the heavenly places.' This does not necessarily mean, for me, that such things as astrology, clairvoyance, spiritualism and various other paranormal manifestations, are to be classified as intrinsically evil. It means that there is at least as much likelihood of evil manifesting in the realms of the spiritual as there is in the familiar social and political scene! It is for this reason that I have decided to engage with that dimension of spirituality that endows human life with meaning and purpose and which, at the same time, provides for moral freedom. It is this that is of importance to counsellors, psychotherapists and others in the helping and healing professions. Such spirituality is beautifully described by Viktor Frankl, the Jewish psychiatrist, in *Man's Search for Meaning*, his moving account of his experiences in Auschwitz and his subsequent development of Logotherapy.

So I had a pretty negative and pathological Script pushing me in one direction, in deference to Freud and his disciples (including Berne, of course); a much more positive personality profile, in deference to Jung and his disciples, drawing me in another; and – overarching the whole lot – the baleful, sinister and utterly incomprehensible influence of stars, planets and zodiacal signs which mysteriously seemed capable of pushing me in either direction! In and amongst all this, surely, I must have some freedom to decide for myself!

But It was transactional analysis psychotherapy, particularly the Gouldings' Redecision model, that gave me an awareness of this freedom, more than the traditional religion I had been brought up with.

* * *

During 1987, whilst I was still on secondment to the Prison Department, Ian and I continued to work together, with valuable contributions from Petrüska Clarkson, Adrienne Lee and others. Eventually everyone agreed that I was ready to face the Final Exam Board again, this time in the confident expectation of becoming at last a qualified transactional analyst.

Examination Boards were held in various European countries and in America, often associated with major training conferences. The examiners all gave their services freely and paid their own expenses but the candidates had a fee to pay to cover administration costs. This time the exams were again held in Germany, not in Heidelberg but in Bad Soden, not far from Frankfurt. The event was convened specially for exam purposes and was not associated with a training conference. On this occasion I travelled alone and got a taxi from Frankfurt airport to Bad Soden, a distance of five or six miles.

Bad Soden is, of course, a spa town and its ambience reminded me very much of Ilkley in Yorkshire, which I knew well. It is clean and attractive with plenty of shops, parks and restaurants. The taxi dropped me at the Kursaal, where the exams were to be held the following day. It was a splendid, modern building in the centre of the town and its facilities for exam purposes were incomparably better than I had experienced at Heidelberg. Most of the candidates and examiners were staying at the Kursaal itself but I was not because Ian, perhaps in deference to his Scots instinct for economy, had booked rooms for us both at a modest guest house a few minutes walk away. Having made sure that my arrival for the exam had been noted, I made enquiries how to get to my digs and walked over, through a little park, with my travelling bag. The landlady was a very pleasant, middle-aged Frau who spoke only a little English but enough to compensate for my limited German and she told me that Herr Stewart had already booked in and would not be back until late. She offered to make me a meal, which I gladly accepted, and then showed me up to my room. Ian had pinned a note to the door explaining that he was at an examiners' meeting and suggested we could meet at breakfast the following morning. So after I had unpacked, I read a book for a while until dinner time and then had an early night.

The following morning after breakfast Ian and I walked over to the Kursaal. The assembly room was crowded now with exam candidates and examiners of many nationalities. Around the walls were pinned papers listing which candidate would appear before which board, in which room and at what time. I found my name on the list for a room called 'Hölderlin' at 10.30. The examiners were Gabor von Varga, Kaspar Wolfensberger, Anita Mosslein and Anna Kohlhass, who was the Chair. Ian gave me a brief indication of what each was like as an examiner. They were all, of course, qualified transactional analysts; Anna, a Certified Trainer, Ian described as 'sharp but straight'; Gabor, I knew slightly, having met him at a conference. He was Hungarian, a Provisional Trainer and a Gestaltist. Ian warned me that though he had a quiet 'front' he might get competitive. Kasper, an ITAA Trustee, also was 'straight' but sharp on theory. Ian did not know Anita. Julie Hay was there as an observer. She was already qualified in the Organizational field and was proceeding now to train as a clinical practitioner. I knew her quite well.

There was a bit of delay in starting and I waited outside the room until Anna Kohlhass appeared and took me in to await the arrival of the others. I was nervous about chatting with her in case I inadvertently provoked a 'woman in a position of authority' response! However, the others were not long arriving and the exam started, gently and unobtrusively with good humour. The room this time was spacious and well-equipped with a wipe-off board, beside which I sat and got my two tape recorders set up in readiness. The examiners were on straight chairs in a line in front of me, with Anna, as Chair, on my right. Julie Hay, the observer, sat separately on my left. The procedure was the same as at Heidelberg, beginning with examination of my documentation and questions about my experience. I was careful this time to avoid even mentioning character disorder or anything that might suggest I thought I was 'somebody'! The case I presented was a piece of work in which a woman I will call Denise was sharing with me her experience of being sexually abused as a child by her older brother and accepting permission to express her feelings. It was the culmination of a good deal of earlier work and Denise had taken off her shoes and had moved over to sit on the floor close beside me. Unfortunately, my tape recorder did not work properly so I could not review the exam afterwards but have to rely on memory and that does not include the verbal exchanges. However, Denise's tears flowed, the session contract was fulfilled and the examiners did not feel the need to hear another tape.

They sat quietly for a few moments, marking their score papers – mainly with fives this time – and then Anna asked them to declare their verdicts, starting with Gabor. With a mischievous twinkle in his eye he hesitated and then said, 'Oh, deferred, of course'. I instantly responded, grinning, with 'Don't you dare!'! He obligingly said, 'OK. Pass.' They all gave me a Pass.

After the exam, as we chatted informally for a few minutes, Gabor said, 'I would like to tell you something, David.'

'You rogue!' I grinned. 'At one time I would have crumbled with that, but not now.'

'Good,' he said approvingly. 'But I was feeling controlled.'

'What ever do you mean?'

He replied, 'You have power, do you know that?'

'No. In what way?'

He said, 'It is something in your voice, in your bearing.'

I was puzzled but recalled Ian's comments a couple of years ago about the Board at Heidelberg feeling threatened by me.

'Good luck,' said Gabor. 'You are a good therapist. Take care.'

I left the exam room, carrying my brief case and tape recorders, with Gabor's words ringing in my ears. I was at last a qualified Transactional Analyst specialising in Clinical Applications! Back in the assembly room

I was decorated with a small gold ribbon on my lapel so that everyone would know I was a Winner but there seemed to be no-one around to whom it mattered. Ian, and most of the others, were still busy in the exam rooms. So I went out into the town on my own and celebrated with a cup of coffee and a piece of torte before finding a public telephone (in a familiar British red telephone kiosk, as it happened) from which I could ring Betty and tell her the good news.

I had long ago decided that when I passed the exam I would buy a present for Betty and a picture for myself to commemorate my achievement. I wondered round the shops looking for something suitable and eventually found for Betty a beautiful square Kashmir shawl, which was fashionable at the time. I then found an art shop and bought for myself a watercoloured engraving of Bad Soden as it had been, probably a hundred and fifty or so years earlier. It has hung ever since at the bottom of our bedroom stairs where, with a frisson of pride, I see it every day.

I was on my own again in the afternoon and decided to go for a walk. I found my way out of the town centre, past a number of sanatoria which testified to Bad Soden's curative purposes, and up a hill into the woods. There were several people taking an afternoon walk with their dogs and I met an elderly German lady who, like me, was walking on her own. She did not speak much English but between us we managed an amusing exchange of information about ourselves. Back in the town we said 'auf wiedersehen' and I went back to the Kursaal. The exams were over by this time and certificates had been distributed at an informal event in my absence. By this time everyone was having an evening meal in a private room in the hotel but Ian and I were not included because we were not resident. However, I was shown where they all were and Alice Stephenson, greeting me as 'Midgley', in her usual way, congratulated me on my success and presented me with the certificate already made out with my name and new status. I was warmly applauded but not invited to sit down and eat with them so I went out alone and found a Chinese restaurant. I hoped Ian might be there but learned later that he had taken a train into Frankfurt. So I ate alone and then went back to the Kursaal where I had discovered there was a Lieder concert taking place. There was a spare seat and, by yet another example of Jung's synchronicity, I found myself sitting next to the German lady I had met in the woods! Together we enjoyed a splendid performance of Schubert's *Winterreise*, after which I walked back to my digs for another early night.

The next day was Sunday but our plane did not leave until late in the afternoon. So I found a little church, Lutheran I think, and worshipped with the locals, singing in German as best I could and trying to follow the sermon. Ian did not accompany me in this ritual of thanksgiving since he had embraced atheism as the appropriate philosophy for an educated psychotherapist. We did not meet again until our flight was called at Frankfurt airport and we travelled back together.

Betty had come for me in the car and was waiting at Middlesbrough station, with Sally on the lead. As I emerged up the steps from the underpass, Sally was so delirious with excitement that her tail wagged her whole bottom as she wet herself with a shower of spray on the concourse floor!

Dr Frank Lake, founder of the Clinical Theology Association, in the garden of Forest Grove House, the CTA HQ at Lingdale, 1981.

Malcolm Sweeting, a tutor for the Clinical Theology Association, David's first psychotherapy teacher and later supervisor.

Gordon Law, David's first sponsor and author of Beyond the Divides in Transactional Analysis – An Integral Approach to Relationships.

Graham Barnes, editor of Transactional Analysis *after Eric Berne, and Gordon's sponsor at that time, with the Eric Berne Memorial Award.*

Dr Ian Stewart (co-author with Vann Joines of TA Today) and founder of The Berne Institute, Kegworth, near Nottingham.

Adrienne Lee, co-director with Ian Stewart of The Berne Institute.

Transactional analyst Raymond Hostie, a Belgian priest; and transactional analyst Dr Margaret Turpin, relaxing at a TA training conference.

Alice Stevenson presenting 'Midgley' with his certificate at the Kursaal, Bad Soden, Germany, 7th November, 1987, watched by Mireille de Meuron from Neuchatel, Switzerland.

David and Professor Alan Guile at their first meeting, Craster, Northumbria, 1991. Mrs Guile and David's mother are in front.

Robert and Mary Goulding, founders of the Redecision School of TA when they received the Eric Berne Memorial Scientific Award, 1975

Gordon Clarke, Education Psychologist, (centre row, left) supervisor for David and founder of Christian Fellowship Ministry, with CFM Christian Counsellors.

Selwyn Hughes (centre) and the staff of CWR's HQ at Waverley Abbey House.

Charles Hocking, Relate Counsellor and David's supervisor (and his line manager, as Assistant Chief Probation Officer, County Durham) with his Finnish wife Pirkko.

Peter Warburton, retired Chief Probation Officer, County Durham.

Peter Warburton and a group of Foresters – retired Probation staff.

Dr John Hawkings, Senior Consultant Psychiatrist, North Tees General Hospital, Stockton-on-Tees.

Jenny Robinson, Director of the Connect Therapeutic Community, Birmingham.

Dr Nicky Miller (third from left), Medical Director of the Teesside Hospice, with members of the staff of this 'anteroom to the Kingdom of Heaven.'

Part Three

IN PRIVATE PRACTICE

13

ROOMS

I took early retirement from the Probation Service at the end of February, 1989, after nearly twenty five enjoyable and rewarding years. The one thing I awaited, before I could feel fully equipped to embark upon a new career as a professional counsellor and psychotherapist in private practice, was accreditation with the British Association for Counselling. I could, of course, have set up in practice without BAC accreditation – or any other qualification, for the matter of that – for the profession was still in its infancy and people were free to advertise themselves as counsellors, psychotherapists, hypnotherapists or a variety of other things, with no recognised qualifications whatsoever. The situation is gradually changing, with encouragement from European professional associations, but at the time of writing psychotherapy has still not become a 'closed shop'. Nevertheless, official recognition and accreditation was crucially important for me personally, not so much as evidence of my clinical competence as because of my peculiar personal needs to be 'somebody and something'! Many others, including my one-time supervisor Malcolm Sweeting, had little patience with such needs and simply did their own thing in their own way regardless of qualifications, although Malcolm was trained in Clinical Theology. No doubt, this was evidence of their 'independence, autonomy and self-sufficiency', whilst I was even yet seeking for 'Positive Strokes'. Sadly Malcolm died suddenly of a heart attack whilst still in his sixties.

During March I received a letter from BAC advising me that my application for accreditation had been accepted and enclosing a certificate that I immediately had framed and hung on my study wall beneath the certificate I had received at Bad Soden. My status was, in fact, even further enhanced a year or so later when the government at last established the United Kingdom Council for Psychotherapy. This had been under negotiation for several years, before standards and criteria were agreed that allowed for the official registration of practitioners using a variety of psychotherapeutic styles, from psychoanalysis and analytical psychology to gestalt therapy, pychosynthesis and, of course, transactional analysis along with many others. So I eventually had a third certificate to hang on my study wall.

The only thing I still lacked was a university degree and, had I come on the TA scene a few years later, I could even have had that as well. Because many countries in Europe required all psychotherapists to be university graduates, some transactional analysis training schools in the UK made arrangements with certain British universities for the award of a Master's degree to those who qualified as I had done, although some additional workshops and written work were required. I have no doubt I was more than capable of completing this work and might in fact have done so at a later stage through the process of APL (Accreditation of Prior Learning) had I been fit enough to travel to The Berne Institute at Kegworth, near Nottingham, to attend the necessary workshops. However, since I was severely disabled by this time with a condition later diagnosed as motor neurone disease, this was not possible. The Child in my head, who longed to hear the echo of my father's voice at last acknowledge me to be a 'top notcher', was disappointed. But not seriously so. Not only had I already achieved sufficient for me to recognise myself as a success, but my father's voice was no longer quite so demanding.

Now I needed rooms. Most people would simply practice from home, especially when they had a study like mine, ideally appointed in a quiet room at the back of the house, overlooking a well-tended garden. In fact, I had already been doing this in the evenings for several years. The problem now was our beloved dog Sally. I eventually found what I was looking for at 4, Yarm Road, Stockton-on-Tees, just across the river and only fifteen minutes drive from home, and arranged a three year lease at a rent I could afford. An artist friend designed me a 'New Directions' logo and a local sign writer made me an impressive sign to install outside the office where it could be seen by all who passed along Yarm Road. It said, 'New Directions – A Private Service for Counselling and Psychotherapy . . . David Midgley, Clinical Transactional Analyst, BAC Accredited Counsellor . . . Consultations by appointment.'

By the 1st August, 1989, I was open for business. All I needed now was clients. I already had a few, of course, but I had decided to work only four days a week to give me and Betty a bit of 'retirement' to play with and ideally I needed to see two clients each morning and two each afternoon – plus, possibly, a client or a group at home in the evening when Betty was there to keep the dog under control. So I worked from Tuesday to Friday each week. Sixteen clients a week was enough, I felt, though some colleagues would see far more, using the familiar fifty-minute hour with ten minutes break between clients. I decided on a full one hour session with a half hour between clients to write up notes, review notes for the next client and have a cup of coffee. I was not, in any event, in business to make a lot of money. I was happy enough to cover my costs and recoup my initial outlay, which was considerable because there was a great deal of refurbishment, decorating and furnishing to be done before I could see clients there. Nevertheless, I was soon earning a good income to add to my probation officer's pension and was able to make a significant contribution to the family budget. To begin with I charged a rather cautious £18 per session and gradually built it up to £35, which was then the going rate in the provinces; and like most therapists, I was willing to negotiate a smaller fee in cases of need. As a matter of therapeutic principle, however, I rarely offered to treat anyone altogether free of charge. People are better motivated to enter into a therapeutic partnership if they are paying a fee.

My case load built up more quickly than I had dared to hope, possibly because qualified counsellors and psychotherapists were a bit thin on the ground in the North East at that time. My first resource was the psychiatrists and GPs in the area, to whom I wrote enclosing details of the service I was offering and a few copies of a leaflet I had prepared for the benefit of potential clients. Since many of the doctors knew me already this did produce some response but not nearly enough. I arranged to see someone in the police, the fire service, local government and in some local industries where there was someone with personnel or welfare responsibilities; and I had small, attractive posters printed which could be displayed on office notice boards. I reckoned I had a valuable service to offer, in particular to over-stressed executives, who might be able and willing to pay me if they knew I was around, so I wrote an article about myself (in the third person) which was published together with my photograph in Executive North East, a journal which was widely read. Entitled, 'New Directions – For People Under Stress' the article said:

'. . . Stress is the dynamic which holds systems together – bridges and buildings, organizations, personalities and relationships. But if the stress gets out of balance and begins to pull in the wrong direction, distress results and the system might begin to fall apart.

'Personal distress . . . might occur because the individual is at odds with his environment – usually the people he lives or works with; or because of conflicts going on within himself. Usually, it is a mixture of different elements. In some personalities the stress itself might provide the driving force or motivation to achievement. But in others it can issue, for example, in a variety of physical disorders such as stomach ulcers or heart disease or in such disabling mental or emotional problems as anxiety states, phobias or depression. Other consequences can be marital disharmony, over-indulgence in alcohol or tranquillisers – or simply a nagging and dispiriting feeling that one is travelling the path of life in the wrong direction.

'But it is never too late to change . . .'

The article briefly described transactional analysis as my way of working, gave a telephone number and offered a copy of my booklet *Taking Charge of Your Own Life*. These various initiatives got me going and after that it really ought to have been plain sailing. But there were several unforeseen obstructions on the line.

I had only just got the business launched when, on the 1st October, Betty had to go into hospital in Harrogate for gynaecological surgery. Our daughter Caroline, who was theatre staff nurse at Harrogate, favoured a certain consultant there. Caroline lived nearby in Knaresbrough with her husband Peter and son Daniel, aged seven, and so was on the spot for visiting and Betty was able to go to live with them for a few weeks whilst she was convalescing. So I was back and forth between Middlesbrough and Knaresbrough until she was fit to come home. I arranged with British Telecom for calls to be transferred to Caroline's number, instead of our home, so Betty could still be telephone receptionist.

She was only just out of hospital, and not feeling much like handling sensitive enquiries for my services, when a middle-aged man I will call 'Alan' rang for an appointment. He was chairman and managing director of a small family electronics firm in York and had read my article in Executive North East. He was exactly the kind of client I was hoping for and Betty fixed an appointment for him. He needed a counsellor rather than a psychotherapist since he was mentally fit; but he was in a moral and emotional turmoil because he had become romantically involved with an attractive woman business associate I will call 'Brenda', who was not long divorced from a husband with a severe drink problem. She was a good deal younger than Alan, childless and unfulfilled, and had unloaded her distress onto him over a business lunch. Being a kind and compassionate man he had listened sympathetically, had actually suggested that Brenda seek counselling and had not really expected to meet her informally again. But Brenda had found his mature warmth very supportive and engineered further meetings. Alan, for his part, found her attention flattering, especially since his wife 'Dorothy' was of a certain age and had recently opted for twin beds. So one thing led to another. The story is so familiar as to need no further detailing but the involvement, which had begun in all innocence, soon dominated the lives of both of them and they began to depend on one another, albeit for different emotional reasons – Brenda probably seeking a father-figure and Alan having his self-esteem enhanced as well as eventually having his frustrated sexual needs met. But he was not, he told Brenda, 'that kind of man'; nor, she had assured him, was she that kind of woman. Nevertheless, they told each other, life was life. When you came to look around 'everybody did it' and if they used common sense and avoided being seen together no-one would know and no-one would be hurt. Though not a religious person, Alan had been brought up with Christian values which were important to him, he was guiltily conscious of having broken his marriage vows, could not sleep at night, found himself becoming unnecessarily irritated with Dorothy and convinced his GP that 'stress at work' was justification for a course of tranquillisers.

The roots of Alan's problem were clearly spiritual, though in no sense overtly religious. He had never asked himself before what life was really all about and had been content to run his successful and profitable business, with his elder son following him, and to enjoy the security of a comfortable home and a dutiful wife who, so far as he could see, was entirely fulfilled with keeping the home spic and span whilst playing bridge with her friends and occasionally looking after their grandchildren. Life was pretty good! He did not need advice or moral guidance. What he needed was simply to talk through the situation, to be prompted to ask questions of himself that he had never asked before and to make his own decisions about what to do next. In fact, it took several months of weekly session before he settled on a frank, cards-on-the-table talk with Brenda that led to her accepting the offer of a job in Birmingham. I had to terminate our work together on my own initiative because Alan was becoming as dependent on me as Brenda had become on him!

* * *

Increasingly, the professional counsellor is fulfilling the role that priests and ministers of religion used to fulfil in days gone by. But it is not quite the same, because the counsellor – the secular counsellor, at any rate – is not part of a supportive community, such as a church, that will continue in relationship with the client long after the need for counselling has finished, and which may have outreaches all over the world where a church member will be welcomed. However, the Institute of Transactional Analysis in the UK is expanding rapidly. It does, in fact, provide a supportive community both for its professional members, its trainees and even for its clients and other interested persons, if they want to be a part of it; and there are numerous opportunities for people who use a 'TA frame of reference' to meet in training workshops and conferences all over the country, in fact all over the world.

I have sometimes wondered whether transactional analysis has actually become a sort of religion for many people, in line with Groder's observation. Like a religion, it has a pretty clear ethical system of beliefs and values, it has its dogma and its 'teachings', based on the work of Eric Berne, as a kind of 'founding father'. He might even have allowed himself to be called a euhemerus. In his book *The Structure and Dynamics of Organizations and Groups*, first published in 1963, Berne defines a 'euhemerus' as 'a dead canon-maker who occupies a special place of esteem in a group.' Following Berne himself, there are, or have been, numerous lesser 'prophets' in the persons of Jacqui Schiff (founder of the 'Cathexis School' of T A), Bob and Mary Goulding, (co-founders of the 'Redecision School); and then Claude Steiner, Taibi Kahler, Stephen Karpman, John Dusay and many others who have made distinctive contributions to the received wisdom which is, collectively, known as transactional analysis. Their writings can almost be regarded as scriptures! And there is a sort of hierarchy of priests and priestesses acting as ministers and 'confessors'; and a growing number of 'bishops' presiding over a growing number of teaching centres where 'neophytes' in the form of student practitioners, meet regularly with their authorised teachers. I myself never set out to qualify as a Teaching and Supervising Transactional Analyst and have been content to remain a sort of minor canon in the TA 'priesthood', looking after my own clients and occasionally teaching about TA and lecturing to those who wanted to learn informally.

There are certain rituals that clinical transactional analysts are expected to observe, almost religiously, such as making clear contracts with their clients, and closing escape hatches. Taking regular supervision from a competent colleague is essential and has, I think, something in common with the provision of 'spiritual direction' in some churches. The 'enquirer' about TA is encouraged to advance from casual interest to the '101 Foundation Certificate'. As an official entry into the world of those seeking independence, autonomy and self-sufficiency, this is almost like a 'baptism' in effect, even if not in procedures, and qualifies the person to proceed to advanced training. The workshops and conferences at which members meet frequently (and at considerable expense) certainly provide fellowship of a quality at least comparable with what I am familiar with in Methodism. I would not call it 'worship' in the conventional religious sense, but there is certainly an element of adoration of those who gave us all this wisdom – not quite gods, but nearly!

In no sense do I wish to satirise transaction analysis. I honestly see real similarities between it and a religious institution and I believe it is this very structure and discipline that I myself have found so attractive. In fact, I have no doubt whatever that TA has contributed as much, and possibly more, to my own personal growth than has the Methodism in which I have been nurtured throughout my life. But the one is no substitute for the other. I guess the Methodism of Wesley's day with its weekly class meetings and Bible studies, was in some respects, more akin to the ethos of TA than it is to the practice of Methodism in most mainstream churches in the 21st Century. But there is a crucial difference. The church is a fellowship for life, regardless of one's personal wealth – though it needs financing like any other organization; its ministers need to be paid and its buildings maintained. But the TA community is, in practice, essentially for those able and willing to pay. When I was obliged by age and infirmity to retire from clinical practice I did, in fact, decide to continue my membership of the Institute of Transactional Analysis, receive its journals regularly, occasionally contribute to them and so keep in touch with old friends. I can continue with this so long as I continue to pay my membership fee. If I were younger and fitter I would love still to attend TA events of one sort and another, regardless of the expense. But I can no longer do so because of my disablement and could not participate even if someone took me, because I can no longer speak coherently and that would be insufferably frustrating. My only means of communication now is by computer keyboard, e-mailing, and my voice synthesizing Lightwriter. But I continue to meet in fellowship with friends at my local church and some of them visit me at home.

Transactional analysis has a clear and unambiguous remit to heal those who are mentally or emotionally sick or whose personal equanimity or relationships are disturbed. This does not, in TA, extend to the healing of physical disorders, though such healing does occur from time to time and can seem almost miraculous, as I have been able to observe in some of my own clients. Church people acknowledge a healing remit, following in the Carpenter's footsteps, and many of us seek to fulfil this by private prayer and the loving care of our fellow members, and also of neighbours or others who have no church connections at all. We are even taught that we have available to us a spiritual power sometimes to heal even physical diseases, though this is rarely sought or used, except in certain Pentecostal and evangelical churches. Training is available to equip churchgoing people with the skills of pastoral counselling and such training is becoming widely available through, for example, the Clinical Theology Association established by psychiatrist Dr. Frank Lake and the Biblical Pastoral Care taught by CWR (Crusade for World Revival) established by Rev. Selwyn Hughes, the Association of Christian Counsellors and similar organizations. Some Christians find experience as counsellors through a secular 'calling', as I trained to be a probation officer and my wife as a social worker, but there is no expectation, as there is in transactional analysis, that we should become 'healers'.

* * *

It was whilst Betty was staying with Caroline and her family that she became aware of a tension in the atmosphere which signalled that all was not well in the marriage. She and Caroline have always communicated well and could talk about this and hope that they would survive the crisis. The main victim was Daniel who was the constant butt of Peter's irritation and continually subject to his father's angry remonstrations. We were very concerned, of course, and to have this situation in my own family was a disconcerting background to my counselling of others who had similar problems in theirs! Sadly, this sort of domestic development has become so common as to be almost the norm! The following year, Peter left home for what he described as 'a trial period' and moved in with Pauline and her children at their home in Boroughbridge. Pauline was also a youth club leader, who had not long been divorced. Caroline knew her slightly and Daniel, on weekend access visits, soon got to know her son and daughter who were around his own age. Peter was as distressed as Caroline about the breakdown and was racked with guilt, returning home from time to time in an effort to find a resolution. But divorce was inevitable. Caroline, for all her close relationship with her mother, preferred to talk with me about the developing situation, either face to face or in many telephone conversations. But eventually she found an independent professional counsellor who helped her through the crisis without the sort of personal investment in the outcome that Betty and I could not have avoided. But Peter was not a person who could readily acknowledge that he needed help.

For a while, Daniel visited him with Pauline and her children at weekends but he did not find the visits anything to look forward to. Peter clearly had no inclination to spend time with him in father-and-son activities and eventually, to Caroline's distress, contact ceased altogether.

Peter had occasionally taken Daniel to see his own parents, Fred and Kath Phillips, but eventually this also stopped. When Caroline eventually discovered what had happened she took Daniel herself to see his paternal grandparents. In due course, and for reasons that were never entirely clear, Peter broke off relations with his own parents also! On the positive side, however, it should be said that Peter gave public service as a councillor in Boroughbridge and eventually was twice elected mayor.

It was a few years before Caroline eventually got married again to Merv Mawer, a single man and a joiner by training, who was in partnership with two of his six brothers in a family building business in Greenhow, near Pateley Bridge. In due course she and Daniel moved there to live with Merv in a house he and his brothers had built themselves and in due course they got married. Merv could not have been a better stepfather for Daniel but it is sad that, as so often happens, he eventually lost touch with Peter his father altogether.

* * *

In the March after I got established in my rooms in Yarm Road, our dog Sally died of a cancer that had been spreading silently and undiagnosed for some time through her bowels, liver and pancreas. For me and Betty it was a traumatic bereavement. For nearly eleven years she had been our constant companion at home, on local walks and on holidays in the Lake District and the Yorkshire Dales. She was mischievous and occasionally bad tempered but full of fun and with a personality all her own. We were devastated. I am totally committed to the view that 'all dogs go to heaven'!

Even that was not the end of problems that beset my first year in private practice. I had suffered for several years from arthritis of the knees, becoming somewhat bowlegged, and eventually my right knee became so painful that walking was increasingly difficult. To avoid inevitable NHS delays, I made arrangements for a private consultation with an orthopaedic surgeon in Northallerton, who had been recommended, and in a very short time he had me in the Friarage Hospital for a right tibia osteotomy. The problem was that the meniscus, a part of the cartilage in the knee joint, had worn down on the outside. The operation involved cutting my right tibia in two with a dome-shaped cut and re-aligning the two halves so that my weight would fall on the inner side of the knee where there was still enough menisicus to cushion it. 'It should last about five years,' the surgeon said. And so it did.

It took a few weeks for me to recover, of course and I could not drive to my rooms in Stockton so when I felt up to it I saw a few clients at home. One of them was a young married man I will call 'Jonathan'. He was referred by his GP with a diagnosis of depression but the doctor felt that domestic problems at home were the root cause and counselling the best prescription. Jonathan was an attractive young man, an accounts clerk with a local firm, but he was clearly very unhappy and had felt unable to work for about three weeks in spite of the GP's medication. He told me of his failure to communicate with his wife about personal matters and he felt she had no understanding of his condition and no sympathy with it. I suspected there was some heavy Game-playing going on here and suggested it might be a good idea if I saw her as well, either alone or with Jonathan. He was not enthusiastic about this proposal, feeling sure she would not co-operate. However, he promised to tell her what I had said and we agreed to explore the matter further the following week.

This was one occasion on which I broke the TA rules, neglecting to ask him before he left, to 'close his escape hatches'. As explained earlier, this involved asking the client to say after me (almost like a marriage vow or taking the oath in court) 'No matter what happens, no matter how bad things get, I will not kill myself or anyone else; and I will not go crazy.' This ritual should be followed – as when Ian Stewart had me do it – by some re-affirmation and clarification that the client fully realised that he was making a decision for himself, not a promise to the therapist. Neglecting to do this can be fatal – and in Jonathan's case it was. I had seen him on the Friday afternoon. On the Monday morning I had a visit from a policeman. Jonathan had hanged himself in his garage in the early hours of Saturday morning! His shocked and distraught wife had found him.

I telephoned the GP and was amazed to hear him laugh and say, 'He made a thorough job of it, didn't he!' I found this response disconcerting to begin with but, on reflection afterwards, I was grateful to the doctor. No doubt he lived with death as a frequent occurence and would have found life intolerable had he retreated into guilt and self-blame every time it happened, for whatever reason. I learned something useful from him and remembered in future to ask clients to close their escape hatches!

14

BURNOUT

After my recovery from orthopaedic surgery my workload quickly built up. By early 1991 about twenty clients were coming to see me each week and I was doing evening group work with some of them in my study at home. But I was also doing quite a bit of lecturing to local colleges where counselling courses were becoming increasingly popular and I set up one-day introductory courses of my own in which I presented the basic principles of transactional analysis to anyone who was interested. Waterstones bookshop, where I was known for their sales of my booklet *Taking Charge of Your Own Life*, displayed advertising flyers, as did the County Libraries, and I usually had twenty or more participants, some of them current clients. Occasionally I had these events at Yarm Road but my group room was not quite big enough for so many people so most of the courses were in rooms I hired from the Local Authority or from the Alcohol Counselling Service or Relate. In addition I had invitations from time to time to speak to specific audiences such as doctors at the Education Centre at South Cleveland Hospital (as it then was) where a programme of post-graduate lectures by qualified specialists was arranged for GPs and hospital doctors. I twice enjoyed the privilege of speaking to them.

At one of the introductory courses there was a young married woman, I will call Jessica, and her husband. Jessica found my teaching helpful and shortly after the course rang for an appointment. She and her husband, though still on good terms, were living separately, for reasons I had no opportunity to explore fully. My first session with her seemed promising; she shared a good deal about her current situation and arranged to come again the following week. But the next day she telephoned and cancelled. I asked why.

She said, 'When I was leaving and you helped me on with my coat you touched my shoulder.'

'Yes?' I acknowledged but puzzled.

She continued, 'And you called me 'Dear'.'

'Oh,' I said, even more puzzled.

She then informed me, 'I am a strong feminist. I think your behaviour was very unprofessional and I do not wish to continue. Will you please send me your notes of the interview.'

'I can't do that, Jessica,' I told her. 'They are confidential and refer to other people besides yourself.'

'I am entitled to see my notes,' she said, rather aggressively. 'I can see my medical notes at the surgery, can't I?'

I did some quick thinking and said, 'I will write to you.'

She seemed satisfied and rang off. But I was alarmed. One reads in the press from time to time of doctors and therapists being charged with indecent assault on their patients, getting struck off their professional registers or even finishing up in prison! To guard against such a contingency I carried a million pounds worth of public liability insurance and had never had occasion to use it. But I was quite ready to use it now. As soon as Jessica had rung off I was onto my Legal Help Line! My client was, of course, entitled to see her notes but not to have possession of them. I was advised that she should be allowed to come to my home and to see her notes in my presence. I should have a witness present, who could be my wife, and the client should bring a witness as well, who could be her husband. I put this in a letter to her and posted it first class. Evidently, she decided it was not worth the hassle and, to my great relief, I heard no more. However, I was very concerned about Jessica. Whilst sympathising with her feminist position I felt it had got completely out of hand and was almost certainly an issue she needed to resolve in therapy so I referred her to a woman colleague. I never heard any more about her.

* * *

Gradually, I became known to a variety of referral agencies including both the Durham and York Dioceses who referred clergy or their families and subsidised or paid my fees. But many of the agencies – now referred to as Employee Assistance Programmes (EAPs) – to which I became affiliated, provided counselling services on behalf of industrial and public service organisations. The agencies usually approached me, having found my name and qualifications in the BAC directory of accredited counsellors. So I had cause to be thankful that I had committed myself to achieving BAC accreditation. The agencies included The Robens Institute Occupational Health Service based in Guildford, ICAS at Milton Keynes, headed by Dr Michael Reddy who had been my first TA teacher, PPP Healthcare in

Reigate, the FirstAssist Group in Hinkley, Leicestershire and, eventually, The Churches Ministerial Counselling Service, run by the Baptist Church on behalf of several Protestant churches including the Methodist Church and the Salvation Army. Also I was pleased to be able to tell one cynical questioner in a medical audience, who thought counselling was 'a lot of nonsense', that I currently had two doctors on my caseload, one of them a consultant, and both referred to me by the BMA Helpline!

One of my most important tasks, however, was as a District Assessor for candidates for the Methodist Ministry, when I felt that Methodism had at last recognised me for what I was and I gladly gave my services free of charge. Unfortunately, I assessed only three candidates before ill-health obliged me to retire from counselling and two of them, a man and a woman, I did not recommend because their motives were at best confused. The third one I recommended with enthusiasm but he himself withdrew. I never heard why, but I guess he found that his evangelical orientation was incompatible with the mainstream Methodist ethos!

* * *

During my many years as probation officer, counsellor and psychotherapist I ran a lot of small groups, rarely more than six or seven clients at a time, and found them to be an excellent way of working with people. The group dynamic, which had been a central feature of Berne's own work, added a valuable dimension to the whole therapeutic processes. Clients were able to help one another, learn from one another and to experience Gamey behaviour and other features of TA as they actually happened in the group. In addition, of course, I could work with several clients at once, which saved time for me; and the relatively modest fee was helpful to them. But this was not 'group psychotherapy' as Berne had practiced it. It was individual therapy in a group setting and was the style of working I had become familiar with during my training. I had usually worked with the clients individually for a while before they joined the group and might see them individually in addition if I felt it necessary.

But the group I found most rewarding – and most exciting – was one that came to be called 'The Road Group'. I have mentioned earlier my interest in the work of M. Scott Peck, the American psychiatrist and psychotherapist whose book *The Road Less Travelled – A New Psychology of Love, Traditional Values and Spiritual Growth*, had been such a spectacular success. I recommended this book to any of my clients who revealed a concern for the spiritual dimension of their lives. This was not, by any means, all of them but certainly the majority. One lady to whom I recommended the book came back the following week having bought the wrong one. It was called *Exploring the Road Less Travelled*, and was a twelve session course developed by Alice and Walden Howard, an American minister and his wife, for the benefit of members of their congregation. It was exactly what I needed and I invited all those clients I thought might be interested (past and present) to attend a meeting one Saturday morning at which I outlined what I had in mind. Fifteen clients attended the meeting and thirteen of them said they would like to join.

I hired a room from Relate and we began to meet on Monday evenings. The group was an instant success and although three had to drop out for one reason or another, there were ten who attended the whole course. They came with regularity and great commitment, several travelling from up to thirty miles away in Durham, Darlington and Barnard Castle, as well as others who lived nearby. Everyone committed themselves to prepare for each session by reading certain chapters of *The Road Less Travelled*, to take personal responsibility for benefiting from the course, to be succinct and explicit in their contributions, to share their true feelings and to respect confidentiality.

The first session was devoted to the basic assumptions that underlie Scott Peck's writing: that 'Life is difficult', and that it is so because it is a 'series of problems' that we often avoid because 'the process of confronting and solving problems is a painful one . . . Yet it is in this whole process of meeting and solving problems that life has its meaning.' As the course proceeded we explored how each of us personally used what Peck calls the tools of discipline – 'delaying gratification, accepting responsibility, dedication to truth and balancing' – the latter meaning the necessity 'to strike and continually re-strike a delicate balance between conflicting needs, goals, duties and directions'.' We explored what it meant for each of us personally to exercise the courage and the discipline of love. We faced frankly the issues of personal growth and how this was related to religion, drawing on an abundance of supportive material from the Bible, many philosophers, poets and other thinkers, and we did homework assignments as well as workshop exercises during the sessions. Throughout the course I did all the work myself (to my considerable benefit) as well as acting as leader.

About half way through the course there was a general feeling that two hours together on a Monday evening was not enough. Could they have a whole day together at my rooms and all bring a packed lunch?

We did that, though my group room was a bit crowded, and everyone got to know each other a bit better. When we had completed the twelve sessions of the course, the expectation that we would never meet together again was disconcerting for everyone and it was decided that we should continue to meet informally once a month on Sunday afternoons in the homes of those who could accommodate us and different group members did a presentation to start discussion. Members began to bring friends along so that for a while the group actually got bigger.

But I was becoming uncomfortable about my own role. These people were now not only clients, they were personal friends, not only with me but also with one another and I was faced with the problem of dual roles, which has now become an important professional issue. I ought, of course, to have withdrawn from the group once the original course was over but I was enjoying it enormously and was as reluctant to stop as they were. Finally, things came to a head one Sunday afternoon when I said to someone who had contributed, 'But what is it that you really want to change about yourself?' It was an entirely appropriate therapeutic intervention but it was somehow out of kilter with the ethos the group had gradually taken on. Another group member – a client I had come to know very well and who, perhaps, felt that her new relationship with me was being threatened – cried out in annoyance: 'David, don't be the bloody therapist!'

The therapist/client relationship had broken down – not for everyone, I'm pleased to say, but certainly for that particular lady. She had, in any event, done all the therapeutic work she needed to do at that stage and she later went on to achieve things she might never have aspired to had we not worked together for so long both individually and in the group. After that, I left them to it and I think my confronter became the effective group leader. On reflection, having looked at myself closely in the course of writing this book, I guess now she was aware of the power I had – which I myself was still not fully aware of – and was reacting in a way I had come to associate with 'women in positions of authority.' In due course she did, in fact, become a women in a considerable position of authority and I guess she felt comfortable with her status. The group carried on meeting monthly for a year or two after that. I never heard at what stage they ceased to meet altogether but I do know that some of them continued to keep in touch with each other. A second Road Group followed but did not continue to meet after the course finished.

I have said quite a bit about The Road Group because it was an important experience for me as well as for my clients and I certainly learned some important lessons from it. Dr Scott Peck was probably the first psychotherapist to achieve international acclaim for his work with clients or patients in the spiritual arena. Later he wrote *The Different Drum – the Creation of True Community, the First Step to World Peace*, a book in which he described the process of community building. He defines a community as 'a group that has learned to transcend its individual differences.'. . . 'and, like marriage, requires that we hang in there when the going gets a little rough.' 'There is', he said, 'more than a quantum leap between an ordinary group and a community; they are entirely different phenomena.'

Experimental community building groups became very popular for a while and I attended a two day event in Leeds in order to experience at first hand what was happening. There were about fifty people present, many of whom had travelled from the other side of the country and had had to make arrangements for overnight accommodation in addition to paying the £100 fee for the course. We were an entirely miscellaneous assortment of people who sat in a circle on straight chairs on an uncarpeted floor in the basement of a community centre. There was an accountant from Bury, three nuns, a Catholic priest, a young man who described himself as 'a celibate homosexual Baptist psychiatrist', a young woman called Judy who appeared to be wearing nothing but a long brown cotton dress and a pair of Wellington boots and had the latch key of her hosts fastened on a string round her neck. During a coffee break I discovered that she was, or had been, a Methodist Local Preacher, as I was, had candidated for the Methodist ministry but had been turned down and now lived, she said, in a wigwam in a New Age community in a Welsh valley! A single, unshaven and rather dishevelled man in his late thirties arrived on a bicycle, having cycled over thirty miles from somewhere west of Huddersfield. He sat between me and a middle aged woman solicitor from Shrewsbury. There was a Sikh shopkeeper, two Muslim women veiled from head to foot, a few teachers and a chemical engineer, amongst many others. We were of all ages, jobs and professions or none. We seemed to have nothing in common beyond having read *The Different Drum* and paid £100 apiece for the privilege of attending. An American man and woman, called Rusty and Diane, both trained by Scott Peck, sat one at either side of the group and acted as facilitators.

We could hardly have been more diverse – and our remit was to learn to love one another! Rusty and Diane told us, with the aid of a flip chart and a bit of brain-storming, how to go about it. It would not be appropriate to attempt to describe in detail what happened during the course of the next two days. Anyone who really wants to know more should read Scott Peck's book, which (together with *The Road Less Travelled*) I count amongst the most significant books on the subject of spiritual growth that I have ever read. Ideally, attend a Community Building Experience and find out at first hand, as I did.

However, I will describe briefly the four stages of community building we experienced, because it is relevant to the process of spiritual growth. The first Peck calls 'pseudocommunity' in which everybody is nice to everybody else. It is pleasant, congenial and, after a while, boring. People run out of nice things to say, especially to people whose attitude, outlook and opinions differ radically from their own. Eventually the 'nice' atmosphere changed and we found ourselves in escalating conflict with people we had never met before. We had reached the stage of community building that Scott Peck calls 'chaos'. This was dynamic and stimulating and people entered into it with such enthusiasm that some even jumped up from their seats and rushed across the bare floor to deal with their opponents at close quarters, with the threat of physical violence if necessary! It reminded me very much of the 'Synanon Game' mentioned earlier as a part of the Asklepieion treatment programme for character disordered offenders in an American state penitentiary. Rusty and Diane were used to dealing with such situations so no blood was spilt. Nevertheless, it became quite scary. One woman got up and left the room, despite an initial agreement that we would all stick with it, no matter what happened. Rusty went after her in a break and she re-joined us. Then came silence. A group can continue fighting pointlessly for only a limited period of time, then follows the stage Peck calls 'emptiness'. The silence was uncomfortably prolonged. Everyone was scared of breaking it in case the chaos started up again. Everyone was feeling vulnerable. Some people even began to cry. Eventually, people began to get up and cross the room to say sorry to those they had been abusing. There were hugs and more tears and a general feeling of relief that all was well once more. Except that we were back in 'pseudo-community'!

Over a two day 'experience' a group will move in and out of the various stages but in due course, if all goes well, the stage of 'true community' is reached. It is best described as an experience of joy, almost like being in love with everyone at once! As Scott Peck writes, 'I have a dim sense that I am participating in a phenomenon for which there is only one word. I almost hesitate to use it. It is 'glory'.'

Scott Peck, although brought up in a Christian environment and even, for a short time, had attended a Society of Friends school, was far from being a Christian in the church-going sense. In fact he had found himself drawn, as have many in the counselling and psychotherapy professions, to Buddhism and other Eastern philosophies that seemed, on the face of it, to be so much more compatible than was Christianity with psychotherapeutic thinking, apart from the contributions of Jung – and Peck was a Jungian psychotherapist. Nevertheless he eventually became a Christian, though non-denominational, and even an evangelist in his own unique and distinctive way. He had 'good news' to tell – which is, of course, what evangelism means. He is on my wavelength. A later book, called *A World Waiting to be Born*, describes how community building has been successfully put into practical effect in business, local government, churches and in management/trades union negotiations.

One member of the first Road Group was a Sikh gentleman, born in India, who had been sent to this country at the age of nine to live with a cousin who had introduced him into an evangelical church. He had had difficulty integrating into the British culture, especially in reconciling his traditional Sikhism with Christianity, and when his parents eventually settled in England as well he was up against strong family pressure to remain a Sikh. But he was so enthusiastic about becoming a Christian that on one occasion he actually asked me to baptise him! I declined, of course, to do this in a private ceremony when I felt that the significance of baptism was to bring him into membership of the Christian community. But he attended a Community Building Experience and eventually went on to train as a facilitator. Years later, long after he had ceased to be a client, he telephoned me to say that he had at last become a Christian and had been baptised – 'properly', by immersion!

* * *

In April, 1992, the year of our Ruby Wedding, we enjoyed our annual week at Hodyoad, the Lakeland cottage we had come to feel was a sort of second home. We were limited in the walking we could now do because we were both getting older and, although I had made a very good recovery from my orthopaedic surgery, mountain climbing was no longer a serious option and, of course, we no longer had Sally to keep us company.

As we were washing up after breakfast on our last Saturday morning and had already packed our cases to set off home, Betty suddenly suffered an intense headache. It felt, she said, as if she had been hit with a brick. She sat on the settee in the lounge, feeling sick with pain, whilst I dashed round to see Judy Cook, our landlady, who lived in an adjacent house. Judy came round promptly, bringing her cordless telephone and rang her GP in Whitehaven. The doctor was in the middle of her surgery but came instantly nevertheless and was with us in less than half an hour. 'A little bleed', she diagnosed and phoned for an ambulance. We were amazed at the speed with which things happened. The ambulance seemed to arrive in less than no time, Betty was bundled into it on a stretcher and I followed in the car to Whitehaven General Hospital. She was put into bed; there were tests, a lumber puncture and various time-consuming procedures at which I could not be present so I was urged to get out of the way, go back to Hodyoad and telephone in a couple of hours to find out the state of play. I was assured that Betty was in no immediate danger, the pain had subsided by then and she was feeling a bit better. So I drove back to our holiday cottage and reported to Judy.

Judy was, of course, preparing for her next intake of guests and I was surplus to requirements so I set off in the car, not quite knowing what I was doing or where I was going. I found myself driving beside Crummockwater through Buttermere and over Honister Pass in the direction of Grange in Borrowdale, the 'heavenly place', to which I had been evacuated at the age of twelve when war broke out. It must have seemed like a sort of refuge from the threat of disaster. However, I stopped in the National Trust car park at Seatoller and made myself sit quietly for a while and think what I was doing. I was panicking, that's for sure! And it was too soon yet to ring the hospital to find out what was happening. The Yew Tree restaurant was nearby so I walked over there and had a pot of tea and a piece of cake by way of calming myself down. Then I went back to the car park and phoned the hospital from a kiosk there. Betty, they assured me, was now quite comfortable and in no immediate danger. She had, however, had a brain haemorrhage and was to be taken, within the next few minutes, by ambulance to Newcastle General Hospital, where there was a specialist neurosurgery department.

I drove back to Hodyoad. Judy was most concerned and felt I was in no fit state to drive all the way to Newcastle so she kindly offered to take me. But I was having none of it. I would be OK, I assured her. She helped me to load our cases and other luggage into the boot of the car and I set off. By the time I arrived Betty was in bed in a side ward. The bleed was quite a small one, due to a burst aneurysm in a blood vessel of the brain called the Circle of Willis, and it had effectively healed itself already. However, there was a possibility that it might recur and the surgeon recommended that he should operate and clip it off. We agreed to this.

So for the next week or so I was back and forth between Middlesbrough and Newcastle and in due course Betty was brought home by our daughter-in-law Mary to spend a while with them at Burniston, Scarborough. It was, in fact, from there that I had commuted to the Community Building event in Leeds.

To have one's dear and utterly indispensable wife at death's door from a brain haemorrhage is traumatic indeed and I was faced again with a deep spiritual need, which I simply could not meet out of my own resources. The first time I had felt like this was when – the day before Caroline's expected birth – I was told by my sales manager, 'David, we are parting company, and we are parting company now!'

And now this. I needed God. Until something like this happens, God can be little more than an intellectual concept, a fantasy, of philosophical interest, perhaps, but having no real meaning or purpose. I had known about Him, of course, ever since I could remember. But it was in the crisis of Betty's brain haemorrhage that God and I became real friends! It was when I experienced my own private 'emptiness' and there was really no-one else to turn to but Him. Also, it was something like the closure of escape hatches; it was as if God was saying to me 'No matter what happens, no matter how bad things get . . . trust me'. I did and, thankfully, Betty made a perfect recovery and was soon back to normal.

* * *

Around this time Malcolm Sweeting decided he wanted to stop his supervision work so he could devote more time to working with clients. In particular he wanted to develop the metaphor work he had learned from David Grove, a therapist he had visited in America for personal guidance and tuition. So I had to find another supervisor. Malcolm's decision, after a life in the Methodist ministry, finally to declare himself an atheist had, in any event, rendered his supervision of the kind of work I was doing, progressively more difficult and confusing for both of us and I was anxious to find a new supervisor who was on my wavelength. I went to see an Anglican priest in Durham who had managed to sustain his Christian faith whilst pursuing a 'sector ministry', as it was being called, as a psychotherapist. But I knew intuitively that he was not my man. He treated me with all the gracious authority of an experienced vicar and there was no doubt that I, with my professional qualifications and my body language (or whatever it was Ian Stewart and Gabor von Varga had noted) was a threat to him. So I went to see Professor Alan Guile and his wife who I had first met with Mother, outside a pub opposite the kipper factory at Crastor. I had not seen them since they both attended one of my introductory courses in transactional analysis. I did not expect that they would be able to offer me the kind of professional supervision I was seeking but I guessed they might well know of someone suitably equipped. In fact they did and referred me to Gordon Clarke who I visited shortly afterwards.

Gordon was exactly right. He was a well-qualified and experienced Education Psychologist in his early fifties with clinical training and experience that was more than a match for mine. He was also a Methodist, though he had not been particularly enthusiastic about religion until after his first wife died of multiple sclerosis, following a long and distressing illness. Gordon had been devastated with her loss and, like me when I almost lost Betty, found himself faced with a need he was unable to meet out of his own resources. So he too had turned to God and had found the transforming friendship that is characteristic of the sincere and committed Christian! He is one of the very few people I have met who had experienced what can only be described as a personal encounter with Jesus Christ. Gordon told me that under the prompting of the Holy Spirit he knew, one day in the early Summer of 1982, that he had to go to the home of his Methodist Minister to obtain the key to the chapel he attended in Yarm. The Minister's wife handed him the key appreciating that Gordon may have a need for prayer in the chapel! He told me that he walked in fear and trembling down the narrow Wynd leading to the chapel. Inside, he was quite alone in this old octangonal building in which John Wesley himself had once preached. As he knelt down to pray at the Communion rail, Gordon became aware of an intense light and presence and he fell down prostrate. He told me that he did not dare to look up. He just experienced tears pouring down his cheeks. Then he was aware of hearing some familiar words: 'My peace I give unto you. . . my peace I give unto you. Not as the world giveth, give I unto you. Let not your heart be troubled, neither let it be afraid.' And his whole being was flooded with peace. Later he found the words in the Gospel According to John, Chapter 27, verse 14.

As a consequence of this profound experience, Gordon decided that he must give up his full time work as a Senior Specialist Educational Psychologist and take a part-time post, giving the rest of his time to counselling people, mainly within Churches, who experienced spiritual and psychological problems. Eventually out of this commitment came the charity, Christian Fellowship Ministry, which in the main offered, free of charge, a Biblically based form of counselling, using a model taught by Selwyn Hughes, the founder of Crusade for World Revival (CWR) a minister and writer of international acclaim whose world-wide ministry is based at Waverley Abbey House, near Farnham, Surrey. Some five years later Gordon got married again, to Ros, a Christian lady who became his true partner in every sense. Eventually, Gordon became a Reader in the Anglican Church!

Gordon's style of supervision was in complete contrast to Malcolm's. Although he welcomed my secular approach using transactional analysis – and even acknowledged the value in learning useful concepts and techniques from me – his own perspective was essentially Biblical. What really mattered to Gordon was what God said in the Bible about human nature, human relationships and human need, and perhaps particularly what Jesus and his apostles taught in the New Testament. My Methodism was simply not accustomed to this sort of explicit use of Scripture as a way of life, let alone as a method of counselling, and it took a lot of getting used to! But I was not usually uncomfortable with it, even when Gordon prayed with me! Prayer became a normal part of our time together. Gordon used none of the highflown pulpit language to address a God who was unequivocally 'out there', separate and somewhat remote from the everyday concerns of life on earth. Gordon's God was not only transcendently in total command of the entire universe, He was also immanently within His creation and in each individual human being, and was very personally there with us in the counselling room! Gordon spoke to God almost 'man to man', in the informal language of normal conversation! I was a Methodist Local Preacher so I knew about all this, of course; but such an experience of closeness with Gordon and closeness with God at the same time, was new to me and I found it immensely refreshing and a wonderful source of strength.

There were times, however, when I was emphatically not on Gordon's wavelength! He was a 'creationist', and I was not! Gordon substantially perceived the Garden of Eden and 'the fall' as historical events when sin came into an otherwise perfect world and corrupted God's perfect creation. Although these differences made for some tension between us at times our relationship was such that we could agree to differ whilst retaining our undoubted respect for each other and our differing theological and professional hats.

Gordon was not only a member of the Association of Christian Counsellors, a well-recognised professional organisation, but at that time was also a member of their Board of Directors. Naturally, he was keen for me to do the necessary extra study and qualify for membership myself. But I resisted this as I knew that I was unequivocally a secular counsellor and to have embraced Biblical concepts in my practice could have been confusing for me, as well as for my clients. Gordon's ministry was primarily, though not exclusively, to church-going people who could be expected to accept his frame of reference. My ministry (and I have always regarded it as a ministry) is essentially, though not exclusively, to the secular world and I am happier with a secular frame of reference, calling on Eric Berne and his followers, as well as Jung, Fritz Perls and others.

* * *

In 1992 the three year lease on my rooms as 4, Yarm Road, Stockton came to an end shortly after Betty's brain haemorrhage and after that, of course, I was happier working from home. My study was an ideal counselling room, comfortably furnished and looking out over the garden at the back of the house. Clients came and went, most of them completing their work successfully, Betty and I had good holidays and life was very congenial. But in 1993 the pressure built up again. One of my clients, a married woman I will call 'Rachel', had been in therapy with me for several months for depression. She was a clever woman and an arts graduate with two teenage children. But in her late thirties, she had begun to feel that she had simply not fulfilled her potential and was striving to match the significance and status of her husband 'Giles', who was a consultant heart surgeon with an international reputation. They were both devout Anglicans but when the Church of England at last decided to ordain women priests Giles was outraged and defected to the Roman Catholics! He was much preoccupied with writing academic books and articles and seemed to Rachel to be insensitive and indifferent to her distress. The marriage was far from harmonious so I had spent time with each of them, both alone and together.

Giles's decision to convert to Catholicism had, perhaps, lost him a lot of friends, since he was a man who did not hesitate to speak his mind, and as a result I guess he felt himself quite isolated and perhaps I was one of the people he felt he could still count as a friend. Because of this, I think, and my own Christian orientation, he invited me to attend his Service of Acceptance at a Catholic church, followed by a buffet reception at their home. For courtesy's sake Betty was invited as well but, understandably, since she knew neither Rachel nor Giles, she had no wish to be there. And she felt strongly that I ought not to go either. Quite apart from the fact that the event, on a Saturday afternoon, was domestically inconvenient, she felt it was quite inappropriate for me to be there, though she had gone with me a few years earlier to a couple of weddings of clients. Betty, who was in many respects a far more professional social worker than I was a psychotherapist, had never been drawn into the sort of friendly closeness with her clients to which I was vulnerable and her disapproval was entirely right. Our disagreement over the matter, however, left me feeling strangely depressed. I recall being, on the Saturday morning, in a bookshop in Middlesbrough where I was waiting for Betty to re-join me after shopping somewhere else, and the memory is curiously preserved, essentially as a very unpleasant feeling. I ought, of course, to have made an excuse and declined the invitation to Giles's Acceptance. But I felt, for some reason, that it was important for Giles's and Rachel's relationship that I should be there. At the reception following the service, however, I was puzzled, and afterwards a bit alarmed, that Rachel, playing hostess, introduced me to everyone as 'my therapist', a relationship I would have expected her to keep quiet about! Whatever was going on?

The depression hung around the following day which, as it happened, was Easter Sunday, an occasion I have always looked forward to as an opportunity to preach about the resurrection. For me this is central to the Gospel, the 'good news' that I shall never die; more central even than the crucifixion, which – whilst able to preach about it with enthusiasm and sincere thankfulness – I have never been able to fully understand. Perhaps no-one can. So on this occasion I felt particularly inauthentic. Fortunately, perhaps, I was preaching that morning from a full script and, as an experienced thespian, I was able to present myself convincingly. But I was troubled in myself because it seemed to me that I had simply been acting, putting on an impressive show. My mind was, in some way, at odds with my spirit. I recall feeling tired and confused.

After lunch I followed my usual routine of taking Mother and Auntie Anne for a drive in the car whilst Betty had an hour two alone at home to catch up on her reading and make tea for us all when we got back. But to-day was to be different. It was to be, as Betty said later, the worst day of my life! I first collected Mother in the car from the Frances Barrett Residential Home and then we drove to Loxley Chase for Auntie Anne. Mother always insisted on sitting beside me in the front, so Auntie Anne was helped into the back by Rita, one of the Care Assistants, who struggled to fasten the seat belt for her. She was unsuccessful but Auntie Anne, characteristically, seized the end of the belt and held it round herself as though it was fastened. The old ladies both said they did not feel like going very far so, instead of a twenty five miles round trip to Saltburn, their favourite spot, I drove through Stokesley and up Carlton Bank. There is a car park and a café at the top and I suggested we all had a cup of tea. Surprisingly, they did not want one. Betty would have tea ready when we got home so they wanted to be on their way. Why I did not simply drive back the way we had come I shall never know. I was tired myself and would have been glad to get home. But for some inexplicable reason I decided to drive back by an alternative route over the moors that I knew would be a bit further, though I did not realise just how much! I could feel myself getting more and more tired and considered stopping in a garden centre car park to take a rest; but decided to press on. We were on a main road and no more than two minutes from home when I fell asleep at the wheel!

Fortunately, I was not travelling fast but I awoke to find the car heading for a wall on the left of the road. I breaked hard and skidded but the car bounced up the pavement and into the wall. I was unhurt and quickly got out. There were three little boys coming from my right on the pavement. Had the crash been only a second later I would have run into them and crushed them against the wall! I asked them to get help and they went to a nearby house. Earlier that same day in South Bank, less than ten miles away, a teenage boy had crashed a car into three little girls, two of whom died instantly and the other had to have both legs amputated! An ambulance and the police arrived at our accident, it seemed, in seconds. Mother, belted in the front seat, was bruised but otherwise uninjured apart from whiplash to her neck – more than enough for a ninety-two year old. But Auntie Anne, with her seat belt still unfastened, was thrown forward; her head was jammed between the two front seats and her right leg hooked over the back seat.

The awful memory is a series of snapshots. The old ladies were put into the ambulance. Why I also was not taken with them to hospital for a check-up is a mystery. In all probability I was so anxious to get home that I insisted there was no need and the police took me home. My own car was a write-off and the wall was in need of rebuilding. However, Betty and I went to the hospital in her car. Mother had been put into a neck brace and Auntie Anne taken to a ward. She had been conscious throughout the incident but her right hip was dislocated and would have to be manipulated back into place under anaesthetic. She survived the operation and we had a jolly time with her afterwards around her hospital bed. But the following morning we were woken up by the telephone at half past six to be told by the Ward Sister that 'Miss Garnham has deteriorated.' I guess she had already died. Had she lived just four more days she would have been a hundred and two.

There were, of course, police enquiries and I was fully expecting that I would be prosecuted for dangerous driving, perhaps even 'causing death by dangerous driving'. The teenage lad in South Bank, I heard later, had finished up in prison! But the police were gracious with me and decided that I had suffered enough, that it was just an accident. Nevertheless, I felt guilty. It was indeed an accident, as friends kept assuring me, but it was an accident for which I was entirely responsible.

About six weeks later Mother died of a heart attack and my grief was exacerbated by feelings of responsibility and guilt. Her heart attack was not directly associated with the accident, for she had been having heart problems for some time. Nevertheless, death must have been hastened by the stress arising from it. It is strange that during her mental illness she had had delusions of visits from the police who, she believed, were 'after' me! Oddly, almost the last significant thing that happened before she died was a visit from a policeman who needed to ask her for details of the accident and what had led up to it. She never told me about the visit; I learned of it later from the staff of the Home. So we had another big family funeral only a few weeks after the last.

My current supervisor at this time was the Rev. Michael Wright, an Anglican priest with an MA in counselling, who had a part-time church appointment but, like Malcolm Sweeting before him, was pursuing a 'sector ministry' as a professionally trained counsellor. Michael was enormously helpful and supportive and, partly as a result, Betty and I were able to open up to each other about our feelings at this time of great distress. But it was Gordon I really wanted to see. He had chosen to restrict his supervision work to CFM counsellors only, but we had kept in touch, and he, hearing of the tragedy, came to see me as soon as he was able. I poured my heart out to him and wept over my guilt. I shall never forget Gordon's words as I told him of the deaths of two dear old ladies for which I was inescapably responsible. He just said, 'It is God's timing'. And then he prayed with me, thanking God for their wonderfully long lives, their love of me and the special times we had had together, reminding me that Betty and I had been able to be a wonderful support to them in their last years.

The responsibility was inescapably mine. But not the guilt of my inexcusable negligence in going to sleep at the wheel of a car, nor the guilt of anything else I had done or left undone throughout my whole life. It was, as Gordon said, within God's timing. God (if the word has any meaning at all) had made me the spiritual being that I am, with all the risks that that entails. Somehow He had taken my guilt upon Himself, suffered for it and cancelled it.

It do not understand this. Perhaps we don't really need to. But I have decided to trust that it is true. I accept it, as we say, by faith – not as a matter of intellectual gullibility, I hope, but in response to my own personal need.

Part Four

NEW LIFE FOR OLD

15

THE ANTEROOM

I can let my body sit here in the summerhouse overlooking the garden whilst my mind is busy about its own business. It is difficult to believe that they are both Me, that this is what I have become. But it is not unpleasant; in fact, I am quite enjoying it. I am in no pain – no physical pain anyway. I even doubt whether I am in any other kind of pain either. Some people might think the frustration of being a mind trapped in a body that will not do as it is told, must constitute an intolerable emotional pain. Perhaps for some people it would, but for me it is not so, at least not at the moment. I am at peace, despite the fact that I had a very nasty fit of coughing this morning at breakfast and continued throughout the next few hours, on and off.

It is an effort to write by hand as I draft the beginning of this final chapter in a pocket notebook. Oddly, I just wrote 'opening chapter' by mistake and have had to cross it out and make the correction! I suppose that was a 'Freudian slip'. Perhaps this really is an opening chapter – not the beginning of the book, of course, but of a new chapter in my life, even though my 'case story', as I have sub-titled it, is nearing its end.

But the truth is that I do not really feel as if I am dying, that my life is now drawing to a close after nearly eighty wonderfully happy and fruitful years. I feel now as if I am even more alive than I have ever been – not physically, of course, or even emotionally. I am more alive spiritually, I suppose – whatever that might mean! It is difficult to describe and probably means different things to different people. I am, in one sense, simply dying – slowly and inexorably of this creeping paralysis called motor neurone disease. But I am also 'dying to live' – that is eager, even desperate, to live, really to Live, with a capital L. Of course I am alive already – living, breathing, conscious of the world around me, heart beating healthily and no blood pressure problems. I am simply dying to live this new kind of life I call 'spiritual'. In fact I have already started to live it, even if only a kind of 'foretaste', as it is sometimes called. I know from present experience what kind of thing it is. But I have this inner assurance that my present experience is no more than a tantalising taste of what is in store.

As I write this in my notebook, I am sitting in our new summerhouse. It is April and the first warm, sunny day we have had this spring. The garden is looking very attractive. Paul, our gardener, has given the lawn its first cut of the season, the forsythia is in bloom, there are pansies and polyanthuses brightening up the borders, daffodils, tulips, heather, aubrietia, doronicums, wallflowers – which have come out early this year with their lovely scent – and several other things. It is very quiet and peaceful.

* * *

I am back in the study, and am busy continuing this final chapter on the laptop. Thank God for computers!

I had better say briefly what motor neurone disease actually is, because many readers might have only a sketchy understanding of it. There are several different kinds of nerve fibres that the body depends on to convey information to and from the brain or different parts of the brain, if the whole system is to work properly. Some neurones are involved, for example, in our physical senses – vision, hearing, smell, taste and touch – some with our thought processes, some with functions like digestion which happen without our giving the matter any attention, and some – the motor neurones – with the movement of muscles over which we normally have refined conscious control. These nerve fibres pass down the spinal cord – which is really part of the brain. So the motor neurones are concerned with conveying information from the brain to those muscles we use to move different parts of the body. The most obvious are the arms and legs, which is why many people with MND have increasing difficulty in walking and manipulating things and this is a big part of my problem, especially mobility. I still have quite a lot of strength in my arms and hands but it is becoming increasingly difficult to manipulate things, like a knife and fork or even a tabloid newspaper. Eating is becoming more difficult because my tongue cannot move food around in my mouth. I choose soft foods as far as possible; but soon everything will have to be pureed before I can eat it at all. And eventually I shall be fitted with a P.E.G (Percutaneous Endoscopic Gastrostomy) and shall then be fed mainly through a tube directly into my stomach.

Fortunately, I can still use a keyboard, though I have to correct more mistakes than I used to and sometimes I clumsily hit two keys at once. I just hope I can complete all the writing I still want to do before I can no longer manage a keyboard.

Rather less obviously dependant on motor neurones are the vocal cords, which enable us to speak, and the muscles of the throat, tongue and mouth that play an important part in speech as well as in chewing food and swallowing. This is an increasing part of my problem.

People manifest MND in a variety of different ways. Some begin, as I did, by having trouble with walking, others find the disease begins in their arms and hands, others in their voices. Breathing difficulties often develop later and when this becomes too severe they might have to go into hospital or a hospice so that they can be helped through the final stages. Nobody yet knows what causes MND and there is still no cure for it, though a lot of research is being done. However, there is the drug Riluzole that helps to slow down the progress of the disease and I have the benefit of that.

I have had to stop driving after sixty years or more and I have not even attempted to play the piano for several years because I did not like the sound of what I heard!

During the early stages, long before I had a diagnosis, I continued to see clients in my study at home; but I was becoming more unsteady on my feet and had several falls both in the house and garden and whilst out walking. Also I continued to take appointments as a Methodist Local Preacher and the occasional public speaking engagement. But my deteriorating speech was making it increasingly difficult for me to preach so, having received a certificate for forty years service in June 2000, I stopped preaching. At the same time I began to phase out my counselling work.

On the 9th March 2001, after about three years of neurological tests of various kinds, I was finally diagnosed as having 'atypical indolent motor neurone disease', because the condition has taken so long to develop. I asked the consultant how long I'd got to live and he estimated two to five years, which is what most patients seem to be told.

It is curious that my diagnosis came on the 9th March. This was not only the anniversary of the date on which I was ignominiously sacked from Thomas Hedleys in 1956, but also the date in our Shakespeare Birthday Book on which I chanced to find a quotation from Henry 4th Part Two which provided me with a title for Chapter 1 of this book – 'Seeds and weak beginnings'. Perhaps I make too much of the concept of 'synchronicity' but it – or something like it – does seem to be reflected in so many events and developments throughout my life that, like the illustrious psychologist Carl Gustav Jung, I simply cannot dismiss it as irrelevant to our pursuit of the truth. There is evidently an 'acausal principle' at work here, which endows life with meaning and purpose, a spiritual dimension, which runs counter to the scientific paradigm of 'cause and effect'.

Anyway, this final confirmation of my diagnosis, which I had long suspected, was more of a relief than a shock. I was terminally ill, however the consultant might put it. In any event I was 74 already and had exceeded my biblical expectations by four years anyway so I could reasonably expect to die of something or other before long. Many of my contemporaries had already succumbed to cancer, stroke, heart disease or some other killer, whilst I had been still as fit as a fiddle and enjoying my working retirement, so I really had nothing to complain about. In fact I probably had several years in hand.

The diagnosis of motor neurone disease opened up a veritable gold mine of public services and a multitude of other resources. I was provided with an assortment of aids to help me get around, grab rails in the house, a three-wheeled rolator walking frame, a wheel chair and many others things. I had already been receiving a day-time Attendance Allowance for a year or two, on account of my arthritis, because it was recognised that I was not fit to be left on my own all day with no-one to make my meals and do my shopping. But once I was diagnosed with MND I immediately became eligible for a fulltime Attendance Allowance because I was now deemed unfit to be left alone at night either. So the money, which keeps being increased, is paid monthly into a building society account, where it accumulates and is converted from time to time into ISAs and things that attract more interest! To begin with I did not spend it, because Betty and I enjoy between us reasonably good superannuation pensions as well as our State Pensions. But later I was able to draw on it to buy in the help I eventually needed.

Immediately after diagnosis we were contacted by the Motor Neurone Disease Association, whose HQ in Northampton is called 'Niven House', after the actor David Niven who also died of MND. The MND Association is mainly concerned with fund-raising for both research and the provision of help and support of many kinds for sufferers and their Carers. There was a Regional Advisor, Hilary Shaw, who came to see us to explain what they could do, and there is a local Branch whose monthly meetings I attended myself to begin with, together with Betty, but later I let her go without me whilst I stayed at home to write. Very soon the Association provided me, on loan, with a portable voice synthesising Lightwriter which, we are told, costs about £2,500; and, as soon as I was ready for it, they made a substantial contribution to the installation of a stair lift. We have a monthly home visit from Sue Gavighan, the Senior

Physiotherapist who gives me a thorough going over, checks my heart, lungs, muscle strength, etc., and every few weeks from Gill Everson, a Speech and Language Therapist, who was instrumental in getting me the Lightwriter. Eventually the NHS provided a powered wheelchair, mainly to help me get around in the house. I am simply overwhelmed with the care and attention we have both received. Several times a year Betty and I attend a Multidisciplinary Clinic with six people, including my therapists, a nurse coordinator and Hilary Shaw from the MND Association, who monitor my progress.

Everyone is also concerned about Betty as my Carer, as well as me, because she is under a great deal of stress, and I go to the Teesside Hospice for a few hours every Thursday, to give her a break. I also go into the In-Patient Unit for a week from time to time so that Betty can go to stay with our daughter Caroline and be free of me altogether. At the Hospice I am spoiled rotten by nurses, therapists and volunteers who major in palliative care – that is, of course, care of the dying, though we don't talk about it! They demonstrate their commitment with a superabundance of affection that I soak up like blotting paper. The Hospice is a sort of anteroom to the Kingdom of Heaven, as the whole of life on earth could be. The hospice is appropriately staffed by angels, both professional and voluntary, and I have never been aware of any who don't merit that description. We also have an art teacher and a computer teacher and facilities for having our hair and our toe nails cut; and there is Eveann who provides aroma therapy, reflexology and reiki – all of which is delightful.

The Medical Director is an attractive young doctor called Nicky Miller. Betty and I went to see her for an assessment a few weeks before I started attending regularly. Nicky and I immediately hit it off. At that stage I was still able to speak a bit, which helped, but the significant thing was that she had been trained in Nottingham as a counsellor and was familiar with the work of Dr Frank Lake whom I wrote about in Chapter 4, and who had developed Clinical Theology. Sadly, he had died so she never knew him personally as I had done, but his name alone revealed that Nicky and I were both Christians and we discovered in the course of a few conversations subsequently that we were on the same wavelength.

The word 'spiritual' means different things to different people. If I can be forgiven for repeating myself on such an important matter, I accept the possible spiritual significance of such extrasensory phenomena as telepathy, clairvoyance and, of course synchronicity, but I do not assume that everything spiritual is necessarily good. I take seriously the reference St Paul makes in his Letter to the Ephesians, Chapter 6, to 'the spiritual hosts of wickedness in heavenly places.' This is not so much my Methodism speaking, as my twenty five years as a probation officer, face to face with people doing 'evil' just for the sake of it, or at least without regard for the happiness of others. In the twenty first century their number seems to be increasing and, despite alternatives to custody, the prison population gets bigger and bigger. Fortunately, the numbers of those who do 'good' just for the sake of it might be escalating even faster! There is no shortage of people who have the happiness of others very much in mind and are eager to give of their time in voluntary service or willing to give generously to worthy causes.

My primary interest as a counsellor is the spiritual significance of meaning and purpose in life, which also can be either good or evil. And I take account of the profound sense, shared by so many throughout human history, that there is continuing experience of life and relationships even after our physical, biological death. Nicky, in her specialist work with terminally ill people, had found that it is not unusual for patients to want to talk about God, or the possibility of an after-life, and it was important for her to be able to meet their need.

The Hospice has an explicit policy on spirituality, which is regarded as an important aspect of holistic care. They define spirituality as: 'A quality that goes beyond religious affiliation, that strives for inspiration, reverence, awe, meaning and purpose even in those who do not believe in God.' I am happy with this definition myself and guess the overwhelming majority of counsellors and psychotherapists will go along with it. The declared aim of the Hospice is 'to encourage the development of non-verbal communication so that through attitude, touch and empathy, relationships which express care, compassion, respect and reassurance are built, recognising the unique value of the individual, the spiritual dimension.' If that isn't characteristic of the Kingdom of Heaven, I don't know what is! And it is, without doubt, characteristic also of counselling and much psychotherapy. There is a lot of common ground.

Even so, physical death is a reality and refusal to face it can be the occasion of a great deal of distress and inconvenience to other people – our families and executors in particular. For this reason we should take the trouble to 'put our affairs in order' in good time before it happens. My colleague Petrüska Clarkson, wrote a valuable article recommending that transactional analysts in particular, and others practicing as counsellors and psychotherapist, should anticipate the possibility of their own unexpected death, which could be by accident or disease, and should arrange to 'bequeath' the continuing care of their clients to a colleague able to take on the responsibility, at least as an interim measure. I must confess that I never did make such an arrangement myself and, of course, all my clients terminated treatment with me long before I was even diagnosed as being terminally ill. Nevertheless, the principle is an excellent example of the care we should all take as responsible professionals.

One of the problems I was anxious not to leave behind was the disposal of books, LPs, audio cassettes, videos and DVDs that have accumulated over the years. My filing system needed sorting out so that other people could find what they needed, a lot of stuff needed shredding, I needed someone to do much of my shopping, to visit the library, the printer and other places I could no longer get to myself, to solve problems with the computer and a variety of other things. So my friend Paul Nash, whose wife, Rosemary, is our minister, has become my part time P.A. Paul is conveniently available for two or three hours a week, is well able to do what I need, is delightful to work with and we have a lot of fun together. Not long after Paul began, Tracy Sargeant, a Care Worker, started to come every morning at eight o'clock. She gets me up, showers me, dresses me and makes my breakfast. She is very helpful, sensitive, efficient, anticipates all my needs and, like Paul, is a lot of fun. Betty too is a lot of fun and she would do all these things if she were equally fit. But sadly, she is no longer as young as she used to be, is being medicated for stroke, blood pressure, an under-active thyroid, glaucoma and (not surprisingly, with me on her hands!) anxiety depression. I tell her she needs a Carer as much as I do! We are very close and she will miss me when, eventually, my flight is called. Meantime, life for me is marvellous, not so much in spite of my MND but, paradoxically, almost because of it! As I said, I am in the anteroom to the Kingdom of Heaven!

Another important job, and one I had to do myself, was to shred quite a number of confidential client files which, for one reason or another, I had not shredded earlier. This was a most traumatic activity because it seemed to be a kind of massacre, almost like killing people I knew and loved, destroying the most intimate details of their lives, secrets and memories that they had shared with me to relieve the pain of being who they once were, so that they could start again, cleansed and renewed, and live thereafter in the new direction they were seeking. This ritual destruction of case records was a kind of metaphor for the death I am now approaching myself! Because these much loved clients are not dead at all, any more than I shall be. Through the cathartic work of confidential sharing and confession, of giving and receiving, which we did together, they are more alive now than they were before we first knew each other.

And so am I, of course, because the work of counselling and psychotherapy is not something one of us does to the other, like a surgeon performing an operation; it is an intimate exchange of our selves in which both of us change and grow. This is not, perhaps, equally true for all practitioners, some of whom prefer to maintain professional detachment. Those more like me sometimes describe themselves now as 'relational psychotherapists'. Like the shredding of clients' files, I guess that when I 'emigrate' I shall leave behind my memories in the obsolete brain of my physical body, where they belong. I guess it will be a kind of spiritual amnesia, rather like someone who, after a serious accident, emerges eventually from a coma with no memories of the past but quite able to deal with present reality.

I guess our experience of the afterlife will involve a change in our awareness of 'time', rather than of being in a different place – a shift from the chronological time of earthly materialism, to the eternity, or 'God's time', of the spiritual dimension. We can sometimes experience 'eternity' even now. As wise old Solomon says in Ecclesiastes Chapter 3, 'There is a season and a time for every matter under heaven: a time to be born and a time to die. . . .' I expect that in the afterlife I shall still be Me, aware of myself and of other people, and of the renewed environment I shall live in. But the distress occasioned by the mess I made of so many things, because of my negative attitude towards myself or others, will simply be forgotten. So, I suppose, will the memory of so many things I have enjoyed. It will be my spirit – my attitude, that is – that will survive. It can be either good, positive and life-enhancing for ourselves and others; or it can be negative and destructive, even 'evil'. I am not the only Christian to have had trouble with the traditional concept of Heaven and Hell, as 'places' to which we go as reward or punishment for our behaviour on earth. My guess is that we will experience in Eternity whatever our spirit – or attitude – has chosen in this earthly life. The problem is that once the choice is made there is no way back – at least, not by being independent, autonomous and self-sufficient! As in the story of the Garden of Eden, the way back is guarded by an angel with a flaming sword!

I find it unhelpful to conceive of the spirit as some vague, ethereal entity, a 'ghost' or phantom. Spirit has substance; it is real and palpable, like a team spirit or a party spirit. You can feel it. This is the spiritual substance that begins here and now and, eventually, I believe, will transcend the death of the physical body. That is why a 'change of mind' – or attitude if, on reflection, it is called for in this life – can have eternal consequences. Such a change is what counselling and psychotherapy – especially transactional analysis – aim to achieve. The Bible translates the Greek word *metanoia* as 'repentance'. But, more prosaically, it means 'a change of mind (or attitude) on reflection'.

Death is a forbidden subject in our society. We treat it as the Victorians (who could talk about death) treated sex! Now we can talk about sex but not about death! We go into denial at the mere mention of it. All my friends assure me that I'll live for years yet, regardless of MND. I am, they say, that kind of person! Up to a point they are probably right because attitude (or spirit), as everyone knows, is a profoundly significant factor in dealing with any illness, including mine.

Personally, I believe that all human beings are born with spiritual vision – with an awareness of a mysterious dimension to life, that grown ups teach their children to refer to in terms of magic and fairies and Santa Claus; and then, when the children get a bit older, admit to them that it is all fantasy – which, strictly speaking, it is. But what we might fail to take into account is that myths, and fairy stories and such things, are often ways of speaking about experiences that are very real but that cannot be discerned objectively. Sigmund Freud used Greek mythology as a frame of reference; Eric Berne, the originator of transactional analysis, preferred fairy stories such as *Little Red Riding Hood*, which were more familiar, as a way of understanding his theory of Scripts or Life Plans. Analogies and metaphors might be the only way of speaking about such things and writers and poets specialise in it. Most good novels aim to do more than just tell a story; they say something profoundly true about the human condition. The best example I know, which clearly illustrates what I mean, is H.G. Wells' classic short story *The Country of the Blind*. It is so important to my understanding of the spiritual life that I will re-tell it in brief, perhaps with some of my own refinements.

A South American climber called Perez was separated from his party in the Andes mountains when he fell more than a thousand feet down a steep, snowy slope. Because of the soft snow he was uninjured apart from bruises but there was no way he could climb back up to join the other climbers and no way they could climb down to him. When he recovered from his fall, Perez found that he was not far above the snow line and saw before him a beautiful valley of green pastures and trees with a background of precipitous mountains beyond, offering no easy way out. However, he could see the houses of a village not far off and he made his way towards it.

The villagers, though naturally apprehensive at first, received him kindly and gave him food and llama's milk and showed him to a hut where he could sleep. It struck him as odd that the hut, like the other buildings in the village, had a door but no windows. In due course he realised that the entire population was blind. He remembered having heard tales of a valley high in the Andes which had been cut off from the rest of the world by some geological cataclysm hundreds of years before. The population had been subject to a virulent disease that had left everyone blind. The disease was inherited and fourteen generations passed during which the people of the community had learned to live in peace and harmony without vision, relying on their other faculties.

Remembering the proverb that 'in the country of the blind the one-eyed man is king', Perez expected that he, being sighted, would have a major advantage over these blind people. But he discovered that it was not so. Having adapted to blindness, the people had developed enormously enhanced faculties of hearing, smell and touch. They could hear a person approaching far away when Perez could not see them. They could identify every individual and even know their mood by their distinctive scent. In close proximity they knew where everyone was by changes in air pressure as they moved about. So Perez was seriously disadvantaged in this community and his efforts to persuade them of the beauty of their valley, the landscape, the mountains, the sky, the clouds, the flowers and many other visible things that brought such joy to him, served only to convince them that he was mad and, in addition, very dull of hearing, smell and touch! He fell in love with one of the village girls but she would not marry him unless he agreed to have his eyes put out so that he would be like everyone else. This he could not do and sadly left the community to set off in search of a way through the mountains, hoping that he might get back to civilization.

The metaphors of light and darkness, sight and blindness are commonplace in the Bible and other religious books and clearly are not intended to be taken literally. Enlightenment is the goal of much religion and mysticism and certainly is sought by Buddhists and others who practice meditation. But we also use such metaphors in everyday speech: 'Do you see what I mean?'

But we humans, I believe, are not born spiritually blind as Wells' fictional people were born physically blind. We are not just highly evolved naked apes; we are spiritual beings, whose lives do have real meaning and purpose that manifests in the love we have for one another and the love that, many believe, comes from 'a power greater than ourselves', as Alcoholics Anonymous put it. People with clear spiritual vision, including many great religious leaders and philosophers, have always had difficulty in communicating their experience to those who lack this faculty and who sometimes regard the visionaries as 'beside themselves'.

The other side of the metaphor is the realisation that human beings whose spiritual vision is weak – or even, apparently, absent altogether – can be like the people in *The Country of the Blind* who had developed acute hearing, touch and smell by way of compensation for their lack of physical vision. Similarly, many people who are 'spiritually blind' develop their powers of reason, logic, scientific understanding and 'common sense' to an extent that leaves many 'spiritual' people quite unable to engage with them in useful debate about spiritual things. The two have no common frame of reference. We might be thought a little crazy! Much of our spiritual sensitivity, and our capacity for intuition, is educated out of us long before we leave school – perhaps before we even get there! I would love to have been able to continue declaring these things from the pulpits of Methodism but my voice was simply not up to it. Because of my deteriorating condition, preaching and counselling both had to stop.

So what was I now going to do with my time? Write – obviously! I had set out at the age of ten to become a writer but it seemed a fruitless struggle after three unpublished novels and a fortune teller's depressing 'prophecy'. From childhood I had wanted to do nothing but write and, probably because of this, had made no serious effort, until I was nearly forty, to get myself educated and trained for a proper career. I did not imagine that the time would come when writing was the only thing I was physically able to do, and even then only on a computer! Had I persisted with my second novel, *Man in a Blue Check Shirt*, and got it published I would, no doubt, have concluded that I was now a writer anyway, in spite of the fortune teller, and perhaps devoted the rest of my life to writing novels instead of training to be a humble probation officer and laying the foundations for what was to follow. But 'a power greater than myself', whether God, *Physis* or the Collective Unconscious, evidently said, 'No, not yet – not for a long time yet. I have other things in mind for you at present.' Had I been allowed to go my own sweet way from the beginning and had not been shunted off onto another line, in a new direction altogether, my life would, in all probability, have been far less rewarding and I doubt I should have enjoyed such opportunities for spiritual growth. I would certainly have gone on writing novels, with the enthusiastic support of Betty who had married me in the expectation that I would eventually become a successful romantic novelist, writing best sellers that had films made of them. But very few writers achieve significant success. In fact, very few can even make a living at it and have to hold down a conventional job of some sort at the same time. I self-published, under my own imprint, a number of small booklets about transactional analysis for professional colleagues. And when I eventually had a book commercially published, by Free Association Books, it was not a novel – so perhaps the clairvoyant I consulted so long ago did have some mysterious access to the unknown future! The book, referred to earlier, is called *New Directions in Transactional Analysis Counselling*, and when six presentation copies and one of the hardback, reached me by post on the 25th November, 1998 (by which time I was 72!) my cup of happiness was full.

Although a specialist book like mine, having a limited market, was far from being a bestseller, the book was well received and got good reviews in several professional journals. A further, and totally unexpected, bonus came a year or so later when my agent sold the Italian translation rights to a publisher in Turin. My cup overflowed!

But I still had a great deal I wanted to write about. I had set out, in *New Directions in Transactional Analysis Counselling*, to share the conclusions I had reached about how to achieve independence, autonomy and self-sufficiency through counselling and psychotherapy. In the last chapter I had even made some preliminary observations about the spiritual dimension of life, though carefully expressed in non-religious terms. But I still had something to say about the simple Christian faith that not only underpinned my living but also energised my work as a counsellor and psychotherapist. I did that in *The Book of Simeon – A Seeker's Way from the Human Predicament to the Ultimate Solution*, which I published myself in 2003. The present book aims to reconcile these two approaches to solving the problems of being human. If I am given time, there is another one to follow even yet!

There is no reason why any thinking person should not embrace both Christianity, or some other religion, and modern science as well, as many scientists do. But for a psychotherapist there is a special problem, wherein lay my dilemma. Christianity is not merely an ethical system, differing relatively little from a variety of other religions; it is, above all else, about a life transforming relationship with a Person who – unlike Socrates and Buddha and many other great teachers of the past – is very much alive now! To establish such a relationship is, I think, what some Christians mean by being 'born again', and those who have this experience, perhaps after leading a dissolute life, begin to think, feel and behave differently – so differently, and so graciously, that people notice! That makes a lot of sense, because to establish such a close, intimate, personal relationship with anyone at all, can be a life transforming experience. In some circumstances we call it falling in love! But to have a life transforming relationship with someone who 'isn't really there', Who is present spiritually but cannot be seen and touched, is another matter all together. Such an achievement seems to me to be a triumph of the creative imagination – and such creativity is, for me, the essential characteristic of the human being, shared by no other animal! It certainly is not accomplished intellectually, by Adult reason and logic alone. I guess it is achieved only through the creative Child ego state, as transactional analysts would call it – the vulnerable, needy, spontaneous Natural Child.

This is where transactional analysis and my understanding of spirituality come together, helped by Berne's concept of *Physis* 'the growth force of nature that makes things grow and makes growing things more perfect.' This, in a nutshell, is my personal 'resolution' of the problem defined in the Preface to this book. The criterion of spiritual maturity is almost the opposite of what some people might think! It is not to be exclusively 'Adult'; it is to acknowledge (whether I am a humanist or a theist) the hungry, needy Child within me – to be willing to become as a little child. Only then can I really welcome the Care and Control of the truly Nurturing Parent within myself or others, or the gracious Fatherhood of God.

My remit as a counsellor and psychotherapist was to help my clients achieve a life transformation by making significant changes in the way they thought, felt and behaved without having a life-transforming relationship with Someone Who – secularly speaking – 'isn't really there', call him God, *Physis*, 'a power greater than ourselves' or anything else you like. The amazing thing was that when my clients did achieve such a transformation (and some, perhaps, did not) the essential ingredient was not so much the counselling or psychotherapeutic techniques I used, important though they were, and certainly not some kind of religious conversion. It was my client's relationship with me! That is a reality all 'relational psychotherapists' will be only too well aware of and it carries a frightening amount of responsibility! I sometimes wonder how many church-going Christians are really aware of it!

* * *

Some readers, those in the helping professions in particular, might be puzzled to find that in a book that has so much to say about the spiritual dimension of life, I have reached the last chapter without any reference to the 'Perennial Philosophy', born of the mystical traditions that have their roots in pre-Christian Gnosticism, and have now re-emerged in the guise of 'New Age'. In fact, I could almost say that that is where I got started – with 'Life Science', as it was called – more than half a century ago. Neither have I mentioned 'transpersonal psychology'. Many helping professionals now use the word transpersonal as if everyone ought to know what it means. The word seems literally to mean 'beyond the personal', but does not appear in my 1979 edition of Collins English Dictionary. However, a computer literate friend got me some print-outs from the Internet that seem to provide a good general account of what transpersonal psychology is all about. It includes experiences of love, empathy, altered states of consciousness, meditation, self-realisation, the higher self, paranormal experiences and a variety of other related subjects – all of which I have experienced to some extent.

Was there anything new here, I asked myself, which I really ought to know more about, that would contribute further to my own spiritual growth and perhaps even equip me for forthcoming adventures in the after-life? The answer I gave myself was, No, there is nothing new. I have no argument in principle with the 'transpersonal', which is of growing interest to many, both within the counselling profession and amongst other thinking people. But I have decided on reflection that, in my case, I simply have no need for it.

* * *

I'm in the summerhouse again, reflecting and remembering. When we first came here in 1966 the garden was uncared for, very rough and uneven, but the house itself had been 'modernised'. The previous occupant, in a fit of cultural vandalism, had ripped out the original Edwardian fireplaces, dumped the rubble at the bottom of the garden and covered it with a layer of topsoil, so that it had the appearance of a rockery. But it was impossible, I discovered, to sink a spade into it to dig it over. In the days of my youthful fitness I had sieved the entire mound through a riddle and hired a skip to take away the bricks and broken tiles.

There used to be an orchard here before the house was built, so to begin with we had two pear trees and two apple trees. But we had nothing much in the way of flowerbeds or soft fruit or a proper lawn. Over the years, with the help of various gardeners and friends, we have knocked it into shape and now it is very attractive and full of colour. All the fruit trees have gone, including a Bramley tree which bore beautiful, big cooking apples; but it got coddling moth in it in the long, hot summer of 1976 and a few years ago it had to come down.

* * *

Betty came and said, 'It's quite warm outside. Would you like to sit in the sun on the patio?' So she brought the wheel chair and I struggled into it and helped her by pushing the big wheels myself because it is not easy for her to push me about unless we are on a very smooth surface. So I am sitting in the sun – with my back to it because I can't do with it in my eyes.

God made me in His own image, so it says, and since He is a creator so am I. It is my creative imagination, possessed by no other animal, which defines me as distinctively human. I am more than just a naked ape that happens to be a bit more intelligent than other apes.

So time, in my imagination, is no more. The past is simply how I happen to remember it, regardless of what other people might remember. The future is whatever I imagine it will be. All is now, intensely now, and always will be, for all Eternity.

The world is full of self-sufficient people – and I'm one, damn it, if the truth is told! I sit relaxing in my private summer sunshine, on my home made chequered patio, backed by sweet peas smiling at me with their multicoloured faces; nine leylandias, eight feet tall by now, protecting me from next door's wilderness – awaiting transformation also and the sound of children's laughter.

And I luxuriate beside a well-trimmed lawn and feast my eyes on pansies, aquilegias, pinks and marigolds and apples just beginning on the Bramley tree, and all is well for autumn, spring and summer, on and on. . . . Here comes the summer salad; here's the wine, the cordless telephone, the comfort, the security, the love that will not let me go.

But what will happen next? Will winter come? Will silent snow descend on everything whilst all my barns stand full?

I'll think of that tomorrow, if I must. The scent of new mown grass intoxicates my soul.

This wine tastes good . . .

Bibliography

Barnes, Graham (Ed.), *Transactional Analysis after Eric Berne*, Harper's College Press, 1977

Berne, Eric, *A Layman's Guide to Psychiatry and Psychanalysis*, Penguin Books, 1971

Berne, Eric, *Games People Play*, Penguin Books, 1971

Berne, Eric, *Transactional Analysis in Psychotherapy*, Souvenir Press, 1975

Berne, Eric, *The Structure and Dynamics of Organizations and Groups*, Grove Press, 1978

Clarkson, Petrüska, *Transactional Analysis Psychotherapy*, Routledge, 1992

Clarkson, Petrüska, *Physis in Transactional Analysis*, (ITA NEWS No. 33)

Dobson, Dr James C, *Dare to Discipline*, Tyndale House, Publishers.

Flugel, J.C., *Man, Morals and Society*, Peregrine Books (Penguin) 1962

Frankl, Viktor E., *Man's Search for Meaning*, Washington Square Press, 1985.

Frederick S. Perls, MD, PhD, *Gestalt Therapy Verbatim*, Real People Press, 1969

Groder, Martin, *Asklepieion: An Integration of Psychotherapies* (in Barnes, Transactional Analysis after Eric Berne, above)

Goulding, Mary and Robert, *Changing Lives Through Redecision Therapy*, Brunner/Mazel, Inc., 1979

Home Office, *The Organization of After-Care*, HM Stationery Office, 1963

Howard, Alice and Walden, *Exploring the Road Less Travelled*, Arrow Books, Ltd., 1990

Jung, C.G., *Synchronicity, An Acausal Connecting Principle*, Princeton University Press, 1973

Keisey, David and Bates, Marilyn, *Please Understand Me*, Prometheus Nemesis Book Company (for Gnosology Books Ltd, 1984)

Lake, Frank, *Clinical Theology*, Darton, Longman and Todd

Lewis, C.S., *Mere Christianity*, Collins, Fontana Books, 1955

Midgley, David, *Who are the Lonely Kids?* (Durham County Probation Service, 1989)

Midgley, David, *Taking Charge of Your Own Life*, (2nd edition), New Directions Publishing, 1983)

Midgley, David, *New Directions in Transactional Analysis Counselling*, Free Association Books, 1999.

Midgley, David, *The Book of Simeon*, New Directions Publishing, 2002.

Peck, Dr M. Scott, *The Road Less Travelled*, Arrow Books, Ltd., 1990.

Peck, Dr M. Scott, *The Different Drum*, Arrow Books, Ltd., 1990.

Peck, Dr M. Scott, *A World Waiting to be Born*, Rider, an imprint of Random House UK Ltd., 1993

Peters, John, *Frank Lake – the man and his work*. Darton, Longman and Todd, London, 1989

Schiff, Jacqui Lee and Beth Day, *All My Children*, M. Evans & Co., Inc., 1970.

Scotland, Lt. Col. A.P., *The London Cage*, Evans Brothers, Ltd., 1957

Stewart, Ian & Joines, Vann, *TA Today*, Lifespace Publishing, 1987

Toffler, Alvin, *Future Shock*, Pan Boooks, 1975

Well, H.G., *The Country of the Blind* (in The Penguin Book of English Short Stories, edited by Christopher Dolley, 1967)